England in the Restoration and Early Eighteenth Century

PUBLISHED UNDER THE AUSPICES OF THE

WILLIAM ANDREWS CLARK MEMORIAL LIBRARY

UNIVERSITY OF CALIFORNIA, LOS ANGELES

Publications of
THE 17TH AND 18TH CENTURIES STUDIES GROUP, UCLA

1.

Seventeenth-Century Imagery: Essays on Uses of
Figurative Language from Donne to Farquhar
Edited by Earl Miner

2.

England in the Restoration and Early Eighteenth
Century: Essays on Culture and Society
Edited by H. T. Swedenberg, Jr.

3

Stuart and Georgian Moments: Clark Library Seminar Papers
on Seventeenth and Eighteenth Century English Literature
Edited by Earl Miner

England in the Restoration and Early Eighteenth Century

Essays on Culture and Society

Edited by

H. T. SWEDENBERG, JR.

Clark Library Professor, 1969-70

1972

UNIVERSITY OF CALIFORNIA PRESS

BERKELEY • LOS ANGELES • LONDON

820.9
S974e

University of California Press
Berkeley and Los Angeles, California

University of California Press, Ltd.
London, England

FOREWORD

When Charles II returned from his travels in May of 1660, he was met with tumultuous acclaim. At Dover he was presented with a Bible which he solemnly declared was the thing he loved best in the world, and when he got to London the carousing was so unrestrained that he was moved (by his advisers, no doubt) to issue a declaration against immoral and riotous behavior. The poets sang with fervor, though not always on key, of the glories now in store for England: justice had returned; Charles was a David come from exile; he was an Augustus who would foster the arts; in short, the golden age was dawning.

True enough a new age was opening, but of course it was to have little in common with the fabled peace and harmony of the golden age; it was rather, like all periods of history, to be full of contradictions and ironies. Probably the Mayor of Dover was unaware of the wry humor in Charles's assurance of his devotion to the Scriptures, but before very long he and many another would appreciate the irony of the little drama played in sight of the white cliffs. Furthermore, the rejoicing in London on the night of the King's entry was not a rejoicing of all men, for doubts and suspicions and bitterness were left over from twenty years of political and religious tumult, and even the most loyal were likely to be anxious about what the immediate future might bring. They had not long to wait. Early in January 1661 Thomas Venner, a fanatical cooper turned preacher, led about half a hundred Fifth Monarchy Men into the streets of London, shouting the slogan, "The King Jesus, and the heads upon the Gates." It was an insurrection, a pathetic one from the perspective of history, but it plunged the city into a turmoil of fear, and most of the available troops were turned out to suppress the rebels. They were shortly enough overpowered, tried, and convicted. Venner, found guilty of treason, was executed before the meetinghouse where he had preached; in accordance with ancient custom he was hanged and cut down alive, his privy parts were cut off, his bowels were removed and burnt, his head was severed from his body, and his body was divided into quarters. The golden age, one can hope, was never quite like that.

And yet glimmers of new light were soon to illuminate the scene; Draconian measures might persist for a long time, but they would eventually pass; and though some might hope to return to the past, it could not be. The Fifth Monarchy Men upset Cromwell as well as Charles II, but they were really insignificant, and the question in church affairs at this time was whether the sober men of dissent and the men of the established church (it was assumed they were all sober) could effect an accommodation in ecclesiastical polity and thus bring peace and union to the church. It was not to be, and the Dissenters continued to be a power to be reckoned with, in spite of the harsh measures of the so-called Clarendon Code, throughout the century and on into the next. Moreover, the Anglican clergy and the church itself, for all its legal power, gradually lost ground, no doubt to the bitter chagrin of the devoted sons of episcopacy. Some were articulate in voicing their frustration, and none so much as the young Jonathan Swift, the most brilliant of all prose satirists of this age.

If the culture of the later Stuarts can be said to have had a single unifying element, it must have been the classicism of Greece and Rome, or so we are wont to think. It was, or used to be said to be, the neoclassic period, and even now when the term has fallen into disfavor, we can safely and politely refer to its neoclassicisms rather than its neoclassicism. Dryden was the English Virgil and Pope the English Homer; Cowley tried to make Pindar his own, as did Gray, who in the process, as Dr. Johnson observed, walked on tiptoe; Plato and Aristotle were giants in the land. Or were they? Apart from the writers and professional scholars, how steeped were the literate in the classics? And what effect did these ancient documents have on the thought and lives of the people, on the men and women who read *The Tatler* and *The Spectator*, for example? Have we assumed too much in our generalizations about a pervasive classicism? Professor Bronson observes that the eighteenth century was the first to be marked by a lively interest in the past. Was it this interest in the Latin past, particularly an interest in and knowledge of Virgil's *Georgics*, which accounts for the burgeoning of poems like *Cyder*, *Wine*, *The Fleece*, and *The Sugar-Cane*, or was their attraction essentially the result of a patriotic concern for English commerce? Twentieth-century sensibility seems unequal to an appreciation of these poems; is the fault in the modern reader, perhaps the result of his nonclassical training, or were the poets themselves at fault both in their conception of an art form and in their execution of it?

The scientific revolution advocated in theory by Bacon and advanced in practice by Harvey moved forward in some semblance of a systematic order with the founding of the Royal Society. If the society solemnly tested the ancient belief that a spider put at the center of a circle of ground horn from a unicorn would be so bewitched that it could not move out, it also sought an accurate and practical method of calculating the longitude at sea. The development of practical ways for improving the lot of man was, in fact, an essential part of its program. And its members did produce some significant discoveries, especially theoretical ones, most notably the astonishing works of the fertile genius of Newton. Yet it should not be forgotten that Newton was also a practical scientist, most surprisingly in the field of alchemy. We are told that while master of the mint he was covertly firing the furnaces in an ardent search for the secret of transmutation—certainly a remarkable hobby for the master of the mint.

But what of the science of medicine, surely as important as any of the arts and sciences to the well-being of society? A glimpse into its pharmacopoeia is afforded by the following advertisement which appeared in *Mercurius Anglicus* for 24–28 March 1680:

> At Tobias Coffee-house in Pye-corner is sold the right Drink, called Dr. Butler's Ale. It is an excellent Stomach Drink; it helps Digestion, expells Wind, provokes Urine, and dissolves congealed Phlegm upon the Lungs, and is therefore good against Colds, Coughs, Phtisical and Consumptive Distempers; and being drunk in the Evening, it moderately fortifies Nature, causeth good rest, and hugely corroborates the Brain and Memory.

Of Dr. Butler's quackery there can be little doubt, but what of the respectable practitioners? One may be permitted to speculate on their education, on their specialized training, on their licensing, and on their professional effectiveness. We remember Pepys's proud display of the stone for which he had been cut; the oper-

ation on the first Earl of Shaftesbury which earned him the nick-
name "Tapski"; the "soft obstetric hand" of Dr. James Douglas;
and Dr. Arbuthnot's friendship among the wits and his practice
among the rich as well as the wits. But how far advanced were
diagnosis, surgery, and internal medicine; and what were the sick
man's chances of recovery?

When the theaters reopened after the Restoration, old plays
were taken from the shelf, refurbished, and acted; but new forms
shortly emerged and took the stage. The best-remembered of
these, of course, is the comedy, a form that may or may not have
held the mirror up to life. It was almost certainly a coterie drama
by and for the elite; nevertheless, many questions have long been
posed about the social and political assumptions behind the depiction of society in this and other types of drama produced from
the time of the Restoration to the Licensing Act of 1737. Certainly as the decades and the monarchs succeeded one another, the
attitudes and the assumptions of the dramatists changed with the
society of which they were a part. The student of the eighteenth
century is still concerned, apart from his study of the drama as an
art form, to know how much dependence he can put in the plays
of the period as a reliable reflection of social history. And he may
well ask how much of the nonliterary data currently being assembled by demographers can be used as a gloss on the drama itself.

The fiction of the early eighteenth century also challenges the
scholar as he attempts to fit it into its milieu. Literary historians
have tended to dismiss most of it as of little consequence and have
concentrated their remarks on the novel, beginning with Richardson; but the record shows that the early eighteenth-century reader
could choose from a plentiful supply of fiction and suggests that
these materials merit a closer examination. Would the people who
were reading the English georgics stoop to read the romances and
the novelle? The question of the extent of the reading public has
long vexed the scholar, and in spite of recent research, it is still un-
answered in precise terms, as perhaps it always will be. Swift was
informed that *Gulliver's Travels* was being read from the nursery
to the council, but then *Gulliver* was a very special kind of book.
What of the French romances? Were they read only by such
young ladies as Mr. Spectator gently chided? And who read *Robinson Crusoe*? Only the nonintellectuals? The answer would seem
to be that fiction was read by all elements of society and that it can
be taken as an index of sorts to the taste of the time.

Finally, there is the matter of satire. One may be permitted to wonder why the fabled peace of the Augustans was so often fractured by satiric blasts of a brilliance never seen before or since. The traditional defense of satire—that it purges in order to cure—is of course relevant (though few such cures are on record), but surely Restoration and early eighteenth-century society was in no more parlous state than that of many other eras. Perhaps it is only that one successful satirist metaphorically begat another until in the 1740s the strain was exhausted. A miasmic gloom pervades some of the satire, most notably *The Dunciad*, but we may doubt that the gathering gloom was as opaque as the works suggest. Pope, for example, was at war not only with the dunces but with many of their betters also; nevertheless he was anything but a misanthrope, whether in Timon's manner or otherwise, and he surely did not believe that all English culture was headed into chaos and old night. His warm and intimate friendship with Lord and Lady Burlington, as delineated by James Osborn, is proof, if any were needed, that the dark side of the satirist also had its obverse of bright cheerfulness and hope for society as represented by his generous, noble friends of good taste. Nevertheless, the satire is there for all to see from Dryden through Pope. The verb *see* is used advisedly. If Hogarth's paintings and prints in series are to be read, much of the best verbal satire of the era should be considered in visual terms, as either emblematic caricature or portrait caricature, to use Professor Hagstrum's terminology.

Many of the issues and questions raised in the foregoing paragraphs, as well as other related ones, are explored in the essays printed in this volume.

In the spring of 1968 the Chancellor of UCLA instituted the Clark Library Professorship, providing for an annual appointment of a senior professor working in the area of the major holdings of the William Andrews Clark Memorial Library. In addition to his other duties, the professor was charged with the responsibility of organizing and presiding over a series of seminars on a general theme, each seminar to be given by a scholar of distinction. The essays in this volume were first presented in seminars at the library before an audience of graduate students, staff, and faculty from UCLA, during the academic year 1969-70. Unfortunately the first paper in the series, "Poetry and Politics: Mighty Opposites," by Professor Maynard Mack of Yale, could not be published in the present collection because the substance of it had already been committed to *The Garden and the City*, a book published by Professor Mack subsequent to his presentation of the paper at the Clark.

I take this opportunity to express my gratitude to the following persons for the honor conferred upon me in my appointment as the first Clark Library Professor: Chancellor Franklin D. Murphy, Vice Chancellor Foster H. Sherwood, and Director Robert Vosper and the Clark Library Committee. I am also grateful to the Clark staff, whose unfailing courtesy and cheerfulness have made my scholarly life serene during the past year and indeed for many a year before it. Finally, I am pleased to acknowledge the meticulous and expert editing which Mrs. Grace H. Stimson of the University of California Press has given to the materials in this book.

H. T. S., Jr.

The Clark Library
3 August 1970

CONTENTS

CONTENTS

I

THE CLASSICS AND
JOHN BULL, 1660-1714

James William Johnson
Professor of English, University of Rochester

During the 1740s, a period sometimes considered to be near the
apogee of British Augustanism or neoclassicism, the fourth Earl of
Chesterfield was steadily inculcating his "natural" son with the
natural principles of the classicist. "Pray mind your Greek particularly," he admonished the eight-year-old boy in 1740, "for
to know Greek very well is to be really learned: there is no great
credit in knowing Latin, for everybody knows it; and it is only a
shame not to know it." Again in 1784 Chesterfield wrote to Philip
Stanhope, then sixteen: "Classical knowledge, that is, Greek and
Latin, is absolutely necessary for everybody; because everybody
has agreed to think and call it so. And the word ILLITERATE, in its
common acceptation, means a man who is ignorant of these two
languages."

These sweepingly elegant assertions about "everybody" (otherwise "the World" or *tout le monde*) certainly have a convincing
ring, coming from the man who united many of the most admired
talents of the mid-century: social, political, diplomatic, and literary.[1] Nevertheless, Chesterfield's confident insistence on a *consensus gentium* in classical matters recalls to us the equally imperi-
ous pronouncements of Edward Lear's Aunt Jobiska, who pref-

---

[1] Lord Chesterfield, *Letters*, ed. John Bradshaw (London, 1926), I, 8, 75, 83–91.

aced her maxims about proper conduct for a pobble with the inevitable phrase, "It's a fact the whole world knows. . . ." By their inclusiveness, such statements incline us to question their validity.

Some modern studies of the role of the classics in eighteenth-century education give apparent support to Chesterfield's generalizations.[2] When closely scrutinized, however, their evidence is seen to be taken from sources not altogether impartial: headmasters' reports to overseers and tracts on pedagogical theory are special favorites. Moreover, this evidence largely concentrates on the practices of Westminster, Eton, Harrow, and Winchester, which were hardly typical or widespread. The student's subjugation to rote teaching, verb parsing, and birching is cited, but the consequences on his intellect and opinions are merely hinted at. The number of students in classics is given, but it is not compared with total population figures. In short, modern studies provide little documentation to prove the universality or the effectiveness of the classics; and in contradiction to them, we have the testimony of writers who lived during the time.

Who read the Greek and Latin authors? Certainly not the female half of the nation, as Chesterfield's definition of "illiterate" indicates. Lady Mary Wortley Montagu was an obvious exception, slipping off as she did to her father's library to read the classics on her own. There were other highborn ladies who elected to wear bluestockings; but such notables as the Duchess of Marlborough and Queen Anne in the first half of the century and the Countess of Upper Ossory and the Duchess of Devonshire in the last half went through life unburdened by classical learning. Somewhat lower in social scale, even those ladies who moved in very literate circles displayed slight, if any, acquaintance with the writers of antiquity. Hester Johnson may have been tutored by Swift, but the memoir he wrote upon her death suggests that he was more concerned with teaching her "the principles of honour and virtue" than Latin or Greek. "She was well versed in the Greek and Roman story," Swift testified, but he implied strongly that Stella knew them in translation, and the *Journal* to her and

[2] See M. L. Clarke, *Classical Education in Britain, 1500–1900* (Cambridge, 1959); Nicholas Hans, *New Trends in Education in the Eighteenth Century* (London, 1951). J. H. Hexter, *Reappraisals in History* (London, 1961), questions traditional assumptions about sixteenth- and seventeenth-century education; see especially the chapter entitled "The Education of the Aristocracy in the Renaissance."

Mrs. Dingley is notably the least allusive to the classics of any-thing Swift wrote.[3] Similarly, Mrs. Thrale became an object of condescension to the learned gentlemen who surrounded her when she broached classical subjects to them. And Fanny Burney seemed to fear that, in the words of Mrs. Malaprop, "Too much learning don't become a young woman"; she not only concealed her brains from her father's circle but actually drew a mild carica-ture of the bluestocking classicist, in the form of the "too satirical" Mrs. Selwyn, in *Evelina*.

In still lower social and economic levels of British society, book learning of the classical kind was remote from the province of women, whatever radical projectors might propose. Steele poked fun at the shopkeeper's wife who affected Greek and he mocked the "female virtuoso" who knew ancient philosophy, while Ad-dison superciliously noted the innocent delight his Greek epi-graphs produced in young ladies who read *The Spectator* and pointedly omitted classical learning as a prerequisite for being a good wife.[4] If Pope admired the good sense of a Clarissa (or Mar-tha Blount), he disdained the dirty intellectuality of a Sappho (or Lady Mary). The daughters of the middle class took these lessons to heart and strove to shine not through erudition but by display-ing the nonliterate femininity of a Sophia Western, Lydia Mel-ford, or Sophy Primrose. In the lowest classes, the fight for exis-tence occupied all the efforts of the hapless female; even the few who schemed or married their way from the depths remained strangers to Greek glory and Roman grandeur. It is doubtful that Moll Flanders and Fanny Hill kept copies of Horace tucked in their pockets to while away the lull between patrons; and Emma Hamilton no more reached the top rungs of the social ladder by quoting Ovid's *Ars Amatoria* to Sir William and Lord Nelson than Nell Gwyn did by addressing Charles II in elegiac distichs.

If the female population of eighteenth-century Britain lived in blissful ignorance of the classics, their menfolk did not fare much better. Certainly none of the lower segments of society knew how to read Latin or Greek. Neither the gazing rustics of sweet Auburn nor the Jemmy Twitchers of underground London felt the need of classical learning, even in their higher avatars like

[3] Jonathan Swift, *Satires and Personal Writings*, ed. W. A. Eddy (New York, 1950), pp. 391–402.

[4] Joseph Addison and Richard Steele, *The Spectator*, ed. Donald F. Bond (Ox-ford, 1965–1967), II, 68–71, 442–445, 582–583.

Stephen Duck and Ebenezer Elliston. Learning's ample page did not unroll for the groveling mechanic or the sooty empiric either. And among the literate middle classes—the de Coverleys and Hardcastles who constituted the country gentry; the Freeports, Bevils, and Thorowgoods who made up the mercantile establishment—a knowledge of the Bible and the common law, of ciphering and taking inventory, was all the education necessary to get a man through life. There was not, we may be sure, an extensive collection of the classics at Harlowe Place; and if Shandy Hall boasted an impressive array of ancient authors and their latter-day commentators, their use by the proprietor of the establishment was hardly a shining testimony to the benefits of a classical education.

To say, then, that firsthand knowledge of the classics was confined to a comparatively small number of the male members of the professional and upper classes in Britain during the eighteenth century may appear to be an elaborate way of indicating what was already plain: that Lord Chesterfield's "everybody" meant "everybody who was anybody" or "the elite." Like Athenian democracy, which declared as equals only some few hundred adult males out of a population of thousands, the neoclassical "republic of letters" was a polity reserved to a select set of men. Chesterfield knew this.[5] So does anyone familiar with English literature. What surprises us is how few were directly acquainted with the literature of antiquity during the era that posterity has dubbed "the classical age of English letters."

Henry Fielding, whose own classical scholarship was worn with such familiarity and good humor, has left a telling description of why classicists were so few. In *The Covent-Garden Journal* (no. 56) he declares that the English are deficient in what he calls "Good Breeding":

For this I shall assign two Reasons only, as these seem to me abundantly satisfactory, and adequate to the Purpose.

The first is that Method so general in this Kingdom of giving no Education to the Youth of both Sexes; I say general only, for it is not without some few Exceptions.

Much the greater Part of our Lads of Fashion return from School at fifteen or sixteen, very little wiser, and not at all the better for having been sent thither. Part of these return to the Place from whence

[5] For Chesterfield's final, and eminently sensible, estimate of classical studies and classicists, see his letter dated 22 February 1748 OS, in Chesterfield, *Letters*, ed. Bradshaw, I, 88–91.

they came, their Fathers Country Seats; where Racing, Cock fighting, and Party become their Pursuit, and form the whole Business and Amusement of their future Lives. The other Part escape to Town in the Diversions, Fashion, Follies, and Vices of which they are immediately initiated. In this Academy some finish their Studies, while others by their wiser Parents are sent abroad to add the knowledge of the Diversions, Fashions, Follies, and Vices of all Europe, to those of their own Country. . . .

Some of our Lads, however, are destined to a further Progress in Learning; these are not only confined longer to the Labours of a School, but are sent thence to the University. Here if they please, they may read on, and if they please (as most of them do) let it alone and betake themselves as their Fancy leads, to the Imitation of their elder Brothers either in Town or Country.

This is a Matter which I shall handle very tenderly, as I am clearly of an Opinion that an University Education is much the best we have. . . .

The second general Reason why Humour so much abounds in this Nation, seems to me to arise from the great Number of People, who are daily raised by Trade to the Rank of Gentry, without having had any Education at all; or, to use no improper Phrase, Without having served an Apprenticeship to this Calling.[6]

The justice of Fielding's remarks is well attested. While such university records as those of Trinity College, Dublin, indicate the presence of an extensive curriculum in the classics, investigations have revealed that this curriculum was largely on paper.[7] Moreover, contemporary accounts—the letters of Gray and Walpole, Gibbon's autobiography, Boswell's journals—confirm a sad fact: the eighteenth-century classicist was most often a self-taught man, like Pope and Shaftesbury, Collins and Johnson, Gibbon and Goldsmith. One who was not interested in classical learning, as Horace Walpole was not, might attend Eton and Cambridge, go on the grand tour, and emerge from the educational process casu-

[6] Henry Fielding, *The Covent-Garden Journal*, no. 56 (25 July 1752). Fielding disposes of women's education in equally pithy terms: ". . . there is very little Difference between the Education of many a Squire's Daughter, and that of his Dairy Maid, who is most likely her principle Companion." Fielding constantly played up the widespread ignorance of the classics even among those who presumably had studied them in school (see, e.g., Bk. II, chap. xi, of *Joseph Andrews*).

[7] See Constantia Maxwell, *A History of Trinity College, Dublin, 1591–1892* (Dublin, 1946), pp. 50–51; W. Bedell Stanford, "Classical Studies in Trinity College, Dublin, since the Foundation," *Hermathena*, LVII (1941), 3–24; M. H. Curtis, *Oxford and Cambridge in Transition, 1558–1642* (Oxford, 1959).

ally admitting his ignorance of Latin, to say nothing of Greek.

Even supposing that an aspiring youth at Oxford or Cambridge persisted in his desire to study the ancients, he was likely to be discouraged by a lazy, indifferent, or bibulous regius professor.[8] Lord Chesterfield has provided an oblique but appalling insight into the status of classical studies in 1748:

Since you do not care to be an Assessor of the Imperial Chamber, and desire an establishment in England, what do you think of being Greek Professor at one of our Universities? It is a very pretty sinecure, and requires very little knowledge (much less than, I hope, you have already) of that language. If you do not approve of this, I am at a loss to know what else to propose to you.[9]

The facts of Thomas Gray's academic career reveal the dismal process by which promising youths drifted, or were shunted, into positions where sloth often substituted for scholarship and where learning, desultorily pursued, might become massive but remain inert.[10] Of course there were some classical scholars in Georgian England who studied diligently, gained wide knowledge, and imparted it through books and lectures. The names of Richard Bentley, Thomas Hearne, and others come to mind. For every Bentley, however, there were half a dozen Thomas Gales, who confined their learning to a circumscribed coterie, or Joseph Wartons, whose love of Greek surpassed their ability to read it, or Thomas Grays, who undertook prodigious researches, satisfied themselves, and passed on to something different without imparting their findings to anybody. At least the Gales and the Grays were scholars of genuine ability. Far more numerous, and far outnumbering the Bentleys and the Grays, were tutors like Dr. Waldegrave, the Oxford don whose "knowledge of the world," Gibbon wrote, "was confined to the university; his learning was of the last rather than of the present age; his temper was indolent; his faculties, which were not of the first rate, had been relaxed by the climate; and he was satisfied (like his fellows) with the slight and superficial discharge of an important trust."[11]

8 Note, e.g., Thomas Gray's remark on a recently deceased colleague: "Brandy finished what port began."
9 Letter dated 15 January 1748, OS, in Chesterfield, *Letters*, ed. Bradshaw, I, 80.
10 William Powell Jones, *Thomas Gray, Scholar* (Cambridge, Mass., 1937).
11 Edward Gibbon, *The Autobiography of Edward Gibbon*, ed. Dero A. Saunders (New York, 1961), p. 78.

Such was the state of classical studies in the eighteenth century. Virtually no women and comparatively few men received any education at all; when available, that education was mechanical, slipshod, or both; it ill prepared the student for further work at the university level; the universities were staffed with tutors whose knowledge was limited and whose interest in teaching was minimal. We may well wonder how such a system managed to produce a Fielding, a Johnson, a Gibbon, a Burke, and a Porson. Moreover, we wonder whether there is any justification in supposing that "classicism" was anything more than a limited phenomenon, affecting only a few writers and having little impact on British (or even English) culture as a whole.

The literary and cultural importance of the classics is possibly best understood by returning to the earliest stages of the "new" classicism in England during the reigns of the last four Stuarts. This era, which has been termed the period "before the Augustans had really begun to be Augustan," was also the period when British physicians were still dominated by Hippocrates and Galen; before Handel had appeared in England, baroque scores in hand; before gardening had started to produce more pentameter couplets than blossoms; before Palladianism had grown into an epidemic; before triweekly journals were littering every London kennel; before the dilettanti had begun to receive crates of headless statues from Italy; before the Adam family were constructing their elegant Edens; and before Sir Joshua Reynolds had begun to commingle plastic and literary terminology. In short, it was a time when classicism as a literary or ideological phenomenon in its "old," humanist version was being modified into its "new" or neoclassical form. Several thoughtful critics have explained the new classicism as an attempt by Restoration writers to impose reason, restraint, and rules upon a disrupted and disorganized society and literature. To an extent, it was decidedly that; but it was not that alone.

The turbulence of the period between 1660 and 1714 has been pictured by contemporary histories, among them Bishop Burnet's *History of My Own Time*. The drama, poetry, prose, and sermons of the era present further evidence of social, political, and ecclesiastical tremors. Certainly there was much of the quixotic and ominous, the confusing and innovational, in events of the time; but there was also a strong element of continuity in thought and attitudes. The alarums and excursions of those five decades

most assuredly demanded that fast answers be provided to urgent
problems; and the Restoration politician, divine, poet, or stock-
jobber usually had to rely upon the same guides available to previous generations: common sense, the examples (often bitter) of
the preceding twenty or thirty years, the Bible, and the literature
of the ancients. For some—a Richard Baxter or a John Bunyan—
the Bible provided all the necessary answers to permissible questions. For others—a Pepys or a Rochester—sensual experience, or
common sense, promised to guide one through life. But for many
others, Dryden among them, the acceptance of common sense and
biblical authority did not serve to meet all exigencies. For them,
then, the question arose of what to accept from the past and what
to reject, of how to combine to best advantage inherited wisdom
and present judgment.

As the personifications of adaptive continuity, certain men influenced the evolving answers to this question. Sometimes critically tagged "transitional figures," these survivors of past crises were
present during the sixties and seventies (and even later) as men in
their prime, or slightly beyond it, exerting political or ideological
pressures on the changing English culture. Educated under the
dispensations of humanist classicism during the reigns of the first
James and the first Charles, they adapted their beliefs to the exigencies of the interregnum; during the reigns of the second
Charles and the second James, they presented to their young contemporaries a variety of classical rationales which in time were
shaped into neoclassicism.

Among this durable group were men both of great genius
(John Milton) and of interesting if small talent (Thomas Killigrew). Some were primarily politicos with a secondary interest
in literature (Edward Hyde); others (Andrew Marvell) were
litterateurs who developed a passionate enthusiasm for public affairs. The continuing if limited influence of some—Sir William
Davenant, for example—is well documented and commonly
known. Indeed, it is superfluous to insist, beyond a simple reminder, on the continuous elements of English culture in the mid-
century. Somewhat more detailed attention to the views of five or
six men, however, suggests how and why Restoration interest in
the classics took its particular form.

In many ways John Evelyn (1620–1706) was an archetypal
figure, not only because his life spanned the period from James I
to Anne, but because his intellect was representative of both the
Renaissance *uomo universale* and the theoretical ideal of the eigh-

teenth century. An expert classicist with learning as deep as it was wide, Evelyn was also a practical man of affairs who dealt with such matters as air pollution and reforestation, an adroit politician, an expert on religious history, a devotee of the new science, an incredibly fecund writer, and a Christian mystic.

To summarize in a few words Evelyn's complexly integrated mentality and to identify the part of classical learning in it are impossible. Nevertheless, Evelyn himself provides a telling glimpse in the entries for 27 and 30 January 1658 in his *Diary*. Pierced to the heart by the death of his son Dick after "six fitts of a Quartan Ague," Evelyn sat down to compose a conventional *memento mortui*, or memoir on the dead. The "prettiest, and dearest Child, that ever parents had," who died at the age of "but 5 yeares & 3 days" after a "long & painefull Conflict" during which the boy was "in greate agonie, whether he should not offend God, by using his holy name so oft, calling for Ease," was, his father wrote,

. . . a prodigie for Witt & understanding; for beauty of body a very Angel, & for endowments of mind, of incredible & rare hopes. To give only a little tast, & thereby glory to God, (who out of the mouths of Babes & Infants dos sometimes perfect *his* praises) At 2 yeare & halfe old he could perfectly reade any of the *English, Latine*, french, or *Gottic* letters; pronouncing the first three languages exactly: He had before the 5t yeare . . . not onely skill to reade most written hands but to decline all the Nounes, Conjugate the verbs . . . learned out *Puerilis* . . . turne English into Lat: & *vice versa* . . . & made a considerable progresse in *Commenius's Janua*: began himself [to] write legibly, & had a strange passion for Greeke . . . Aesop . . . Euclid. . . . He had learn'd by heart divers Sentences in *Lat*: & *Greeke* which on occasion he would produce even to wonder. . . . God having dressed up a Saint fit for himselfe, would not permit him longer with us, unworthy of the future fruites of this incomparable hopefull blossome: such a Child I never saw; for such a child I blesse God, in whose boosome he is. . . . Thou gavest him to us, thou hast taken him from us, blessed be the name of the Lord. . . .

On the *Saturday* following, I sufferd the Physitians to have him opened. . . . Being open'd they found a membranous substance growing to the cavous part of the *liver*, somewhat neere the edge of it for the compasse of 3 Inches, which ought not to be; for the Liver is fixed onely by three strong ligaments, all distant from that part . . . & indeed *Liver* & *Splen* were exceedingly large &c. . . .[12]

[12] John Evelyn, *The Diary of John Evelyn*, ed. E. S. de Beer (London, 1959), pp. 385–387. See Evelyn's memento on the death of his daughter on 14 March 1685 (*ibid.*, p. 797). Fielding parodies the paternal eulogy on a child's classical learning and promise in Bk. IV, chap. viii, of *Joseph Andrews*.

When this specimen of a conventional genre is compared with later ones—say, Swift's memoir on Stella—we see the perfect embodiment of a fused intellect in contrast with a fragmented one. Evelyn suffered no dissociation of sensibility. He could record a transport of religious ecstasy or an inventory of objets d'art in a French palace with equal aptitude. He could converse unselfconsciously with Samuel Pepys or Sir Isaac Newton, catechize Margaret Blagge Godolphin, or correct Richard Bentley's Greek to his face. He was equally at home in church or at a meeting of the Royal Society. In his synthetic universality, Evelyn could combine the temporal and the timeless, past and present, empiric data and mystical vision. To him, then, the worldly wisdom of the ancients was a preamble to the cosmic disclosures of Christ's incarnation, a record of the continuity of human experience, a supplement to the limited experience available to a man through his senses, a confirmation of the human condition. He accepted the classics for what they contributed to himself as a man and to the collective values of the human race.[13] And when he was faced with inherent contradictions between classical authority and sense experience or Christian revelation, he maintained his intellectual equilibrium by straightway resolving them.

Two of Evelyn's longtime friends and fellow scholars furnish some interesting comparisons and contrasts, with Evelyn and with each other. All three appear on the surface to possess impeccable training in Greek and Latin literature, a universal curiosity, a vast range of knowledge, and a capacity for synthesis. But the unity of Evelyn's world view could not be maintained by Méric Casaubon and Thomas Hobbes, whose particular theoretical emphases demanded somewhat different attitudes toward classical study.

Both Casaubon and Hobbes were drilled in the old-fashioned methodology of humanist scholasticism, and each continued to smell of the inkhorn for the rest of his life. In many ways Méric Casaubon (1599–1671) is to all appearances so typical a scholar of the Renaissance variety as to seem an anachronism in the court of Charles II. The inheritor of the manuscripts as well as the ideas and techniques of a line of sixteenth-century polymaths, including his father Isaac, Casaubon spent his long lifetime in England writing on subjects dear to his predecessors, collating texts, trans-

[13] Evelyn's criteria are implicit in his account of Bentley's consultation with him about the attack on Epicurus in the first Boyle sermon, 17 April 1692 (see *Diary*, ed. de Beer, p. 953).

lating the ancients, and occasionally producing pamphlets that garnered all data, pagan and Christian, to solve some doctrinal matter his forerunners had overlooked.[14] His writings nevertheless contain significant innovations in their attitudes toward the classics.

In the first place, Casaubon's ostensible dedication to using the pagan authors in justification of revealed religion was deceptive; he actually preferred pagan ideology to Christian. A churchman and eventually a prebendary at Windsor, Casaubon would sit reading a volume of Pliny or Diodorus during the sermon. His published writings were orthodox, but his conversation eventually led even the broad-minded Charles to remark that Casaubon was the oddest man, who would believe anything so long as a heathen writer vouchsafed it but who doubted everything in the Scriptures. All the great names of the preceding century—Scaliger, Lipsius, Vossius—had used the ancients in doctrinal causes of one kind or another. Méric Casaubon also did so, but he denied the necessity of Christianizing the Greeks and Romans for the sake of justifying some human institution or other—the church or the monarchy—and he thereby separated the spiritual, political, and in time the social pretensions of classical study from its chief value, which Casaubon asserted to be entertainment.

In *A Letter to Peter du Moulin, D.D., Concerning Natural experimental Philosophie, and some books lately set out about it* (Cambridge, 1669), Casaubon gave fullest expression to his antiquarianism. Du Moulin had sent Casaubon a volume describing the empirical posits of the Royal Society, including their discreditation of Aristotle's scientific treatises.[15] Alert to the implications of the new science, the old scholar penned one of the first broadsides in the battle of the Ancients and the Moderns. Many of his particular arguments are the standard ones: he halfheartedly argues that the sacred documents of Christianity are written in Greek and Latin, as well as in Hebrew, and that discrediting the ancients will lead to a lapse in the study of those languages and thus to ignorance of Christian texts, and will thereby encourage the increase of freethinking and atheism. Other of his points are in

---

[14] For a fuller discussion of Casaubon's contributions to neoclassicism, see James William Johnson, *The Formation of English Neo-Classical Thought* (Princeton, 1967), pp. 156–162.

[15] Casaubon does not name the book, but it was probably Thomas Sprat's *The History of the Royal-Society of London* (1667).

the same reactionary vein. In his desperation to protect his beloved ancients, however, Casaubon assails not only the Royal Society but Johann Comenius' trilingual textbook, the *Janua* (which little Dick Evelyn had made so much progress in), rather hysterically declaring Comenius a projector who would destroy classical learning and "make every man wise." Casaubon's obvious belief that classicism should be an elitist cult takes on even more limited implications when he argues that life without the classics would be vain and empty, that one must have ancient history, mythology, and literature to fill up his time. Casaubon's position toward the classics is, therefore, a severely restrictive one, denying all practical application and placing Greek and Latin literature in the category of playthings for antiquarians.

Thomas Hobbes (1588–1679) might seem a mirror opposite to Casaubon. Hobbes was accused of wanting to destroy all reliance on the classics; his detested opinion, stated in the *Leviathan*, was often quoted against him: "Though I reverence those men of ancient times, that either have written truth perspicuously, or set us in a better way to find it out ourselves; yet to the antiquity itself I think nothing due. For if we will reverence the age, the present is the oldest." This sophistic reasoning, taken far too seriously and inclusively by Hobbes's critics, was compounded by his assertion that if he had read as many books as other men, he would know no more than they did. Construed as a criticism of all classical learning by a freethinker and atheist, these sentiments are obviously a criticism of antiquarianism, not a criticism of classicism. Hobbes's insistence on experiential criteria never took the form of denying all ancient knowledge. As Hobbes himself said, he reverenced those ancients who wrote the truth or set the reader in a better way to find it.[16]

Like Casaubon, Hobbes severed classical study from the doctrinal and institutional ties that humanism had carefully knotted. What he wished to do was use ancient literature as empirical data upon which he could draw in constructing his systems of government, ethics, and psychology. By appropriating Epicurean-Lucretian physics, Hobbes certainly was not being anticlassical. Nor was he averse to using facts from Greco-Roman historiogra-

[16] For further comments on Hobbes's classicism, see Samuel I. Mintz, *The Hunting of Leviathan* (Cambridge, 1962), pp. 2–6. See also Hobbes's *Analysis of Aristotle's Rhetoric* (Oxford, 1833).

phy to support his political theorems. Hobbes's essential point about studying the classics was that classical learning should be used in practical ways. This functional emphasis was indeed antithetical to Casaubon's antiquarianism, although, realistically speaking, Hobbes was just as much a scholastic speculator and theorist as Casaubon; and Hobbes's personal interest in the classics for which he made translations and redactions—Thucydides, Aristotle, Homer—was as idiosyncratic as Casaubon's. But where Casaubon's classicism assumed a comprehensive and undiscriminating use of the ancients for the pleasure of the individual, Hobbes's classical rationale asserted a selective use for wide social and political purposes. Thus, Casaubon's retrospectively oriented "defense" of the classics stood in genuine opposition to Hobbes's prospectively directed criticism of antiquarianism. Ironically enough, it was the views of Hobbes, the Evil Genius of Malmesbury, which his classicist critics ultimately absorbed into their own attitudes toward classical study.

Not, however, Abraham Cowley. In the works he wrote after 1660, Cowley first attempted to combine Hobbesian and Casaubonian posits; but this endeavor led him to take still a different stance. In the preface to *A Proposition for the Advancement of Learning* (1661), Cowley promises to be joining the ranks of the empiricists and defenders of the new learning. He cries out, along with Charleton, Dryden, and many others, "Hence, loathéd Aristotle!" but then hastily goes on to show that his feelings are most ambiguous: "Not that I would disparage the admirable wit and worthy labors of many of the ancients, much less of Aristotle, the most eminent among them; but it were madness to imagine that the cisterns of men [i.e., books] should afford us as much, and as wholesome waters, as the fountain of nature." Nature, he explains, is the phenomenological universe; his proposed academy would include a curriculum heavily weighted in the sciences: mathematics, anatomy, chemistry, architecture, and so forth. Yet, as he continues to detail his theory, it becomes obvious that Cowley is still strongly tied to the old scholastic methods of humanism. The students would read Theophrastus and Dioscorides on plants; Aristotle himself on animals, morals, and rhetoric; and a host of other ancient writers, poets equally with natural scientists. Students would be required to declaim in Latin. And they would inhabit a remote and sylvan academy accommodating only two hundred pupils. Cowley's interest in Hobbesian experimentalism is conjoined with Casaubonian elitism.

The ode, *To the Royal Society* (1667), ostensibly lauds a group dedicated to experimentalism, activism, and practicality, along with the new learning; however, Cowley's metaphors indicate his increased ambivalence toward these criteria. Nature has become a remote garden, accessible only to the inquisitive and courageous few who invade it to taste the fruit of knowledge. This figure is decidedly ambiguous, particularly in the year that brought *Paradise Lost* into print. And the comparison of the members of the society to Gideon's army emphasizes the militancy and the involvement necessary to battle for science in a time inimical to its aims.

With the publication of *Several Discourses by Way of Essays, in Verse and Prose*, in 1668, the year after his death, it is obvious that Cowley's withdrawal into the Surrey countryside led him to abandon his remaining interest in politics, the new science, public welfare, and secondary education. The theme of the *Discourses* is "the choice of life" or, as Cowley phrases it, "we are here to discourse, and to enquire what estate of Life does best seat us in the possession of" the "Liberty of a private man." This liberty is synonymous with Epicurean practices: one must remove himself from the active, political life, take up a solitary and unknown habitation in the garden, and please himself with intellectual activities. For Cowley, these activities consist to a great extent in reading and studying the ancient writers. As he quotes Cicero, Seneca, Horace, and their fellow pagans, Cowley plainly has approximated the elitism, if not the antiquarianism, of Casaubon; but his extolling the life of contemplation in opposition to that of involvement has the effect of using the classics to oppose the participation of educated men in public affairs:

Now because the soul of Man is not by its own Nature or observation furnisht with sufficient Materials to work upon; it is necessary for it to have continual recourse to Learning and Books for fresh supplies, so that the solitary life will grow indigent, and be ready to starve without them. . . . But this you'l say is work for the Learned, others are not capable either of the employments or divertisements that arrive from Letters; I know they are not; and therefore cannot much recommend Solitude to a man totally illiterate.

The implications of Cowley's apolitical and selfish use of the classics were not lost on John Evelyn, to whom Cowley dedicated "The Garden," the most avowedly Epicurean section of the *Discourses*. Evelyn could not have been much pleased by the piece. The idea of indulging a dilettante classicism at the expense of public service, he believed, was a dangerous doctrine to be preaching to Englishmen in the 1660s. Too many intelligent and educated men had sought country retreats: in the forties and fifties to escape the Civil Wars and Puritanical strictures and again in the sixties to avoid metropolitan riots, plagues, and fires. Evelyn saw clearly the political and national consequences if they continued to do so and if the contemplative life became idealized. In a pamphlet published in 1667, *Publick Employment and an Active Life Prefer'd to Solitude, and all its Appanages, by J. E. Esq.*, he declares that the Puritans' neglect of public business "had like to be the *Catastrophe* even of this our *Nation*" and goes on to say that the "Common-wealth . . . would fall to universal confusion and solitude indeed, without continual care and publick intendency." To support his argument Evelyn culls dozens of examples of civic dedication and its effects from ancient literature, praises Augustus as an active leader whose "excellent Government . . . rendred that age of his so happy above others," and remarks that those Roman rulers who gave up public responsibility for a life of retirement and ease became "subjects of Tragedy and Satyr."[17]

If Evelyn did not originate either his arguments or the use of historical analogies to illustrate present events, he did manage, in *Publick Employment*, to combine most of the beliefs that were to grow into the congeries of ideas associated with the new classicism. He also managed to disarm a greater threat to classical study than the combined Puritanical distrust of pagan learning, the disdain of Charles and his courtiers for the life of the mind, the growing reaction of educated men against the stultifying rigidity of schoolmaster classicism, and the self-isolation of scholars like Casaubon and Cowley. It was the conviction of the prestigious Edward Hyde, Lord Clarendon, that classical learning was essentially irrelevant to modern life.

Although he himself was a classical scholar of parts and a life-long devotee of ancient literature, Christian as well as pagan, Lord

17 John Evelyn, *Publick Employment and an Active Life* . . . (London, 1667), pp. 1–8, 11–12, 14. For the sentiments of Cowley's which may have provoked Evelyn's reply in the pamphlet see Abraham Cowley, *Essays, Plays and Sundry Verses*, ed. A. R. Waller (Cambridge, 1906), pp. 377–386, 394, 420–428.

Clarendon was chiefly a shrewd and realistic politician. He had attempted to refute Hobbes with scriptural authority and scholastic logic in *A Brief View and Survey of the Dangerous and Pernicious Errors to Church and State, In Mr. Hobbes's Book, Entitled The Leviathan* (1676); his experience had convinced him of the fallaciousness of ancient authority. Privately Clarendon continued to read the chronological speculations of Scaliger, Ussher, and Marsham, but he wrote in his essay, *Of the Reverence due to Antiquity*, that although the "Custom is so universal, amongst those who wrestle to support the Strength of every Opinion in Religion, to appeal to the Judgment and the Practice of the Primitive Times . . . yet there was never any Difficulty reconciled and determined by that Judicatory." It would seem—although the imperfect dating of his essays makes this conjectural to some extent—that Clarendon began with a standard confidence in the classics shared by those in his generation, found his trust shaken by the varying postures of Hobbes and Casaubon, and at last denied the applicability of all ancient literature because it was "dark and obscure." In *A Dialogue Concerning Education* he commented that Greek and Latin were "the Key to Knowledge" and proposed that a royal academy be established to propagate classical learning. But in *An Essay on an Active and Contemplative Life: And, Why the one should be preferred before the other,* and in the late *Of Humane Nature* (written after his fall from power, in 1668), Clarendon attacked the methods of the schoolmen, which snarled and perverted language and learning, and declared that "as we are liable to be misled in the forming our Practice of Judgment by the Rules and Measures of Antiquity, with reference to the civil and politick Actions of our Lives, so Antiquity will be as blind a Guide to us in Matters of Practice or Opinion relating to Religion." Despite his doubt of their usefulness, Clarendon did suggest that the classics perhaps were of some interest as records of human affairs, that they could be read in French or English translation without the pain of learning dead languages, and that reading increased wisdom.[18]

[18] See Edward Hyde, Earl of Clarendon, *A Brief View and Survey of the Dangerous and Pernicious Errors to Church and State, In Mr. Hobbes's Book, Entitled The Leviathan* (London, 1676), pp. 30–35, 67–69; *An Essay on an Active and Contemplative Life: And, Why the one should be preferred before the other* (Glasgow, 1765), pp. 52–53; *The Miscellaneous Works of the Right Honourable Edward, Earl of Clarendon,* 2d ed. (London, 1751), pp. 103–104, 218–240, 313–398.

Evelyn shared Clarendon's preference for the active before the contemplative life, but he also believed that to a considerable extent the political experience of the ancients, recorded in history, was a serviceable guide to the present. Evelyn's exemplary heroes from the past (Epaminondas, Themistocles, Lycurgus, Cato, and others) were admirable for their constructive roles in public affairs. He flatly insisted that the political arena was a highly suitable setting for the display of virtue and Christian conduct, and that there was no finer deed or career than "building some august Fabrick or Publick Work."[19]

By the close of the 1660s, therefore, the monistic attitude toward the classics which had characterized humanist education in the early century and had survived the hostility of the Puritans in mid-century was beginning to separate into distinctive schools of thought.[20] All of them more or less agreed that spiritual matters could not be authoritatively settled before classical tribunals, that attempts to justify political institutions on the basis of ancient ipse dixits were of doubtful merit, that the rote methods of learning promulgated by the schoolmen were disgusting, but that the classics did possess wisdom which moderns would do well to assimilate. As the theorists disputed, the poets of the sixties were using ancient history to embellish their panegyrics and dedications to the aristocracy, to add mythic dimensions of heroic idealism to their verse and plays, and finally, after 1665, to satirize and reprimand their ease-loving monarch. The audience for the poets was almost as small as for the classical theorists, being limited to literate, interested nobles and citizens who lived in or near London. John Evelyn and Anthony à Wood agreed from their differing perspectives that the Restoration aristocracy as a group was as ignorant of the classics as the vast majority of the townspeople.[21] The cultist aspects of classical knowledge, then, were pronounced in the sixties; and the literary composition that used classical referents—whether play, poem, sermon, or pamphlet—appealed largely to the elite rather than to the populace.

19 Evelyn, *Publick Employment*, pp. 78–82, 102.
20 For education before 1660, see Foster Watson, *The English Grammar Schools to 1660: Their Curriculum and Practice* (Cambridge, 1908); John Mulder, *The Temple of the Mind: Education and Literary Taste in Seventeenth-Century England* (New York, 1969), pp. 13–31.
21 See James R. Sutherland, *English Literature of the Late Seventeenth Century* (New York, 1969), p. 15; Anthony à Wood, "John Wilmot," in *Athenae Oxonienses* (1691–92).

In 1670 John Eachard's *The Grounds and Occasions of the Contempt of the Clergy and Religion* opened the decade with witty but severe blows at several previously sacrosanct targets. Asserting that the clergy were generally contemned, by gentry and common folk alike, Eachard pointed to the deficiencies of traditional classical education, criticizing its pedantry and lack of usefulness in the common business of life, as well as its snobbery and virtual commitment to penury of scores of young men otherwise better employed. Why, he asked, should "it be unavoidably necessary to keep lads to 16 or 17 years of age *in pure slavery to a few Latin or Greek words?*" Comenius' *Janua*, which Casaubon feared would destroy classical learning, Eachard characterized as a "fine game to cheat [a youth] into the undertaking of unreasonable burdens," like memorizing Latin terms for "all the instruments in his father's shop." Youths of mean station and "low and pitiful" parts were coerced into the schools by parental ambition and pedagogical vanity; there they served time until they were declared qualified to teach or preach, whereupon they spent the rest of their contemptible lives as dishonest clergy instead of as honest field hands. Eachard's solution was to make classical scholars only of those boys who possessed genuine ability, to give the others readings from the classics in translation, and to establish a community, if not social equality, by means of simple and good English among congregations where farmers and shepherds, plowmen and hedgemenders, king's commissioners and peace justices, listened together. Eachard wanted to eliminate false pedantry and at the same time to extend the benefits of ancient wisdom:

I am not sensible that I have said anything in disparagement of those two famous tongues, the Greek and Latin; there being much reason to value them beyond others, because the best of human learning has been delivered unto us in those languages. But he that worships them purely out of honor to Rome and Athens, having little or no respect to the usefulness and excellency of the books themselves, as many do —it is a sign he has a great esteem and reverence to antiquity; but I think him by no means comparable, for happiness, to him who catches frogs or hunts butterflies.

Eachard's version of a sensible and widespread classicism may not have revolutionized school practices. Dr. Busby continued to smack his pupils into the correct Greek accent as he had done since 1638 and was to do until his death in 1695. But the opinion gradually increased that the end of reading the classics was to gain a humane wisdom and that in many instances translations might serve as well as the originals. Obadiah Walker took up this refrain in *Of Education, especially of Young Gentlemen* (1673), and still later John Locke countenanced it in *Some Thoughts Concerning Reading and Study for a Gentleman.*[22]

The increased number of English translations of Greek and Latin masterpieces after the Restoration began to take on significant dimensions during the 1670s, although there was still hardly a classic in every British purse or pocket. The humanists had translated Greek works into Latin; before 1660 a significant number of Greek and Latin classics had made their way into English: Hobbes's Thucydides and Aristotle, John Ogilby's Virgil and Aesop, Evelyn's Lucretius and Epictetus, and Sprat's versification of Thucydides, to name but a few. In the sixties Ogilby added his *Iliad* and *Odyssey*; Hobbes continued to interest himself in Homer; and a sizable group of university classicists became aware of the profits to be made from sales of translations. By the mid-seventies Ogilby had been joined by Joshua Barnes, who began translating Greek tragedy and adapting Ctesias, and still later by Thomas Creech, Sir Roger L'Estrange, Laurence Echard, and John Ozell, among more illustrious and more obscure names. The availability of classical translations did much to make John Eachard's proposals feasible.

English drama also began to show more pronounced Greco–Roman interests in the late 1670s than before. The heroic modes brought back from France at the time of Charles's Restoration emphasized legendary or fabulous themes from the Orient, the Middle East, Iberia, and the Americas. Of course there were a few dramas treating Greek or Roman events—Dryden used Alexander the Great and Maximin in two plays—but Davenant, Boyle, and Howard preferred the Solymans, Pizarros, and Herods as their protagonists. It was not until about 1674, when Nathaniel Lee's

22 For a more traditionally oriented essay on educating children, see Henry Wotton, *An Essay on the Education of Children, in the First Rudiments of Learning, Together with a Narrative of what Knowledge, WILLIAM WOTTON, a Child six Years of Age, had attained unto, upon the Improvement of those Rudiments, in the Latin, Greek, and Hebrew Tongues* (London, 1753). Written in 1672, this document stresses the intellectual and cultural, as well as the behavioral, benefits of studying ancient languages even as it continues to emphasize etymological techniques. The young prodigy was that selfsame William Wotton who was later embroiled in the Phalaris controversy (see William Wotton, *Reflections upon Ancient and Modern Learning* [London, 1694]).

first play, *Nero*, appeared, that Greco–Roman tragedies came into their own. The delay was partly owing to the waning of the heroic drama early in the decade. The heroic ideal grew increasingly trite as its dramatic possibilities were exhausted and as the King proved himself unsusceptible to improvement through steady exposure to heroic models, and the disasters of the late sixties had further disillusioned the audiences of the time. Certain ominous events of 1673–74 prepared them psychologically for plays of a more somber hue which instructed them about the course of historical events while entertaining them with the exotic and flamboyant devices of the earlier heroic plays. The playwrights of the late seventies—Lee, Otway, Crowne, and of course Dryden—wrote a succession of classically inspired tragedies that made the next ten or fifteen years a period of dramatically intense concentration on Greco–Roman themes. From Otway's first play, *Alcibiades*, in 1675, playwrights went on to Augustus Caesar, Titus and Berenice, Vespasian, Alexander the Great and his loves, Mithridates, Theodosius, Lucius Junius Brutus, Caligula, and many others. We have only to see Dryden's development of interest beginning in 1677 with *All for Love* and continuing to *Cleomenes* in 1692 to gain some sense of the importance of the classics in stimulating drama and of the drama in popularizing ancient history. The connection of these plays to the increasingly dominant rationale of neoclassicism is implicit in Dryden's Antony, who perfectly illustrates Evelyn's maxim that the Roman ruler who gave up public duty for retirement and ease was a fit subject for tragedy—or for satire.

In the first half of the 1680s both tragic and satiric uses of classical sources were popular; larger numbers of pamphlet buyers and playgoers were absorbing the didactic results of neoclassical stress on history teaching by example. The sequence of satires by Dryden in 1681–82 makes the most subtle and imaginative use of the classics: *Mac Flecknoe* cleverly manipulates material from Livy and Virgil; *The Medall* incorporates elements from Diodorus Siculus and Pliny; and the serious verse essay, *Religio Laici*, openly appeals to Plutarch, Seneca, and Cicero for standards. Among the tragic plays of the time, Otway's *Venice Preserved* (1682) and Rochester's *Valentinian* (acted in 1684 at court, published in 1685) combine a satiric contrast between present culture and Roman glory with a tragic irony that assumes the destructive parallels between the respective courses of Roman and of English history.[23] The art of translation was steadily improving as the classics in English dress were read by more and more people. Roscommon's, Creech's, and Oldham's translations of Horace, Lucretius, Ovid, and others were triumphantly peaked by Dryden's *Sylvæ* in 1685, with a preface that was the most important justification of the classics so far produced by a popular writer. The continued use of classical analogies for honorific purposes was typified by Dryden's poems on the death of Charles and the birth of James's son, while Samuel Johnson's *Julian* pamphlets against James extended the technique of vilifying by classical parallels.

The most prophetic development in the use of the classics for applicable wisdom in the 1680s, however, was the pronounced bifurcation of its lessons. By the mid-eighties classicists in general were agreed that the great virtue of ancient learning was that it threw light on eternal human nature and provided patterns of experience, individual and collective, which might guide both private and public behavior. The belief that ancient history was a valuable mine of political experience informed the theories expounded in Algernon Sidney's *Discourses Concerning Government* (1680) and Henry Neville's *Plato Redivivus* (1681). These, and subsequent explorations of political systems—notably Walter Moyle's *Essays*, which were not published until 1726—affected the emerging polity after William and Mary ascended the throne and the British constitution came to resemble the polities envisioned by Plato, Aristotle, Polybius, and their disciples.[24] In a very basic way, the classical theory of balanced government as it was embodied in British politics provided the atmosphere in which John Bull was born.

While the public application of ancient wisdom was taking a direct and single course, the private or ethical use was still being debated. Sir William Temple, who had withdrawn to his gardens at Moor Park in 1681, produced a series of essays that extolled the contemplative life with a persuasiveness that Cowley, as a scholarly recluse, could not command. Temple knew of the Epicurean controversy in the sixties; he was surely acquainted with the writings of Casaubon, Cowley, Evelyn, and Clarendon on the issue.

23 Andrew Marvell had already polished this method of ironic contrasts in his *Last Instructions to a Painter* (1667), which is the prototype not only of the mock-heroic but of the satiric heroic couplets which Dryden popularized in the 1680s. For the neoclassical use of historical analogies, see Johnson, *Formation of English Neo-Classical Thought*, chap. 2.

24 Zera S. Fink, *The Classical Republicans* (Evanston, Ill., 1945).

Nevertheless, Temple argued, in his essay *Upon the Gardens of Epicurus; or, Of Gardening, in the Year 1685*, that despite the urges of ambition and riches the best life was that of withdrawal and contemplation. Since his own diplomatic career had been just short of brilliant and he was still sought after by William III, Temple's Epicurean arguments were especially forceful. They threatened once again to substitute a selfish, dilettantish use of classical learning for private purposes in place of a dedication to public benefits.

Temple was attacked by many opponents, perhaps most sharply by Gilbert Burnet in his *History*: "He was a corrupter of all that came near him. And he delivered himself up wholly to study, ease, and pleasure."[25] But the most thorough refutation of Temple's hermeneutic classicism is to be found in John Evelyn's *The History of Religion*. Although this work was not published until the nineteenth cenutry, it reveals the arguments used against Temple which established a countersystem of opinions in later neoclassical literature. As early as 1667 Evelyn criticized Epicurean ethics in his *Publick Employment* essay, where he defined the "hero" in politically and morally active terms. The man who "conflicts with the regnant *Vices* and overcome[s]," said Evelyn, is a hero "as surely as the conqueror of armies, defender of his country, and freer of the oppressed." In the section of *The History of Religion* entitled "Christianity Contrasted with Other Religions," Evelyn elaborated upon this view. He declared Christians superior in heroism to all the vaunted and admired pagans of antiquity: Socrates, Alcibiades, Trajan, Cato, and the rest. He described the valor of faith, praised the Christian who entered public affairs, and generally equated Christianity with altruistic service in contrast with the egotistic passivity of the contemplative man.[26] In subsequent years Evelyn's Christian hero served as one alternative for neoclassicists like Steele, who found the gentlemanly Epicurean overly pagan, or like Swift, who questioned the political and institutional consequences of withdrawal.

In the last decade of the century the essential tenets of the new classicism were plainly embodied in major events. The classics in

[25] See Jonathan Swift, *Prose Works*, ed. Temple Scott (London, 1898–1908), X, 344–345. Swift commented marginally that "Sir William Temple was a man of virtue, to which Burnet was a stranger."

[26] John Evelyn, *The History of Religion. A Rational Account of the True Religion. By John Evelyn. Now First Published* (London, 1850), II, 170–179, 213–271. See also Evelyn, *Publick Employment*, p. 40.

translation received a final seal of approval when Dryden published his *Satires* (1693), containing the classical models for future times: Juvenal and Persius. The *Third Miscellany* added Ovid; the translation of Virgil (1697) provided an English verse *Aeneid*; and the *Fables* (1700) turned the century with more translations of Ovid and Homer. Other English translations by Dryden's colleagues included L'Estrange's *Aesop*, while Tonson was urging a bright young classicist at Oxford—Joseph Addison—to translate Herodotus and Plato. The old scholastic insistence on reading works in the original tongues was significantly modified by the 1690s, when excellent and ingenious translations by some truly creative poets were broadening the appeal of the ancients to modern readers.

The event of the first Boyle sermons also indicated how far from humanist criteria the new classicists had come. The sermons were delivered by Richard Bentley, the most prestigious classicist of the day, who conferred with Sir Isaac Newton and John Evelyn in writing his synthesis of all wisdom, past and present, scientific and revealed, Christian and pagan, "to demonstrate the superiority of Christianity." Superficially like the polymathic syntheses, Bentley's sermons were the last great attempt to use the classics in the service of Christianity (though they were far from the last such efforts); but Bentley succeeded in demonstrating the inferiority of Epicurus, Cato, Seneca, and Plato to divine revelation, and the overall effect of his work was to place the classics in a distinctly separate category from Scripture. The neoclassicist thenceforth valued the pagans for their worldly wisdom but sought the Scriptures in matters of the supramundane. Despite the efforts of Stillingfleet and Newton to maintain a fusion between secular and religious historical data in their chronological exercises, the historical and the biblical became dichotomous, though not contradictory. Swift's *Sermon on the Excellency of Christianity* is a typical specimen of how the relationship operated.

If the classics were parted from religion, however, they were wedded even more closely to politics, as the formation of the Kit-Cat Club implied. The membership of literary-political clubs in the nineties suggests how widely diverse were the men brought together by a mutual interest in letters and public affairs. Noblemen, physicians, cits, printers, M.P.'s, scholars, merchants, and schoolmasters commingled. They were all literate, with uneven degrees of classical expertise; but they shared some common assumptions derived from Florus, Livy, Plutarch, and Nepos about events in time, political history, and proper civic conduct. Their fellowship was one indication of how diffused classical precepts were helping to mold the social and political structures that would guide Georgian culture.[27]

By the end of the century the traditional grammar schools had changed very little. Conservative schoolmasters maintained the rote procedures that Eachard had objected to thirty years before and that Steele would assail ten years later.[28] The founding of new schools, however, including Dissenting academies, permitted experimentation, and even the sons of printers and bricklayers were able to learn the classics in translation. Furthermore, the universities began to change by replacing declamations and lectures with the tutorial. Left on their own to study Greek and Latin, young students might become savants, dilettantes, or ignoramuses in the classics. Fielding's diatribe composed forty years afterward showed the ignoramuses gaining ground, but the savants remained at about the same number and the gentlemen classicists increased, having Temple as their ideal.

Concomitantly, antiquarianism as such came to be more and more despised. The dryasdust pedant was scorned both for his narrowness of intellect and for his refusal to be concerned with worldly matters. The Phalaris controversy epitomized the way in which young men who were to become statesmen, peers, bishops, and deans within the next twenty years were secularizing the classics for social and cultural, as well as political, purposes. They were combining learning and scholarship with the gentlemanly ideal called *sprezzatura* a century earlier but *sophrosyne* in their day; and if that meant labeling the most eminent classicist of the era a pedantic fool, they were willing. Even those who sought to extend the charismatic appeal of the classics to common—not to say vulgar—consumers were sometimes accused of pedantry. John Dunton and Charles Gildon were skewered with their cohorts of the Athenian Society in Settle's *The Athenian Comedy*; surely the democratization of the classics could not be more ludicrously affirmed than by casting John Dunton as a fin-de-siècle Casaubon.

[27] The argument about a standing army, which went on from 1688 to 1714 and after, was a particular issue involving military policy in which classical analogies were furnished pro and con by a strange assortment of writers: Defoe, Moyle, Prior, Swift, Addison, Steele, and so on.

[28] See W. A. L. Vincent, *The Grammar Schools: Their Continuing Tradition, 1660–1715* (London, 1969).

The reign of Anne saw the young men of the nineties growing into formidable Augustan maturity and continuing to perfect the classical assumptions agreed upon earlier. The ties of many works composed between 1700 and 1710 to precedent attitudes are obvious: *Of Contests and Dissentions in Athens and Rome, The Christian Hero, The Sentiments of a Church of England Man*— these and other works contain the same dominant themes that had been current in the time of William and Mary. And a glance at the chief works published during Anne's last four years—*The Spectator, Characteristicks, The Examiner, Cato*—reveals that the use of the classics for public edification and private exempla was now firmly established in its popular variations. The extent of popularity may also be judged by observing the audiences to whom Addison, Steele, Shaftesbury, and Swift addressed themselves: a variegated group quite unlike the noble readers to whom Davenant, Dryden, and Howard appealed.

Despite their widened circulation through translations, fictional adaptations and allusions, prose and verse propaganda, and sermons, and despite the prevalence of the neoclassical public and personal rationales, there never was a universal enthusiasm for the classics in England. Addison tried as hard to make the classics fashionable as he did morality: he asserted the love of Latin "among our common people" and love of Greek "in the fashionable world," lovingly explicated his Greek and Latin mottoes, and told anecdotes about rural congregations that based their churchgoing on how much Latin the parson could incorporate into his sermon. Addison also fair-sexed it constantly to popularize Greco–Roman plays and to flatter the reader into loving ancient history and culture.[29] Yet, when his *Cato* was acted in 1713, many of the playgoers were forced to buy Theobald's reader's digest of Roman history to find out who Cato and Caesar were.

In *The History of John Bull* pamphlets, printed in 1712, Arbuthnot sketched the national character of England in terms surprisingly close to those of Dryden in earlier days and to those of Goldsmith in later days. John Bull, said his creator, was "an honest plain-dealing Fellow, Cholerick, Bold, and of a very unconstant Temper . . . very apt to quarrel with his best Friends. . . . his Spirits rose and fell with the Weather-glass, but no Man alive was

---

[29] *Spectator*, I, 392, 405; II, 359–60; III, 55. Compare Addison's earlier views, penned while he was studying at Oxford, in *A Discourse on Ancient and Modern Learning* (London, 1739).

more careless, in looking into his Accounts, or more cheated. . . . a Boon-Companion, loving his Bottle and his Diversion." After being gulled and cheated for years by Lewis Baboon, Nicholas Frog, and Humphrey Hocus, at last John Bull, who had formerly relied on oaths and a stout oaken cudgel to deal with his enemies, discovered a new way of responding to Dutch treats and French tricks:

John receiv'd this with a good deal of *Sang froid*; *Transeat* (quoth John) *cum caeteris erroribus*: He was now at his Ease; he saw he could make a very good Bargain for himself, and a very safe one for other Folks. My Shirt (quoth he) is near me, but my Skin is nearer. . . . Though John Bull has not read your Aristotles, Plato's, and Machiavels, he can see as far into a Millstone as another: With that *John* began to chuckle and laugh, till he was like to burst his Sides.[30]

John Bull's bluff reliance on proverbial wisdom is given an ironic twist by his quoting Horace even as he disparages the need of classical learning. Whether or not it was a Latin scrap from some forgotten sermon, John's ancient maxim had become a part of his total outlook.

If the common Englishman in 1714 was unaware of the extent to which his society had been formed through the influence of the classics during the preceding half century, his ignorance in no way lessened that influence. English government, politics, military affairs, school curricula, literature, popular entertainment, and manners all bore the imprint of Greek and Roman models. If comparatively few Englishmen could read the languages containing the ancient wisdom that had been transmuted into modern practices, and if the "republic of letters" remained a glossocracy, nevertheless the nation of shopkeepers had absorbed many an ancient aphorism and considered it "common sense." Had he but known it, honest John Bull would have been quite startled at how greatly his ability to see into a millstone had been determined by the views of his betters—Jonathan Bull, Esquire; Sir Jonathan; Dr. Bull; and My Lord Bull—and how greatly their views depended upon the Aristotles and the Platos.

[30] John Arbuthnot, *The History of John Bull*, ed. Herman Teerink (Paris, 1925), pp. 239–240.

II

THE LIMITS
OF HISTORICAL VERACITY IN
NEOCLASSICAL DRAMA

John Loftis
Professor of English, Stanford University

Perhaps no part of the *Poetics* had more important consequences
for the neoclassical theory of literature than that in which Aristotle explained, in a famous paradox, that poetry has more truth
in it than history, at least in the specialized sense that it is more
general in its application to human affairs than history, which is
limited to the specific and thus idiosyncratic occurrences that are
its subject. In writing about imaginary individuals, poets can
achieve a kind of universality, since—as Samuel Johnson never
tired of saying—men are the same in all places and times. Many of
the central attitudes and doctrines of neoclassicism are corollaries
of Aristotle's discrimination between the province of history and
the province of poetry: the circumscribed conception of originality in literary composition, for example, and the pervasive doctrine of decorum in characterization, so influential in shaping
notions of genre in Restoration and early eighteenth-century drama. Extending Aristotle's argument further than he took it, a
theorist might assert that a poet, if he were completely successful
in assimilating his materials to a universal theme, would produce
a work that lacked a historical dimension.

In fact, the setting in time and place is nearly always apparent
and nearly always functional in determining the meaning of a

work. Literature and literary criticism as well are time bound. And I cannot wish it otherwise. For literature in its mixed nature —part art, part documentary record—provides the emotional dimension of the past; it is a record not so much of the great events of the past as of what men thought about them: the human response to them, the interpretation of them in a given point in time and space.

The function of literature as historical record can be illustrated, I think, even in the writings of the neoclassical formalist critics who were most insistent that the poet concern himself with the universal. The ancients, Thomas Rymer wrote in *The Tragedies of the Last Age* (1677), "found that *History*, grosly taken, was neither proper to *instruct*, nor apt to *please*; and therefore they would not trust History for their examples, but refin'd upon the History; and thence contriv'd something more *philosophical*, and more *accurate* than History." [1] Still Rymer, like René Rapin before him, revealed the moment in time in which he was writing, deducing, for example, the doctrine of decorum in characterization from the assumption that the seventeenth-century conception of the hierarchical ordering of society was valid for all times and all places. He wrote a royalist form of literary criticism, objecting on principle to the portrayal of dramatic characters in a manner he deemed inappropriate to their social rank; one of the reasons his criticism now seems so wide of the mark lies in the fact that we cannot accept the social and political assumptions on which it was based. Certainly Dryden found Rymer's arguments persuasive, even if he did write, though not publish, a rejoinder to Rymer. In several of Dryden's serious plays, written before Rymer's essays were published as well as after, there is an imposition of European models of government and society, and of conceptions of decorum, on non-European cultures.

Any consideration of historical veracity in neoclassical drama must take into account the contemporary literary theory and the progressive modification of it. There is steadily a tension, more obvious in comedy than in tragedy, between the claims of accuracy in portrayal of English life and the demands of a sophisticated body of literary theory. The tension affected both the drama and the theory of drama. One of the disruptive elements in neoclassicism as an operational force in the eighteenth century

[1] Curt A. Zimansky, ed., *The Critical Works of Thomas Rymer* (New Haven, 1956), p. 23.

was, I think, an intensified concern for reportorial accuracy, as well as a change in the social reality to be reported.

Here I shall examine the relationship between drama and the contemporary life that, directly or indirectly, provided its subject, considering in turn the uses of drama in the study of history and the uses of history in the study of drama. Because I must be brief, I shall attempt at the outset to formulate the questions to which I shall suggest modes of approach. Above all, I shall seek to avoid a circular argument, that is, the uncritical acceptance of the drama as a record of the society that produced it or, conversely, of the nonliterary record of that society as an infallible guide to the interpretation of the drama. More specifically, I shall examine the means that are available, in the study of drama, for separating literary artifice from the useful historical evidence found in the observation of society.

What kind of valid historical information, if any, can we expect the drama to yield? Conversely, what is the usefulness of the history of England to the student of drama? What changes in social and political organization conditioned the development of drama? What changes occurred between, say, the reigns of Charles II and George II in the conception of the dramatist's obligation to historical veracity? And what were the consequences of those changes for the drama and for the neoclassical theory of drama? It goes without saying that comprehensive answers to these questions would require a series of volumes. I can merely address myself to the problems of method they present. Several of the problems were recently called to my attention by a historian of English social structure, Peter Laslett, to whose conversations and writings I gratefully acknowledge an obligation. I shall later make reference to some of the preliminary findings he is about to announce from the researches of the Cambridge Group for the History of Population and Social Structure.

In the preface to *Historia Histrionica* (1699), James Wright described one of the uses of the drama:

Old Plays will be always Read by the *Curious*, if it were only to discover the Manners and Behaviour of several ages; and how they alter'd. For Plays are exactly like *Portraits* Drawn in the Garb and Fashion of the time when Painted. You see one habit in the time of King *Charles I.* another quite different from that, both for Men and Women, in Queen *Elizabeths* time; another under *Henry* the Eighth

different from both; and so backward all various. And in the several
Fashions of Behaviour and Conversation, there is as much Mutability
as in that of Cloaths.

The perennial claim that drama is history, more precisely social
history, is one that falls within the limits of almost self-evident
validity. Yet there are limits to the usefulness of drama as a record
of society, narrower limits than are sometimes acknowledged,
and the failure to acknowledge and describe them can render
suspect the validity of a potentially important body of historical
information. Far from wishing to discredit literary evidence as a
source of historical information, I hope rather to help make it
usable by limiting the claims made for it and by describing some
of the methodological difficulties inherent in its employment.

We must differentiate at once between the permanent in human experience, which is not the subject of history because it
does not change, and the aspects of experience which do indeed
change. The coexistence in a play of strict honesty in the depiction of human nature with limited honesty in the depiction of the
contemporary scene provides a common difficulty, one that is
apparent in Restoration drama. The best Restoration comedies,
those, say, by Etherege, Wycherley, Congreve, and Vanbrugh,
carry in the colloquial idiom of their dialogue and in their determined avoidance of emotional cant an impression of authenticity.
If the dramatists were so honest in analyzing the emotional ambiguities of courtship, we reason, ambiguities that we know are
faithfully represented because we have experienced them, then
the dramatists must have been similarly honest in representing
the society they saw about them. The conclusion may be justified
—but how do we know that it is? How do we know that Restoration comedy does not portray, in Charles Lamb's phrase, "a
utopia of gallantry," a fantasy land having no close relationship
to any society that ever existed?

The problem of verifying, or more precisely of correcting, the
dramatist's view of society is troublesome, but it is not hopeless.
Despite the difficulties and dangers in using literary evidence for
social history, the potential value of that evidence cannot be
ignored. Neoclassical drama provides a voluminous record of society written by intelligent and well-informed men. The comic
dramatist does nothing at all, John Dennis wrote in reference to
Molière, "if he does not draw the Pictures of his Contempo-

raries." [2] Restoration and eighteenth-century comedy includes a large body of conversation, much of it directed to what the dramatists saw about them and only tangentially conditioned by the dramatic medium. Both comedy and tragedy turn on themes that represent judgments about contemporary life. Yet methodological difficulties need to be clarified, and so do problems of objectives.

Before turning to details, may I suggest several modes of approach to the relevant problems of method and objective:

1. Comparison of the record of society provided by dramatists with the evidence made available by subsequent historical research, including the demographical research of the twentieth century.

2. Comparison of that record with comments on it made by the dramatists' own contemporaries.

3. Formulation of the social and political assumptions of the dramatists, collectively and individually, which conditioned their interpretation of what they saw about them.

4. Formulation of the literary theory and conventions, and the progressive changes in them, within which the dramatists wrote their plays.

The resourcefulness of modern students of social and demographic history—I refer specifically to Peter Laslett and his associates at Cambridge University—has yielded information even about that most elusive of subjects, the history of sexual permissiveness. That the sexual attitudes controlling Restoration comedy are unrepresentative of those of the nation at large in the later seventeenth century has often been noted: Professor Miner has said as much in one of the best critical discussions of the subject.[3] How unrepresentative they are has recently been suggested in statistical detail. The comedies of Etherege and of most of the other important Restoration dramatists depict a society of sexual freedom, for men under a very liberal code, and for women as well except for young true wits like Harriet in *The Man of Mode*, who are the matrimonial prizes to be carried off by the likes of Dorimant. Restoration playwrights are rarely pornographic; except perhaps for Aphra Behn and later Colley Cibber, they avoid

[2] *Remarks on a Play, Call'd, The Conscious Lovers, a Comedy*, in John Dennis, *Critical Works*, ed. E. N. Hooker (Baltimore, 1939–1943), II, 259.

[3] *Restoration Dramatists*, ed. Earl Miner (Englewood Cliffs, N. J., 1966), pp. 2–8.

lascivious titillation by merely alluding to and not dramatizing sexual adventure. Yet they frequently assume extramarital sexual experience, for men if not for all women, as a condition of life; and certainly, as Jeremy Collier charged at the end of the century, they are ready enough to forgive the licentiousness of their male characters, to depict libertines appreciatively and provide rich heiresses for them at play's end. Yet Peter Laslett's study suggests that there was in fact less sexual license in Restoration England than in almost any other period of English history.

Laslett's evidence is largely derived from records of illegitimacy, based on ratios of births out of wedlock to total number of births. Using figures derived from parish records, where illegitimacy was customarily noted, Laslett concludes that bastardy rates in Restoration England were at a lower level than in most of the periods for which data are available.[4] To be sure, illegitimacy ratios for the peerage are somewhat higher than those for the country at large, though not strikingly so.[5] Given the social orientation of Restoration drama, the peerage figures have more relevance here. They may be higher merely because illegitimacy, of considerable importance in property settlements, was more carefully recorded for noble families. Neither set of figures, however, is consistent with the impression conveyed by an uncritical reading of Restoration drama that the age was one of libertinage. Apparently John Evelyn and Daniel Defoe were more representative of the sexual mores of the later seventeenth century than were Samuel Pepys and the Earl of Rochester or the comedies of Etherege, Dryden, and Wycherley.

The disparity between historical fact, as suggested by the statistical tables on illegitimacy, and social conduct as revealed by the drama cautions against the uncritical use of literary evidence, but it does not, I think, invalidate that evidence. Restoration comedy began as a courtiers' drama, a coterie drama directed to the tastes of the King and the noblemen and gentlemen surrounding him, a group so small as to be statistically insignificant. Charles II's sexual behavior is scarcely debatable, nor for that matter is the Duke of Buckingham's, the Earl of Rochester's, Sir Charles Sedley's, and

[4] Peter Laslett's statistical tables are published in the French translation of his book *The World We Have Lost* (New York, 1966), under the title, *Un monde que nous avons perdu* (Paris, 1969), p. 146.

[5] See Thomas Hollingsworth, "The Demography of the British Peerage," *Supplement to Population Studies*, XVIII (1964). Reference from Peter Laslett.

Samuel Pepys's, to name but a few conspicuous members of the theater audience. The records of bastardy, in short, merely provide an added dimension to what we have known all along, that Restoration comedy gives only a partial and selective view of English life.

Here is but one among many possible illustrations of the usefulness of demographic research in deterring unwarranted generalizations based on the dramatists' portrait of society. The historians of population can save us from other, perhaps more subtle, misapprehensions about the reliability of literary evidence, as, for example, on the age at which young women were married. Because we all remember Shakespeare's Juliet, and because we occasionally encounter other girls who married in their early teens, we assume that marriage in extreme youth, for women at least, was not uncommon. Yet the firm evidence of marriage licenses reveals that early weddings were rare indeed,[6] that brides in England, if not in the Italy of *Romeo and Juliet*, were as a rule older than twentieth-century brides. Indeed, in the totality of Renaissance and Restoration drama, the number of very young brides is not large. The detail, in itself unimportant, points to a conclusion worth making: reliable historical conclusions cannot be drawn from uncorroborated literary evidence that is narrowly based. Still, the dramatists' observations on what they saw around them and the conclusions of modern historians are mutually enlightening.

One of the liveliest topics in recent debates among social historians has been social mobility, a subject that is central to Restoration and early eighteenth-century comedy. Preoccupation with rank and status, as in the writings of, say, Wycherley, Vanbrugh, and Steele, is a distinguishing quality of the comedy of manners, a dramatic form that is concerned above all with social relationships, between classes as well as between individuals. In fact, the individuals are frequently intended to represent the classes, of status or of occupation, to which they belong. The dynamics of the social and financial change that produced the tensions animating the rivalries portrayed by the dramatists are now better understood, thanks to social historians, though many uncertainties remain. Professor Lawrence Stone, for example, has described in statistical detail "the inflation of honours" that preceded the Civil War; the large expansion in the numbers of titled

[6] Laslett, *The World We Have Lost*, p. 83.

persons stemmed in part from the selling of titles to raise money for the crown.[7] The consequences of all this are reflected in the prominence of foolish knights, such characters as Dryden's Sir Martin Mar-all, in early Restoration comedy. The loss of prestige in the rank is pointed out by Dapperwit in Wycherley's *Love in a Wood* (II.i): "your true wit despises the title of Poet, as much as your true gentleman the title of Knight; for as a man may be a Knight and no Gentleman, so a man may be a Poet and no Wit." We are easily convinced of the truth of his remark as we observe Sir Simon Addleplot in the play.

In an analysis of social mobility in sixteenth- and seventeenth-century England,[8] which is comprehensively documented in non-literary sources, Professor Stone makes no reference to the drama. Much of what he says, however, supplements and often corroborates observations made by dramatic characters. Compare, for example, Professor Stone's comment on the rise in status of professional men and businessmen with a famous statement on a related subject by Mr. Sealand of Steele's *The Conscious Lovers*. The twentieth-century historian describes a structural change in society as

the rise of the commercial and professional classes in numbers and wealth, and their consequent acquisition both of a share in political decision-making and of social recognition. . . .

Along with their admission to the political nation went a rise in their social status. There was a slow but steady shift of attitudes on the part of the landed classes, a growing recognition that the previously anomalous occupational categories [merchants, lawyers, clergy, and administrators] formed a series of semi-independent and parallel status hierarchies.[9]

The eighteenth-century dramatic character (IV.ii) asserts that

we Merchants are a Species of Gentry, that have grown into the World this last Century, and are as honourable, and almost as useful, as you landed Folks, that have always thought yourselves so much above us.

Professor Stone helps us to believe what Steele's normative character says; Steele helps us to understand the personal and emo-

[7] Lawrence Stone, "The Inflation of Honours," *Past and Present*, no. 14 (Nov. 1958), pp. 45–70.

[8] Lawrence Stone, "Social Mobility in England, 1500–1700," *Past and Present*, no. 33 (April 1966), pp. 16–55.

[9] *Ibid.*, pp. 52–53.

tional consequences of the changes that are the subject of the modern analysis. Mr. Sealand's boastful remark was not after all unprovoked.

The search for corrective or validating evidence is not limited to twentieth-century investigations. Neoclassical drama was written against a background of critical commentary. The responses evoked by the drama from contemporary critics, some of whom forthrightly described "distortions" of the social realities the dramatists purported to represent, provide at once a source for social history and a check on present-day assumptions about historical veracity in the drama. Because the body of contemporary commentary on neoclassical drama is very much larger than that on English drama in any earlier period, we can compare our own response to the plays with those of the first audiences as it is impossible to do, say, with Renaissance drama.

In reading dramatic criticism, as in reading the plays themselves, one must take into account the prejudices of the writer and the literary strategies—raillery, hyperbole, satire—he employs. Jeremy Collier, for example, in his famous polemic of 1698 repeatedly censures dramatists for distorted representations of occupational groups and social classes such as clergymen, merchants, lords, and squires. Because he is both voluminous and specific, Collier provides information about the distance between drama and social reality. Yet the interpretation of his comments requires an allowance for his own bias, imperceptiveness, and special purpose. In his denunciation of Vanbrugh's *The Relapse*, to illustrate, he insists that the country squire of the play, Sir Tunbelley Clumsey, is not at all representative of his class in real life: "This Gentleman the *Poet* makes a *Justice* of *Peace*, and a *Deputy Lieutenant*, and seats him fifty Miles from *London*: But by his Character you would take him for one of *Hercules*'s Monsters, or some Gyant in *Guy* of *Warwick*."[10] How, we ask in wonderment, could even so fanatical a critic as Collier have failed to recognize that Vanbrugh had employed broad stage caricature in the service of satire? And yet Collier, his critical obtuseness notwithstanding, in the long paragraph devoted to Sir Tunbelley and his dealings with Lord Foppington suggests, even while denouncing Vanbrugh, the relationships between the squirearchy and the

[10] Jeremy Collier, *A Short View of the Immorality and Profaneness of the English Stage* (London, 1698), p. 215.

nobility, a subject that has recently been of intense interest to social historians.

A better example of the usefulness of criticism as a criterion of historical veracity is provided by the comment on Etherege's characters in *The Man of Mode*. It leaves little doubt, I think, that to contemporary observers the characters seemed to represent, no doubt with literary heightening, the exclusive society in which court wits were the principal figures. Dryden, who wrote the epilogue to the play, thought fit to include in it a disclaimer that Etherege, in his title character, had any one person in view. "Yet none Sir *Fopling* him, or him can call," Dryden wrote. "He's Knight o' th' Shire, and represents ye all." Indeed, one hostile critic, Captain Alexander Radcliffe, isolating as a special fault the close correspondence between the dialogue in Etherege's comedies and the conversation he heard about him, censured Etherege

> for writing superfine,
> With words correct in every Line:
> And one that does presume to say,
> A Plot's too gross for any Play:
> Comedy should be clean and neat,
> As Gentlemen do talk and eat.
> So what he writes is but Translation,
> From Dog and Pa[r]tridge conversation.[11]

In other words, the plays lack originality of contrivance and rely for effect merely on a faithful rendering, with stylistic improvement, of the conversation of town gallants at the fashionable Dog and Partridge Tavern. In the face of this kind of contemporary testimony, we may ask, can the social historian afford to ignore Restoration comedy?

Some members of the early audiences of *The Man of Mode* identified characters with prominent persons. Peter Killigrew, brother of the leader of the King's Company, reported in a letter written just three days after the first performance the "generall opinion" that Sir Fopling represented "Mr. Villiers, L⁽ᵈ⁾ Grandisons eldest son," and that Dorimant represented the famous Duke of Monmouth.[12] The latter conjecture would, to say the least,

[11] *News from Hell*, in *The Ramble* (1682), p. 5. Quoted from H. F. B. Brett-Smith, ed., *The Dramatic Works of Sir George Etherege* (Oxford, 1927), I, lxx.
[12] Joseph Spence, *Observations, Anecdotes, and Characters of Books and Men*, ed. James M. Osborn (Oxford, 1966), II, 638.

seem improbable, and in any event it is contradicted by the reports of others, notably John Dennis. Dennis's remarks repay quotation, not for their literal accuracy (for Dryden's denial of specific correspondences with living persons seems accurate), but for the general impression they convey of a resemblance between Etherege's characters and the court wits:

Now I remember very well, that upon the first acting this Comedy, it was generally believed to be an agreeable Representation of the Persons of Condition of both Sexes, both in Court and Town; and that all the World was charm'd with *Dorimont*; and that it was unanimously agreed, that he had in him several of the Qualities of *Wilmot* Earl of *Rochester*, as, his Wit, his Spirit, his amorous Temper, the Charms that he had for the fair Sex, his Falsehood, and his Inconstancy; the agreeable Manner of his chiding his Servants, which the late Bishop of *Salisbury* takes Notice of in his Life; and lastly, his repeating, on every Occasion, the Verses of *Waller*, for whom that noble Lord had a very particular Esteem. . . .

Now, as several of the Qualities in *Dorimont*'s Character were taken from that Earl of *Rochester*, so they who were acquainted with the late Sir *Fleetwood Shepherd*, know very well, that not a little of that Gentleman's Character is to be found in Medley.[13]

This testimony of a contemporary (Dennis was born in 1657), the more plausible because of its specifics, is useful in assessing the historical veracity of the play, whatever may have been Etherege's intentions in writing it. Dennis obviously thought of *The Man of Mode* as a faithful representation, within the conventions and limitations of dramatic form, of the life, not of a large number of Englishmen, but of the very small group that had given a distinctive cast to Restoration literature and society.

Dennis admired *The Man of Mode* and was seemingly untroubled by the sexual permissiveness implied in the authorial approval of Dorimant's conduct of life. Although insisting that Sir Fopling is a cautionary figure intended to arouse aversion, an opinion that is scarcely debatable, Dennis refrains from so describing Dorimant, defending him rather by historical reference to the easy morality of Restoration courtiers. Yet even in Restoration drama there is dissent from the insouciant acceptance of sexual indulgence and from the habits of mind by which it was

[13] *A Defence of Sir Fopling Flutter*, in Dennis, *Critical Works*, ed. Hooker, II, 248–249.

rationalized. The permissive attitude of the King and the court wits dominated Restoration comedy, though not to the exclusion of contrary opinion. A dissenting comment on the sexual license, embodied in a successful play, will exemplify the usefulness of the drama for the historian of society and of thought.

An organizing principle of *The Man of Mode* is the love chase or, perhaps more accurately, the sexual chase; in Dorimant's courtship (though not in Young Bellair's) lust excludes affection except perhaps for Harriet. A modern psychologist would call Dorimant a Don Juan, that is, a predatory lover, seeking a variety of sexual gratification as well as pleasure in his triumphs from which sadism is not totally absent. Only a few months before the appearance of *The Man of Mode*, but after the stage type that Dorimant represented had been firmly established and five months after Wycherley had provided in Horner a classic—and diabolical —exemplar of it, the first important rendering of the Don Juan legend in English had appeared in Thomas Shadwell's *The Libertine*. Shadwell stands apart from other leading Restoration dramatists not only in the breadth of his social sympathies, but also, as *The Libertine* and other works reveal, in his moral judgments.

If *The Libertine* includes in its depiction of the insatiate lust of an unprincipled adventurer and even in its episodes much that is familiar in the Don Juan legend, the texture of the play is distinctive to Shadwell. *The Libertine* seems to embody Shadwell's response to contemporary drama and to the life of the court wits who were its subjects. His Don Juan is more vicious, more aggressively evil, than any other well-known representative of the tradition;[14] the extent of his depravity, as well as that of his two constant companions, makes his sin something more than primarily sexual wrongdoing. Most Don Juans kill only as required by the exigencies of their love intrigues; the English Don John kills as well for profit and even for sadistic pleasure. Wholesale murder, including parricide to enable him to succeed to his father's estate; incest with his sisters, alluded to as adventures of Don John's past; calculated robbery on more than one occasion—all these crimes change the familiar figure of legend from a man in the grip of lust, driven to violence by necessity and postponing religious observance for present pleasure, to an incarnate demon, sinning on principle, rejoicing in the excesses of his iniquity. Shadwell's Don John, like Milton's Satan, acts from calculated principle; unlike

[14] See Leo Weinstein, *The Metamorphoses of Don Juan* (Stanford, 1959).

Satan, he is an atheist, as he carefully and repeatedly explains.

It is as though Shadwell, moralist and avowed disciple of Ben Jonson, were dramatizing, fully and schematically, assumptions allegedly present in plays written by his contemporaries depicting with genial approbation the lives of the court wits and demonstrating the logical and inevitable consequences of their behavior. In the absence of contemporary comment on the subject, I offer this interpretation tentatively; and yet I think it fits the observable relationship among *The Libertine*, many other Restoration comedies, and the lives of several of the principal court wits. Don John, the atheistic philanderer, represents an extreme embodiment, perhaps even a caricature, of moral qualities intermittently revealed, or allegedly revealed, by a score of young sparks of Restoration comedy who, as libertines like him, were committed to the unscrupulous pursuit of women. And we have only to think of the Duke of Buckingham and the Earl of Rochester to recall that Shadwell may have had targets as well in contemporary life. A few years earlier, in the preface to *The Sullen Lovers* (1668), Shadwell had complained that in recent comedies the "two chief persons are most commonly a Swearing, Drinking, Whoring, Ruffian for a Lover, and an impudent, ill-bred *tomrig* for a Mistress"; it is easy enough to find characters from earlier comedies he may have had in mind. Don John was perhaps his response, a dramatic demonstration of what he regarded as the ultimate consequences of freethinking in religion and libertinism in courtship as exhibited in restrained form by the "fine gentlemen" of Restoration comedy. In any event, Etherege's Dorimant of a few months later, like Wycherley's Horner of a few months earlier, if more witty and less vicious than Don John, is not totally unlike him in his relations with women and his freedom from religious inhibition. The small circle around King Charles, it would seem, did not lack its critics, even among the dramatists.

The social biases of the dramatists, related, as already suggested, to neoclassical theory, are for the most part clear and apparent, and they must be taken into account if we are to arrive at the drama's "refractive index" (to use a phrase employed by R. G. Collingwood in a different context).[15] The playwrights of Charles II's reign were nearly all royalists writing for a small audience in-

[15] Collingwood (*The Idea of History* [Oxford, 1946], p. 70) uses the phrase in an exposition of Vico's theory of history.

cluding the King and his courtiers. They can be expected to provide, not a comprehensive and objective view of English life, but rather a view from the vantage of bureaucrats and gentlemen and noblemen who shared the King's interpretation of recent English history. Political animosities aroused during the interregnum and exacerbated by transfers of property, some of them irreversible, had not yet cooled; they found expression in comedy: in the satirical edge of dramatic dialogue, in the harsh depiction of character types—citizens and Puritans who were inimical to courtiers—and even in the shape of the plots, contrived as many of them were for the discomfiture of citizens and Puritans. We would search Restoration comedy in vain for a fair-minded portrayal of Englishmen who had supported Oliver Cromwell, some of them still alive and presumably not totally penitent. Among the major dramatists only Thomas Shadwell broadens the social range, providing engaging portraits of men outside fashionable society and, as I have said, venturing criticism of gentlemen not confined in its application to social affectation. Shadwell is a solitary instance of a playwright whose vision transcended the prejudices of the court circle, and even his plays impose severe limits on social toleration. For example, the London merchant he idealizes in *The Squire of Alsatia* proves to be the son and brother of rich country squires. Restoration drama is a record of the prejudices, preoccupations, manners, and social values of a group that was numerically small. Yet because the dramatists' angle of vision is well defined, the optical calibration needed to correct it can be made with a certain confidence.

The value of drama as historical record is the more obvious in comedy, but it can be seen in tragedy as well. Tragic dramatists supplied less literal comment on the times, since characters and locales were associated with remote times and places; and yet they too wrote with an awareness, albeit a prejudiced awareness, of the passing scene. The themes of tragedy from the Restoration to 1688 are, with a few significant exceptions, royalist; the term "Tory" applies for the period after the Popish Plot. Consider, for example, the dramatic treatment of the implausible episode that convulsed the nation after Titus Oates committed audacious perjury in 1678. At least two of the best tragedies of the later seventeenth century, Nathaniel Lee's *Lucius Junius Brutus* and Thomas Otway's *Venice Preserved*, have political themes that derive from the Popish Plot, the former providing a Whig commentary on the constitutional issues posed by it, and the latter, a Tory commentary.[16] Again, the biases of the dramatists are so obvious that we have no trouble in correcting for them, gaining thereby an insight into the patterns of current political thought and into the passionate emotional dimension of the theoretical debates. *Lucius Junius Brutus* (1680) provided a cautionary example of royal tyranny in Tarquin and, in the title character, a devoted admirer of the rule of law a full decade before Locke published *Two Treatises of Government*. As Locke's editor has demonstrated, the *Two Treatises* were written about 1681, roughly the same time as the play, though they were revised after the Revolution and before publication in 1690.[17] Lee's political theme was too bold to be tolerated, and his play was promptly and permanently prohibited by order of the Lord Chamberlain. On the other hand, Otway's theme in *Venice Preserved* was acceptable. The political meaning of the play is much more subtly revealed than is that of *Lucius Junius Brutus*, and yet, as the subtitle, "A Plot Discovered," implies, *Venice Preserved* turns on an episode that in 1682 would have had inescapable relevance to the Popish Plot. The play's theme of political conservatism, of the need for stability in government even at the cost of corruption and injustice, yields an insight into the frame of mind that could accept the inequities of Restoration England rather than risk the horrors of revolution.

When revolution did come in 1688, the themes of tragedy changed abruptly.[18] In reading the plays as evidence of contemporary political attitudes we must adjust the angle of our corrective lens to take into account the altered assumptions of the dramatists, reenforced as they were by the operation of censorship. Again the correction for the dramatist's prejudices is easy to make, and having made it we can gain from the tragedies knowledge of English thought. We must remember, however, that we are looking, not for comprehensive or objective representations of opinion, but rather for passionate dramatizations of the working out of political propositions that were acceptable to the government.

The neoclassical dramatists are prejudiced witnesses, and their prejudices must be recognized in any attempt to evaluate the ev-

16 John Loftis, *The Politics of Drama in Augustan England* (Oxford, 1963), pp. 15–17, 18–19.

17 John Locke, *Two Treatises of Government*, ed. Peter Laslett (Cambridge, 1960), pp. 45–61.

18 Loftis, *Politics of Drama*, pp. 22–25.

idence they supply. We do not, in courts of law, bar witnesses who are well informed on certain aspects of a subject from giving testimony because they are prejudiced or because they do not know all aspects of the subject. Rather, we listen to what they have to say, make allowances for their point of view and their limited knowledge, and check their assertions with such other evidence as is available. We should, I think, proceed in the same manner in evaluating historical evidence from neoclassical drama. The playwrights' prejudices are after all easy to discern and make allowances for. Moreover, there is a considerable body of relevant evidence that does not originate in the drama against which their portrait of society may be checked.

Thus far I have been concerned with the means of historical verification and correction available in the study of neoclassical drama, as well as with the usefulness of that drama in historical study. I have drawn my examples mainly from plays written in Charles II's reign. Another, more strictly literary, aspect of the problem has to do with the changes evident in the early eighteenth century in the dramatists' perception of the relationship between their plays and the life around them. Neoclassical formalism in drama, as expressed by Rymer, Dryden, and Dennis, for example, included, in its insistence that the poet concern himself with general types, some aristocratic assumptions, notably that the hierarchical ordering of society, with relationships among social classes as they were envisioned in the mid-seventeenth century, was universal and permanent. By the time of the Hanoverian succession, however, some observers began to realize that interclass relationships were not necessarily permanent and that the portrayal of occupational groups, as well as dramatic genres, had to undergo modification if the drama was not to have an anachronistic relationship to the society that provided its subject. The effort to bring literary practice into closer touch with social reality proved to be disruptive of neoclassical theory, in comedy first and later in tragedy. That it did not completely annihilate neoclassicism is attributable to the pertinacity of older conceptions of decorum and genre, which had not entirely disappeared by century's end, and perhaps have not disappeared even at the present time.

As I have elsewhere argued,[19] the history of comedy in the later

[19] John Loftis, *Comedy and Society from Congreve to Fielding* (Stanford, 1959).

seventeenth and early eighteenth centuries reveals the gradual transformation of character types, notably those of businessmen, to approximate more closely their equivalents in contemporary life. The transformation, slower than the parallel change in society, was conditioned by political controversy. It involved an interaction between social structure and dramatic convention which has relevance to the nature of historical veracity in drama. Neoclassical comedy provides an instance of the correction of what Bernard De Voto, referring primarily to the modern American novel, has called "the literary fallacy."[20]

The correction came slowly, and it did not occur without modification of the structure of comedy and deterioration in its quality; but its pervasiveness lends the support of literary evidence, I think, to Professor Stone's finding of a "slow but steady shift of attitudes on the part of the landed classes, a growing recognition that the previously anomalous occupational categories formed a series of semi-independent and parallel status hierarchies." It is readily apparent that the emerging conception "of semi-independent and parallel status hierarchies" was not compatible with the neoclassical conception of decorum in characterization, based as it was on the assumption that all members of society, and in consequence all dramatic characters, belonged to a single status hierarchy. The writings of Steele in comedy and, later, of George Lillo in tragedy explicitly reject neoclassical assumptions about characterization on the ground that those assumptions did not correspond to observable facts about contemporary societal organization.

Changes in the conventions of representing social and occupational groups were part of the eighteenth-century dramatists' efforts to achieve greater historical veracity. More important in its ultimate literary consequences is the relaxation, in some instances even the abandonment, of the neoclassical insistence that the dramatist concern himself with general truths rather than with particulars. This change is evident in many ways in eighteenth-century drama: in an increased allusiveness to specific persons and events, in greater originality and intricacy of plots, in stronger individualization of dramatic characters. Professor Watt has explained the consequences for the novel of an intensified concern with the unique experience, and the corollary abandonment of conventional plots and character types, in the literary effort to

[20] Bernard De Voto, *The Literary Fallacy* (Boston, 1944).

convey an impression of authenticity.[21] Although he does not discuss the drama at length, much of his argument is relevant to it, and I am indebted to him for the conceptual framework I bring to the history of eighteenth-century drama. In the altered relationship between dramatic convention and contemporary life evident in the plays of Henry Fielding, altered, that is, from the relationship customary in earlier neoclassical drama, we can observe a formal development in the drama analogous to that in eighteenth-century prose fiction.

The increased allusiveness of drama to contemporary persons and issues becomes striking when we turn to the plays written in opposition to Sir Robert Walpole. The best-known plays of Gay and Fielding, the most distinguished of the opposition dramatists, are properly considered experimental drama: ballad operas and stage burlesques, topical and satirical reviews of England in the 1720s and 1730s. The liveliest vein of dramatic writing in these years is in these "irregular" plays, many of them musicals, and it is of their nature to carry a heavy load of topical allusion. In the best of them all, *The Beggar's Opera*, the topical is so adroitly assimilated into the dramatic situation as to provide no barrier to our untutored and spontaneous delight; our original delight is merely reenforced by historical study—and it is significant that the plays of the literary opposition require historical study as do only a few Restoration plays—when the full import of social comment and political satire becomes intelligible. Our response to Fielding's plays, however, is otherwise. Several of them can scarcely be read without an initiation into the current preoccupations of court and town. Fielding's plays pose an uncommonly difficult critical problem in their combination of inventiveness with—in the absence of commentary that can be provided only with historical study—unintelligibility. The problem is not unlike that posed by Pope's *Dunciad* (a poem requiring a duncelike attention to historical detail if it is to be understood), to which indeed several of Fielding's burlesques bear a thematic resemblance.

Fielding's assessment of the state of literature was scarcely less severe than Pope's, and in fact *The Author's Farce* is a kind of dramatization of conditions in London as enterprising booksellers, with an eye to the growing market for books, organized hack writers into a factory system for the production of cheap literary wares. In the play Dash, Blottage, and Quibble are shown "writing

[21] Ian Watt, *The Rise of the Novel* (London, 1957).

at several Tables" in the house of their employer Bookweight, their conversation, as they search for rhymes with the aid of Bysshe's rhyming dictionary, burlesquing an aspect of literary life which came under Pope's attack.

There is a connection, I think, between the intensified allusiveness and the altered conception of originality in plots and characters of eighteenth-century drama on the one hand, and, on the other, a change in the conception of literary property which is evident in Pope's *Dunciad*. An important target in the poem is plagiarism, especially the extensive borrowings of contemporary dramatists. We all remember Pope's early pronouncement about literary property, so quintessentially neoclassical, in *An Essay on Criticism*, the couplet about true wit as familiar thoughts given superlative expression. Dryden had written in a similar vein in *Of Dramatick Poesie* when comparing Ben Jonson's borrowings to the conquests of an invading monarch; he reaffirmed his opinion much later, in the preliminaries to *Don Sebastian*, when he replied defensively to Langbaine's attack on him in *Momus Triumphans* for plagiarism. Langbaine may have lacked generosity of spirit and critical perceptiveness, but his conception of literary property, much more sharply defined than that customary earlier, was to become widespread in the eighteenth century. This altered conception, as I have suggested, is latent in *The Dunciad*. And whether Fielding consciously formulated it or not, his five-act comedies, at least those he wrote after his apprenticeship, show a conception of originality closer to that we associate with the later novel than with the earlier neoclassical drama. As we examine these plays in their relationship with the contemporary life they purportedly record, we must take into account a tacit change in the theoretical assumptions controlling the depiction of society. In other words, *The Modern Husband*, for example, has a different kind of historical veracity from that evident in *The Man of Mode*, and the difference has consequences for the development of drama, just as it does for our reading of the drama as a record of society. In his later five-act comedies, Fielding no longer attempted, at least in his central characters, to portray representative types.

If possible variations on the formalized pattern of Restoration comedy had largely been played out by the end of the seventeenth century, other promising veins in comedy had been opened. Even *The Way of the World*, by consensus the ultimate perfection of Restoration comedy, reveals an innovative quality in the intricacy of its plot, in the depth of the moral evil explored, and in the complexity and the individuality of several of its characters.[22] The depravity of Fainall and of Mrs. Marwood and the resulting difficulty of Mrs. Fainall's position are unconventional aspects of the comedy of that time; we are more accustomed to finding them in the later novel than in the earlier drama. Even before *The Way of the World*, Vanbrugh's *The Relapse* has about it a quality that may, perhaps anachronistically, be described as "novelistic": a departure from comic conventions of plot and character in a manner anticipatory of the mid-eighteenth-century novel. It is idle to speculate as to how much of the play's unconventional quality is owing to its rapid composition and its origin as a parody of *Love's Last Shift*, how much to Vanbrugh's premeditated design. (*The Relapse* presents theoretical problems analogous to those encountered in Fielding's *Joseph Andrews*, which like Vanbrugh's play originated in parody and was to some undetermined extent a work of brilliant improvisation.) In any event, Vanbrugh's Amanda and Worthy seem curiously incongruous with the other characters of the play—Miss Hoyden, Sir Tunbelley Clumsey, Lord Foppington, and the rest—who are cut to familiar Restoration patterns. Within a single play we find two different modes of representation of life: generalized portraiture of social groups and human types, heightened and exaggerated for comic and satirical effectiveness, and particular portraiture of individuals with problems unique in late seventeenth-century drama. Amanda's obstinate and high-minded virtue, enduring to the end of the play and in face of Worthy's plausible claim on her affections, suggests something of the idealism of Richardson's heroines, and Worthy's final soliloquy is difficult to reconcile with the comic and satiric tone of the play.

Although the characters of comedy, unlike those of the novel, retain their conventional and adjectival names, they acquire, at least by the time of Fielding, an individuality of motive and a variety of occupation which separate them from the true wits and the would-be wits of Restoration comedy; and the dramatic fables in which they act out their roles become more varied than those of the love-game comedies of Dryden, Etherege, and Wycherley. If dialogue becomes less witty, it also becomes stylistically closer

    [22] See Clifford Leech, "Congreve and the Century's End," *Philological Quarterly*, XLI (1962), 275–293.

to the language men speak, and the settings of the plays cease to be so exclusively the fashionable areas of London. The extent of innovation in early eighteenth-century comedy has been obscured by the fact that the subsequent history of comedy is not more impressive. Yet the reasons for the later failures are at least in part the consequences of the Licensing Act. In any event, Fielding, the best dramatist of the 1730s, anticipated in his five-act comedies themes and methods that he later developed more fully in his novels.

Fielding's *The Modern Husband* (1731) holds special interest in this respect, for it seems, in retrospect, to represent a movement in the drama toward the form of the novel. However qualified a critical assessment of the play must be (a stronger case for it can be made than has yet been attempted), it is strikingly original in conception,[23] as the novels, more specifically the last of them, *Amelia*, are original. From the time of Vanbrugh and Congreve comedy had included complex characters embroiled in difficult domestic situations. Even so, *The Modern Husband*, preoccupied with fullness and honesty of characterization in persons other than true wits, with matrimonial problems, and with problems of economic survival, represents a break with the conventions inherited from Restoration comedy. Fielding retained the neoclassical conception of comedy as instructive through the depiction of corrupt, cautionary characters, but he can scarcely be said to have retained a generic conception of comedy as witty or humorous. It is as irrelevant to criticize this grim play, in which the title character lives by pimping for his wife, for its failure to evoke laughter as it would be so to criticize *Amelia*. The neoclassical conception of decorum in characterization is abandoned in the treatment of the debauched and despicable Lord Richly, formerly a purchaser of Mrs. Modern's favors, now grown weary of her and attempting, with her bribed assistance, to seduce the virtuous Mrs. Bellamant. Mr. and Mrs. Bellamant anticipate the marital problems of Captain Booth and his wife Amelia of the novel. (The specific detail of Captain Booth's quest for assignment to an active regiment is here represented, not by Mr. Bellamant, but by Captain Merit, who is forced to the humiliation of attending Lord Richly's levee.)

Even in its amplitude, *The Modern Husband* seems—again in

[23] See Wilbur L. Cross, *The History of Henry Fielding* (New Haven, 1918), I, 118–119.

retrospect, in the light of subsequent literary history—novelistic. It is a very long play with several concurrent lines of action, none of them following the predictable patterns of earlier love-game comedy; and in its conversational review of problems and paradoxes of contemporary life it reveals a social commitment coupled with an analytical method which to a modern reader is likely to recall Shaw. (May I add parenthetically that Shaw's curiously high praise of Fielding may have been occasioned by the five-act "comedies" rather than by the irregular plays, as is commonly assumed. In any event, *The Modern Husband* and also, perhaps, Fielding's *The Universal Gallant* represent as close an approximation as we will find in eighteenth-century drama to Shaw's iconoclastic dialectic.) Years before the Licensing Act of 1737 terminated his career as a dramatist and thus led him to write novels, Fielding had broken with earlier conventions in plotting as well as in characterization and in dramatic dialogue. Yet however full of promise in the sense of dramatic innovation *The Modern Husband* may be, it is a qualified success, its character relationships too numerous and complex to be fully assimilated, the sordidness of its subject not fully compensated for by analysis of character and society. Fielding had not yet worked out solutions to the problems that confronted him in consequence of his break with precedent in the conventions within which he sought to comment on the life about him.

What are the limits of historical veracity in the dramatic commentary Fielding provided? It is already apparent that in reading his plays as social record we must make allowance for his altered conception of comedy. Etherege took seriously the neoclassical admonition to prefer representative types, and if in his true wits he achieved characters that are, in Samuel Johnson's phrase about Shakespeare, "just representations of general nature," he was content to draw characters other than his witty young lovers with broad strokes. Like Sir Fopling, who in Dryden's opinion represented all fops, some of Fielding's characters are also generalized types: Captain Merit, for example, and perhaps Lord Richly. Just as he did later in his novels, in his plays Fielding placed side by side broadly drawn caricatures and characters of unpredictable originality. Mr. Bellamant, in his financial difficulties and in his relationships with his wife, his mistress, and his son, has the uniqueness of life, and thus he cannot be considered a just representation of a typical gentleman in George II's England. Fielding's innovation comes not in the individualization of major characters alone but also in the range of personality and occupation he brings to them. They are as little representative of occupational and social classes as persons we meet on the street.

And so we return to Aristotle's paradox about poetry and history. The historical in Fielding's plays takes precedence in a curious way over the poetical: in his experimental drama, in the form of allusion to living persons and controversial issues; in his five-act plays, in an intensity of concern with moral and social corruption which precludes the employment of major characters who are representative types or who remain within the limits of expectation established in neoclassical drama. His themes may represent a generalized commentary on what he saw about him; his major characters are individuals.

Fielding's generalized commentary on the life about him is to be read, I think, in his themes, in the total impression conveyed by his plays, rather than in his characters. As Dennis implied in 1698, most of the Restoration dramatists, Wycherley excepted, had focused attention on their characters: "Mr. *Wycherley* being, indeed, almost the only Man alive who has made Comedy instructive in its Fable; almost all the rest, being content to instruct by their Characters."[24] Thirty years later Fielding too provided instruction in his fables and, to use a more inclusive word, in his themes. He was as thoroughly committed as earlier dramatists to the criticism of what he saw about him, but he chose to pass his judgments, not merely in characters representative of social, occupational, and personality types, but in the depiction of unique situations and unexpected, and therefore unrepresentative, individuals.

Fielding's plays are imaginative constructions, of course, and any value they possess as historical record was presumably unintended on the author's part. Yet whatever their difficulties, Fielding's plays provide a remarkable record of Walpole's England: not a comprehensive and objective record, it goes without saying, but in their themes—and his themes are emphatic—an uninhibited commentary on what seemed to merit the attention of a man with a sensitive social conscience. The historian of the 1730s can no more neglect Fielding's plays than he can neglect the prints of Hogarth to which Fielding himself made illuminating reference.

24 John Dennis, *The Usefulness of the Stage*, quoted from Gerald Weales, ed., *The Complete Plays of William Wycherley* (New York, 1967), p. xiii.

It is obvious that we cannot trust the plays as reliable guides to the historical reality of contemporary life without taking into account Fielding's angle of vision and other forms of evidence, eighteenth-century and modern in origin. The plays provide no quantitative information, no information, for example, concerning the numerical incidence of a man's pimping for his wife. They do not yield the kind of information we can derive, to illustrate, by comparing vital statistics in London with the records for the consumption of gin. But they can reveal, as the statistics cannot, how an intelligent and sensitive man responded to London life in the gin age; they can reveal, that is, the emotional dimension of sociological fact. They record in their judgments on society, if we make allowance for the heightening inherent in the literary process, what an articulate man thought he saw about him. If we conceive of history as a dialogue, as the meeting place between a modern intelligence and a body of evidence surviving from an earlier time, the plays assume importance because they are, unlike such forms of evidence as vital statistics and tax reports, not merely the raw material for historical judgment but are, within the changing conventions of drama, themselves judgments. In Fielding's plays the modern historian encounters an intelligence at the far side of two centuries trying to tell him something, an intelligence with prejudices and limitations that must be taken into account but one nevertheless cooperating in the dialogue that is history.

III

FICTION AND SOCIETY IN THE EARLY EIGHTEENTH CENTURY

Maximillian E. Novak

Professor of English, University of California, Los Angeles

In an issue of *The Spectator* dedicated to a discussion of the power of love to refine human passions, Richard Steele published a letter from an "enamour'd Footman in the Country to his Mistress." The footman was formerly a bully, but love had tamed his manners and reading his master's romances had transformed his style. The letter begins, "Remember your bleeding Lover, who Lyes bleeding at the Wounds *Cupid* made with the Arrows he borrowed at the Eyes of *Venus*, which is your sweet Person." Continuing in this vein, the footman added some social commentary on love and class as he remarked on the presence of a London visitor who had come to marry the master's daughter. "Oh! dear *Betty*," he wrote, "must the Nightingales sing to those who marry for Mony, and not to us true Lovers!" Steele revised the letter to read as an expression of simple passion untainted by the style of romances. The last passage is made to read: "Our Young Lady, and a Fine Gentleman from *London*, who are to marry for mercenary Ends, walk about our Gardens, and hear the Voice of Evening Nightingales, as if for Fashion-sake they courted those Solitudes, because they have heard Lovers do so. Oh *Betty*! could I hear these Rivulets Murmer, and Birds Sing while you stood near me, how little sensible should I be that we are both Servants, that there is any thing on Earth above us."[1]

Granted that Steele's style is superior to the footman's, there are still many questions that might be asked about Steele's essay. What was a footman doing reading romances? Why would he think to express himself through the style of those romances in making love to Betty? Was it acceptable for a footman to comment on a "mercenary" marriage in the family he served? And how did those "murmuring Rivulets" get into the letter? In this brief paper I will be asking more questions than I will be answering, but I want to examine three areas that have always seemed to me to raise difficulties in discussions of fiction and society in the early eighteenth century: first, the way in which histories of the novel have influenced our view of all the fiction written during the period; second, the question of who read what; third, the manner in which the fiction of the period influenced and was influenced by social change.

Perhaps nothing has complicated these problems so much as the tyranny of literary history. When the editor of the periodical, *Bibliothèque Universelle des Romans*, which first appeared in 1775, stated his reasons for issuing a monthly journal of world fiction, he explained simply that fiction gave the best picture of national manners through the private history of a few citizens. And after this justification for fiction on simple sociological grounds, he proceeded to divide fiction into eight classes, including everything from religious fiction to fairy tales, and in subsequent volumes printed selections from works as different as *Amadis of Gaul*, *Guzman de Alfarache*, *The Adventures of David Simple*, and *Almahide*. This catholic taste in fiction is still present in Dunlop's *History of Fiction*, published in 1814.[2] Modern literary history dates, for the most part, from the late nineteenth century, when theories of evolving biological and social forms were popular. To have viewed the drama as evolving from the plays of a primitive like Shakespeare to some higher form might have been difficult, but the genius of a Tolstoy or a Flaubert made such a theory possible for fiction. It is locked into Baker's *History of the Novel* and is reflected in a title like Francis Stoddard's *The Evo-*

---

[1] *The Spectator*, ed. Donald F. Bond (Oxford, 1965–1967), I, 305–308 (no. 71).
[2] Dunlop merely divides fiction into "the *serious*, the *comic*, and the *romantic*," pointing to the futility of any genuinely detailed analysis of a novel like *Tom Jones* (John Dunlop, *The History of Fiction* [Edinburgh, 1814], III, 363, 372).

lution of the Novel. In such works Defoe appears either as the inventor of a primitive form of novel or as a Neanderthal of fiction quickly shoved aside by a Richardson. If a sociological theory is needed to explain this development, a brief recourse to middle-class creators, middle-class heroes, and middle-class audiences is usually sufficient.

Ian Watt's influential *Rise of the Novel* must be regarded as the most sophisticated statement of this position. He is not concerned with writers like Mrs. Behn or Mrs. Manley, but with those who contributed toward the development of a particular form that was rooted in the rise of economic individualism and found its expression in realistic prose fiction. Like Eric Auerbach, Watt placed an inherent value on circumstantial and psychological realism, suggesting that the essential differences between the novel and earlier fiction might be found in these new elements of realism. In taking this position he has much in common with Marxist critics like Lukacs, Kettle, and particularly Ralph Fox, who identified realism as a specific product of the capitalist mentality.[3] While Watt's subsequent analysis of individual works of fiction draws on a variety of critical methods, much depends on his thorough examination of the social structure of the reading audience and on his discussions of the "Protestant ethic" as expounded by R. H. Tawney and Max Weber.[4]

Brilliant as *The Rise of the Novel* is, it simply does not describe with any accuracy what we know of prose fiction in the early eighteenth century, and in some ways it may prove less helpful than Northrop Frye's *Anatomy of Criticism* which, appearing in the same year, treated the novel as a segment of a larger body of prose fiction which included the romance, the confession, and the anatomy.[5] Frye's categories may be open to question, but they do allow us to take into account the multitude of fictional forms to be found in the beginning of the eighteenth century and the dominance of a form that was usually called a "novel," or what, for want of a better name, I shall call a novella. The older novellas of

[3] Ralph Fox, *The Novel and the People* (New York, 1945; first publ., 1937), pp. 37–39.

[4] See Ian Watt, *The Rise of the Novel* (Berkeley and Los Angeles, 1957), pp. 63–74.

[5] Northrop Frye, *Anatomy of Criticism* (Princeton, 1957), pp. 303–326. Frye's work has led directly to books like *The Nature of Narrative*, by Robert Scholes and Robert Kellogg, and to the general tendency to examine fiction rather than the "novel."

Cervantes and Scarron were still being reprinted,[6] but the twelve volumes of *Modern Novels* published by Bentley in 1692 each contained from three to four works of about two hundred pages each, most of which had been published in the past decade. Among them was one masterpiece, Madame de Lafayette's *The Princess of Cleves*, and a variety of forms, secret histories, fictional memoirs, and even dialogues of the dead. Most were translations from the French, and most have an identifiable style.[7]

It is worth glancing at these novellas for a moment to curb our tendency to search for the traditional realistic novel among them, a tendency that still lurks behind recent interest in pre-Richardsonian epistolary fiction.[8] As Congreve stated in the preface to his novella, *Incognita*, novels, compared with the imaginative flights of the romance, "are of a more familiar nature; Come near us, and represent to us Intrigues in practice, delight us with Accidents and odd Events, but not such as are wholly unusual or unprecedented, such which not being so distant from our Belief bring also the pleasure nearer us."[9] Mrs. Manley, describing her particular type of novella, usually called a secret history or a scandalous chronicle, argued that this type of fiction, unlike the romance, should move at a rapid pace with few digressions. She agreed with Congreve that the novella, in its treatment of the passions, was similar to the drama, and that the form had greater appeal because of its avoidance of the marvelous.[10]

In giving *Incognita* a carefully worked out plot, Congreve unquestionably produced one of the finest examples of the genre in English, but the emphasis on dramatic plot and on twists of fortune or providence was common to all,[11] particularly to the brief novellas that appeared in almost every number of Peter Motteux's *Gentleman's Journal* in the 1690s. When someone wrote to ask

[6] See especially *A Select Collection of Novels in Six Volumes*, ed. Samuel Croxall (London, 1720–1722).

[7] For a discussion of the influence of Italian and Spanish models on the French *nouvelle*, see Frédéric Deloffre, *La Nouvelle en France à l'Age Classique* (Paris, 1967).

[8] See, for example, Robert Day, *Told in Letters* (Ann Arbor, 1966); and *The Novel in Letters*, ed. Natascha Würzbach (Coral Gables, 1969).

[9] William Congreve, [*Works*], ed. Bonamy Dobrée (London, 1925–1928), II, 5.

[10] Mary de la Rivière Manley, "To the Reader," *The Secret History of Queen Zarah*, in *Prefaces to Fiction*, ed. Benjamin Boyce, Augustan Reprint Society no. 32 (Los Angeles, 1952).

[11] See, for example, *Victorious Lovers; or Love Victorious over Fortunes*, in *Modern Novels* (London, 1692), Vol. IV.

why he printed them, he replied, "As for Novels, I need not Apologize for them otherwise than by saying that the Ladies desire them; besides they are short, and, as often as possible, not only true but Moral."[12] Many of these were relatively comic tales of contemporary life; even so, the tears of a heroine are always described in terms like "a flood of liquid Gems."[13] Such a style may have been, as Ian Watt thought, antithetical to the realism of the novel form, but it was certainly pervasive. The rivulet that suddenly appears in Steele's corrected version of the footman's letter is part of a landscape common to both the romance and the novella. Addison's Leonora, an ardent reader of romances, has landscaped her estate with a "little Rivulet which runs through a Green Meadow, and is known in the Family by the Name of *The Purling Stream.*"[14]

In Richard Blackburn's novella, *Clitie*, there are numerous scenes like the following:

A Woman lying on a Bank of Flowers, making her Arm (more white than Snow) her Pillow; her curling Hair being negligently o're her Face, which as the friendly Wind remov'd away, made him perceive a Cheek more beautiful and fair than ever he had seen before; but what mov'd him most . . . was the other fair Hand, that ever and anon was imploy'd with a Handkerchief, in wiping away those Tears which fell in streams from her Distilling Eyes.[15]

Those tears are as symptomatic of these novellas as the landscape, and there are probably as many weeps per page in *Clitie* as in any sentimental novel of the latter part of the eighteenth century. Darbelle, Clitie's faithful lover, weeps as easily as Harley in Mackenzie's *The Man of Feeling* and faints with more style.

Such works tell us little about society except to remind us that the fictional world into which people want to escape has a fairly permanent set of props. They remind us that no theory of fiction that fails to take these works into account can be quite valid, and they also show us just how different the best works of fiction written at the time are from the standpoint of their response to social reality. Diana Spearman has tried to suggest that whatever view of society we may get from the fiction of Defoe, Richard-

[12] *Gentleman's Journal*, II (Feb. 1963), 38.
[13] *Ibid.*, I (Jan. 1692), 25.
[14] *Spectator*, I, 158 (no. 37).
[15] *Clitie*, Pt. III, p. 200, in *Modern Novels*, Vol. X.

son, and Fielding, it is certainly neither very middle-class nor very accurate. It is a relief to be told that the real meaning of *Clarissa Harlowe* does not, as Christopher Hill suggests, lie in its grasp of the technical problems involved in getting a peerage for Clarissa's brother and that Defoe, far from being an echo of a nebulous middle class, was actually a social outcast writing about criminals.[16] But Mrs. Spearman demands too much of fiction. As Northrop Frye remarks, "the ideas of literature are not real propositions, but verbal formulas which imitate real propositions."[17] Fiction that presents a mirror image of society approaches the genuine case history; the fictionist might as well follow the suggestion of C. Wright Mills and step aside for the imaginative sociologist.[18] A work of fiction with a mixture of good social observation and with some fairly clear and not entirely inconsistent statements about society would qualify as an important piece for the present discussion.

Richard Altick has summarized the literary situation for fiction in 1740 among women readers: "Old-fashioned romances like *The Grand Cyrus* and *Astrea*, however lengthy, could not solace her indefinitely, and when she finished them she had nothing further to occupy her. . . . The time was ripe for a Richardson, and when *Pamela* appeared (1740–41) its success and that of the novels that followed it revealed the extent of the female audience which for several decades had been waiting for something to read."[19] When we examine the sheer amount of fiction available during this period, however, we know women had plenty to read even if they needed the "solace" of sentimental love stories. The long-winded French romances, though abandoned by their creators, were still read. In 1810, reviewing Charlotte Lennox's *The Female Quixote*, a novel about a woman affected by French romances as Cervantes' hero was by chivalric romances, Mrs. Barbauld remarked that "most young ladies of the present day, instead of requiring to be cured of reading those bulky romances, would acquire the first information of their manner from the work designed to ridicule them."[20] Nevertheless, Charlotte Lennox, writ-

16 Diana Spearman, *The Novel and Society* (London, 1966), pp. 29–32.
17 *Anatomy of Criticism*, p. 85.
18 C. Wright Mills, *The Sociological Imagination* (New York, 1959), pp. 16–18.
19 Richard Altick, *The English Common Reader* (London, 1957), p. 45.
20 Anna Barbauld, ed., *The British Novelists*, 2d ed. (London, 1820), XXIV, iii.

ing in 1752, had obviously read them all and must have thought there would be a sufficiently large audience to understand her allusions.[21]

There was certainly nothing unusual about the reading and the library of Leonora, as described in *The Spectator* of 12 April 1711. She owned *Cassandra, Cleopatra, Astraea, Le Grand Cyrus*, and a copy of *Clelia*, "which opened of it self in the Place that describes two Lovers in a Bower." Her library also boasted "A Book of Novels" and Mrs. Manley's *The New Atalantis*, but Leonora's general behavior followed the précieuse prescriptions of the old romances. Addison's attack on works that "divert the imagination" is clearly directed at them rather than at novellas, which is not surprising since many of the brief pieces of fiction in *The Spectator* bore some resemblance to the novellas of the *Gentleman's Journal*, and Addison even ventured on a parodic "Ante-diluvian novel" in two numbers.[22] Yet Leonora's romances continued to appear in library catalogues of the period along with others like *Polexander* and *Parthenissa*.

The old romances contained much that was completely absurd, but they were certainly not lacking in subtle discussions of love. Like *Pamela* and *Clarissa*, they lent themselves to indexing for their sentiments, and although Charlotte Lennox attacks them for their bad effect on the imaginations of impressionable young ladies, she takes her perfectly serious discourse on raillery directly from Madeleine de Scudéry.[23] In no sense can the novella be regarded as an "advance" over the romance. A story like "The Jealous Lover" from *Artamenes* lost all its subtlety when in 1702 it appeared, drastically cut and in English dress, in the epistolary novella, *The Adventures of Lindamira*.[24] The problem with the

[21] Several characters in *The Female Quixote*, in addition to Arabella, the slightly deranged heroine, have read extensively in romances. By 1785, however, the old romances were apparently "despised" as well as ignored; Clara Reeve described them as "the books that pleased our grandmothers . . . dull,—heavy,— and uninteresting" (see *The Progress of Romance*, Facsimile Text Society no. 4 [New York, 1930], Pt. I, pp. 68–69).

[22] *Spectator*, IV, 595–598; V, 1–3 (nos. 584, 585).

[23] Cf. Madeleine de Scudéry, *Artamenes; or Cyrus the Great*, trans. F. G. (London, 1653–1655), Vol. II, Pt. IX, Bk. III, pp. 137–139; and Lennox, *The Female Quixote* (1752), II, 122–124.

[24] Cf. *Artamenes*, Vol. I, Pt. III, Bk. I, pp. 63–83; and *The Adventures of Lindamira*, ed. Benjamin Boyce (Minneapolis, 1949), pp. 120–125. Mlle de Scudéry's original is remarkable for its subtle presentation of Leontidas' uncontrollable jealousy and the way in which it destroys his chances of gaining the

romances was that all their subtlety was expended in developing a theory of love and passion, while their treatment of character and plot was extraordinarily artificial. The novellas retained the stylized landscape, the emphasis on love and the passions, and frequently even the idealized hero and heroine. They also retained names like Philander, Celintha, or Cleophil (as Congreve signed himself in *Incognita*), Mrs. Manley explaining that *"Names of Persons ought to have a Sweetness in them, for a Barbarous Name disturbs the Imagination."*[25] But their authors cut the dialogue, the digressions, and the number of characters and, as both Congreve and Mrs. Manley stressed, frequently concentrated on one episode.

The chances are that those who read novellas were likely to have dipped into a romance, but who were these readers? Mrs. Manley stated that the romances were read with "surprizing greediness," that the "Fury" for them was like a drug addiction.[26] She suggested that the same was true of readers of novellas, but modern scholars have been more moderate in judging the extent of the audience for fiction. A recent summary presents a traditional picture of that audience:

It probably excluded the poor, the learned, or the intellectual, the religious, and the commercial "lower middle class." (There is no question that other members of the *economic* "lower middle class," such as the very numerous group of upper servants, were readers of popular fiction.) It included many members of the nobility and gentry, the bourgeois rich, the young, and the fashionable; and although the tastes of women may have dominated its choices in fiction, it also included many men.[27]

Leaving aside the question of literacy for the moment, one might well wonder how this list of readers was compiled. Is it true that intellectuals did not read fiction? Did they read fiction when they were young intellectuals? When we speak of an audience for a work, surely we cannot mean anything but those people who actually read it, whether they liked it or not. Pope was mildly ironic

love of Alcidamia, who insists on an element of play in courtship. Alcidamia can confront Leontidas only after he reluctantly agrees to turn his discourse with her into "Raillery." Incapable of sustaining control over his emotions, Leontidas is finally rejected by Alcidamia as an impossible lover.

[25] *Queen Zarah*, sig. A3ᵛ.
[26] *Ibid.*, sig. A2.
[27] Day, *Told in Letters*, p. 77.

about Mrs. Manley's tremendously popular *New Atalantis*, but Lady Mary Wortley Montagu could hardly wait to get her hands on the next volume.[28] The Baron in *The Rape of the Lock* is an ardent admirer of Mrs. Manley, and if Pope did not share that admiration he was, nevertheless, unquestionably a member of Mrs. Manley's audience.[29]

Some attempt has been made to describe certain works as "popular fiction" as opposed to fiction for an elite audience, but such a distinction, unless carefully defined, does not hold up under close analysis.[30] *A Tale of a Tub* and *Robinson Crusoe* are cases in point. A recent critic seems to have been uncertain whether to include Defoe in a study of "popular fiction," whereas another assures the reader that the medieval romance, *Guy of Warwick*, was republished in the eighteenth century "for exactly the kind of readers for which *Robinson Crusoe* was written."[31] What prompts this remark is Charles Gildon's well-known attack on *Robinson Crusoe* in 1719, in which he identified Crusoe with Guy of Warwick, stating, "There is not an old Woman that can go to the Price of it, but buys thy Life and Adventures." To Gildon, Crusoe was a "Mob Hero," "a *Pyecorner* Hero! one a foot with *Guy* of *Warwick*, *Bevis* of *Southampton*, and the *London Prentice*."[32] Oddly enough, Gildon compared *A Tale of a Tub* with the same works, except that he substituted *Amadis of Gaul* for

[28] Mary Wortley Montagu, *The Complete Letters*, ed. Robert Halsband (Oxford, 1965–1967), I, 15–19.

[29] Pope's criticism of Mrs. Manley in *The Dunciad* was, of course, far more direct.

[30] A work such as Q. D. Leavis's *Fiction and the Reading Public* (London, 1932), which deals with the gradual debasement of taste in popular fiction up to the thirties, seems peculiarly dated today. Either the crisis in western European culture which concerned Mrs. Leavis has passed or we face too many other crises to regard cultural crises as of prime importance. Doubtless Mrs. Leavis would argue that the event she feared has already arrived and that modern fiction is in a hopeless state. Writers like Bellow and Nabokov, however, are likely to have their novels at the top of the best-seller lists without bowing to popular demands for fiction more compatible with daydreams and wish-fulfillment fantasies.

[31] John Richetti, *Popular Fiction before Richardson* (Oxford, 1969), p. 179; Spearman, *Novel and Society*, p. 101. Richetti refuses to discuss Defoe's fiction in detail because Defoe was actually a creator of "pseudo-documentaries rather than 'novels' in the eighteenth-century sense." His refusal is difficult to understand, since he treats criminal biographies and other works that are even further from fiction.

[32] Charles Gildon, *The Life and Surprizing Adventures of D— De F—*, in *Robinson Crusoe Examin'd and Criticiz'd*, ed. Paul Dottin (London, 1923), pp. 71–72.

The London Prentice.[33] One of the earliest attacks on *A Tale of a Tub* accused it of corrupting the lower and middle classes, beginning with the plumber who bought it by mistake.[34]

The question of literacy is important for solving the problem of how many members of the lower classes were capable of reading fiction, but an analysis of signatures on marriage documents can hardly tell us who read what.[35] It is impossible to say how many shoeblacks César de Saussure observed in 1726 pooling their resources to purchase a newspaper would have read fiction.[36] The price of a newly published work like *Robinson Crusoe* would have been prohibitive for a worker,[37] but now, thanks to R. M. Wiles, we know something of the extent to which books were published in numbers.[38] *Robinson Crusoe* and *The Arabian Nights* were also serialized in newspapers throughout England. And if, like James Lackington at the end of the century, a worker had been willing to do without a meal, he might have been able to buy a battered secondhand copy of a novella. Some might even have been willing to join Lackington in quoting Turgot to the effect that "more grand moral truths have been promulgated by novel writers, than any other class of men."[39]

I have no desire to throw the entire question of audience into greater chaos than now prevails. Certainly a poet like Pope conceived of himself as writing for the few who were learned enough

---

[33] Charles Gildon, *The Golden Spy* (London, 1709), sig. A7ᵛ.

[34] William King, *Observations on A Tale of a Tub* (London, 1704), pp. 3–4. The power of Swift's work over relatively unsophisticated readers is testified to by William Cobbett, who told how he was so completely fascinated when he started to read *A Tale of a Tub* at the age of fifteen that he missed his dinner and had to sleep outside in the park (see Altick, *English Common Reader*, p. 39).

[35] For the outlines of such a project, see R. S. Schofield, "The Measurement of Literacy in Pre-Industrial England," in *Literacy in Traditional Societies*, ed. Jack Goody (Cambridge, 1968), pp. 310–325.

[36] César de Saussure, *A Foreign View of England in the Reigns of George I. & George II.*, trans. Madame Van Muyden (London, 1902), p. 162: "Workmen habitually begin the day by going to coffee-rooms in order to read the latest news." For similar reports see Altick, *English Common Reader*, p. 40.

[37] Watt, *Rise of the Novel*, p. 41; K. I. D. Maslen, "Edition Quantities for *Robinson Crusoe*, 1719," *The Library*, 5th ser., XXIV (1969), 149–150.

[38] R. M. Wiles, *Serial Publication in England* (Cambridge, 1957). See particularly his account (p. 46) of *All Alive and Merry*, which printed novels at the rate of a farthing a number. As early as 1710 a work called *The Records of Love or Weekly Amusements for the Fair Sex* was offering brief novellas at 2d. a sheet or 1s. 6d. a quarter.

[39] *Memoirs of the Forty-Five First Years of the Life of James Lackington*, 13th ed. (London, n.d.), pp. 133, 245.

to appreciate his allusions. And certainly Defoe wrote that "If any man was to ask me, which would be supposed to be a perfect stile, or language, I would answer, that in which a man speaking to five hundred people, of all common and various capacities, ideots or lunaticks excepted, should be understood by them all in the same manner with one another, and in the same sense which the speaker intended to be understood, this would certainly be a most perfect stile."[40] When, however, a recent critic writes that the fiction of the period, judged by the standards we expect of literature, "can best be described as fantasy machines, which must have appeared to the educated literate elite of the eighteenth century precisely what comic books and television seem to the contemporary guardians of cultural standards," he is simply failing to make distinctions.[41]

Even a work like *Guy of Warwick* appeared in various forms, from chapbooks of a few pages to those of a hundred and fifty pages. The same is true of *Robinson Crusoe, Colonel Jack,* and *Moll Flanders,* which were rapidly abridged and then put into chapbook form. In this form Moll Flanders no longer appears to be guilty of incest, and, far from breaking the law by returning to England, she dies in full prosperity and penitence in Virginia.[42] The well-known lines,

> Down in the kitchen, honest Dick and Doll
> Are studying Colonel Jack and Flanders Moll,[43]

[40] Daniel Defoe, *The Complete English Tradesman* (London, 1727 [1726]), I, 26.

[41] Richetti, *Popular Fiction,* p. 9. What evidence Richetti adduces for his assertion that the eighteenth-century audience had "fewer cultural levels" (p. 12) than the modern audience is difficult to discover. He may have fallen into the error of believing that Pope's rhetorical device of dividing the literary world of the eighteenth century into two camps—one populated with his enemies, fools or starving hacks writing for the ignorant lower and middle classes, and the other with his friends, men of genius writing for a cultural elite—creates a true picture of the literary scene.

[42] See, for example, *The History of the Famous Moll Flanders* (Newcastle, n.d.), British Museum Cat. 107b. L.2 (b). Many of the changes were made to save space. Instead of the elaborate psychological analysis explaining Moll's agreement to marry her lover's brother, the reader is given the simple reason that Moll was pregnant.

[43] *The Flying Post; or Weekly Medley,* 1 March 1729. For a similar judgment on Defoe's fiction, see Peter Longueville, *The Hermit* (London, 1727), p. v. The tendency to assume that Defoe's fiction, including *Robinson Crusoe,* was read almost exclusively by the "lower" ranks of society is more an exercise in literary criticism than a careful observation of Defoe's audience. The same comment would have been made about any writer of realistic or picaresque fiction. In his

unfortunately fail to stipulate the editions, but unless Dick and
Doll, like Steele's footman, borrowed a copy from their master or
mistress, they were probably reading something they could afford
—something rather different from what Defoe wrote.

All that we really know is that a great deal of fiction was available and that the strange mixture of Locke and Malebranche
alongside Mrs. Manley and de Scudéry in Leonora's library does
not appear to have been unusual. The library of Dr. Francis Bernard, sold in 1698, had almost every kind of fiction obtainable at
the time, from imaginary voyages to novellas, and a large number
of learned works. In a catalogue of libraries of a divine, a lawyer,
and a physician, sold in 1722, may be found Swift's *Tale of a Tub*,
"Crawford's Novels," *Persian Tales*, *Turkish Tales*, and Sorel's
Comical History of Francion listed with philosophers like Locke,
Pufendorf, and Thomas Burnet.[44] Ten years later, in another
catalogue, we find *The New Atalantis*, *Gulliver's Travels*, *Robinson Crusoe*, and Croxall's six-volume collection of "novels."[45]
Certainly almost everyone who could afford a library read some
form of prose fiction.[46]

To construct a general model of social and historical change for
the first half of the eighteenth century and fit most of the fiction
into that pattern would not be difficult. The reign of Queen Anne
was filled with party strife, and the Triennial Act produced a
continual focus on politics. We might expect that fiction would
tend to be disorganized and satirical. After 1714 England settled
down to a period of internal peace under an assured Protestant
succession. Social lines were hardening, as evidenced by the Peer-

discussion of the picaresque, from *La vida de Lazarillo de Tormes* to *Histoire
de Gil Blas de Santillane*, Lengelet du Fresnoy (*De l'Usage des Romans* [Amster-
dam, 1734], I, 196–198) maintained that such works violated the neoclassical ideal
of a generalized image of nature. He compared writers of picaresque fiction with
the Dutch realists in general and with Rembrandt in particular, arguing that such
artists were inferior to painters like Van Dyke.

[44] *A Catalogue of the Valuable Part of the Libraries of the Reverend Mr.
Maurice Vaughan . . . ; of a Counsellor at Law and of a Physician* (London,
1722), pp. 3, 5, 30, 32.

[45] *A Catalogue of the Libraries of Mr. Bishop . . . Mr. Hitch . . . and Dr. Castle*
(London, 1732), p. 47.

[46] The library of Anthony Collins, sold on 18 January 1731, reveals the degree
to which a man of philosophical temperament could find fiction suitable to his
taste. As might be expected, Collins owned books on imaginary voyages, like
Joseph Hall's *Mundus Alter et Idem* and *Gulliver's Travels*, but he also possessed
Defoe's *A New Voyage Round the World*, some epistolary fiction, and *Gil Blas*.

age Bill of 1719, but a writer like Defoe, who glorified the social mobility of England in his *Tour through the Whole Island of Great Britain* and *The Compleat English Gentleman*, might well have produced a fiction based on a Whig myth of open opportunity. As English trade began to flourish, writers turned to fiction containing a great deal of exploration and voyaging. By 1740, however, social lines had hardened to the extent that a new assertion of the superiority of moral virtue over rank became necessary. Writers might tend to satirize the venality of a society they seemed incapable of changing and retreat into various forms of withdrawal from the competitive world, whether a physical and moral withdrawal to the country or a withdrawal into seemingly impossible happy endings.

That such an interpretation suffers greatly from hindsight I do not deny, but before examining the social responses of some of the writers of fiction I would like to glance briefly at the way fiction may have influenced society. In *The Spectator* of 21 December 1711, Lydia writes a bantering letter to Harriot, upbraiding her for being in love after six months of marriage and for speaking well of the country. Instead of a reply from Harriot, we are given a letter from plain Mary Home, who upbraids Lydia for her false sophistication. Mary Home's refusal to play the role of a correspondent in an epistolary novella suggests that the language of contemporary fiction might have spilled over into everyday life or at least into everyday letters. The following passages are quoted from letters written by Defoe's future son-in-law, Henry Baker, to Sophia Defoe:

O how I now repent the hours I have lost, those unhappy happy hours! when all alone with you, but overawed, I durst not tell my flame. And yet I hope they were not wholly lost; surely then, my eyes, my silence, my confusion told it: for even silence speaks, and love declares itself a thousand ways without the help of words. Ah! how can I bear this absence! Absence did I say? How Lovers rave!

My Sophy, ah, how I languish for thee! What soft sensations seize me! . . . Methinks . . . I snatch thee to me, and devour thy lips, strain thee with breathless raptures to my bosom, till feeble mortal nature faints, unable to endure bliss so excessive, and sinks with joys Celestial.[47]

[47] Thomas Wright, *The Life of Daniel Defoe* (London, 1931), pp. 374, 379. Baker's "breathless raptures" did not prevent him from engaging in a protracted battle with his future father-in-law over Sophia's dowry.

64 FICTION AND SOCIETY

Another Sophia, Sophia Western in *Tom Jones*, seems to have been influenced by novellas at a time when she and Mrs. Fitzpatrick were young Miss Graveairs and Miss Giddy, and even Tom Jones has his moments of speaking like a hero from a contemporary novella. Fielding may not have been so guilty of a failure of realism as some have supposed, though on hearing this kind of language we might agree with Belinda in Congreve's *Old Bachelor*, who called such a speech "a Whine" and complained that her lover spoke so much of "Flames and Stuff" that she could not bear to look at fires.[48]

Much of the fiction that exploited the type of love fantasy of which Henry Baker's language was so much a part had little direct relation to the immediate social milieu. Some of this fiction was erotic, as was a large part of the writings of Mrs. Haywood; some of it was highly moral, as were the productions of Mrs. Aubin. In the first two decades of the century the purely imaginative function of the romances was being usurped by the flood of "Tales" inspired by the publication of *The Arabian Nights* in 1706 and followed by *Persian Tales*, *Chinese Tales*, and *Peruvian Tales*. Novellas avoided marvelous genies and concentrated insistently on the marvels of love. When Mrs. Manley turned several stories that had appeared in William Painter's Elizabethan collection, *The Palace of Pleasure*, into contemporary novellas, she began with a passage that appears nowhere in the original but tells much about what she conceived those stories should be like:

Of all those Passions which may be said to tyrannize over the Heart of Man, Love is not only the most violent, but the most persuasive: It conducts us through Storms, Tempests, Seas, Mountains and Precipices, with as little Terror to the Mind, and as much Ease, as through beautiful Gardens and delightful Meadows: A Lover esteems nothing difficult in pursuit of his Desires: It is then that Fame, Honour, Chastity and Glory, have no longer their due Estimation even in the most vertuous Breast. When Love truly seizes the Heart, it is like a malignant Fever which thence disperses it self through all the sensible Parts; the Poyson preys upon the Vitals, and is only extinguished by Death; or, by as fatal a Cure, the accomplishment of its own Desires.[49]

[48] Congreve, [*Works*], ed. Dobrée, I, 45, 49 (Act II, scenes iii, viii).
[49] Mary de la Rivière Manley, *The Power of Love* (London, 1720), p. 1. See also Mrs. Manley's extended description of the sudden reversal from love to hatred so common in contemporary drama (p. 201): "Her Heart was immediately open to Wrath, Indignation, Madness and Revenge. All the Furies of Hell

Most of Mrs. Manley's additions, intended to underscore the conflict of the passions aroused by love, are in this manner.

In her scandalous chronicle, *The New Atalantis*, published in 1709, Mrs. Manley creates a vision of an entire society governed by varying degrees of irrational passion and self-interest. As Defoe was to do later, she exploits the various arguments on natural law which might permit a freer type of relationship than traditional marriage, and in narrating her bits of contemporary gossip as fictional tales, she includes love incidents involving everything from lesbianism to incest. Mrs. Manley presents a variety of fictional points of view, including those of a Country Woman and Mrs. Nightwork, a midwife, to reveal some of the secrets of the upper classes from a lower-class perspective. Pierre Bayle's confident claim that no romance would ever have a heroine with a "big Belly" was certainly not true of contemporary novellas exploiting the approach of scandalous chronicles like *The New Atalantis*.[50]

Mrs. Manley's fiction reveals much about contemporary society, but she seems to have been quite incapable of rendering her serious ideas in fictional form. The end of her *Secret History of Queen Zarah* dissolves into a fascinating essay on society, including one statement that supports what Peter Laslett has written concerning the difference in physical appearance between the rich and the poor. The rich have "good Nourishment, and the Juice of Nice Meats, which mixes with the Blood, . . . and renders them more proper for the Functions of Nature." Their dietary habits change their entire appearance, putting an "odd Fire and Liveliness in their Eyes, which distinguishes them from other Persons, whose Stupidity is perceiv'd by their dull and languishing Eyes."[51] Swift thought Mrs. Manley a fairly capable writer, but either she was unable to weave ideas into her fiction or she did not believe it worth doing. After twelve pages of expository prose, she resumes her typical style and returns to the scandalous life of Zarah, otherwise known as Sarah, Duchess of Marlborough.

---

entred like a Torrent into her Breast, and in a moment expell'd her native Softness; Love hid his Face and would be seen no more; he took wing with all his Train and Dependents, and flew for ever away from that Hospitable Heart where he had been so fondled and tenderly entertain'd."

[50] Pierre Bayle, *The Dictionary*, trans. Pierre des Maizeaux, 2d ed. (London, 1734–1738), III, 866.

[51] Mary de la Rivière Manley, *The Secret History of Queen Zarah* (London, 1743), p. 89.

Apparently Mrs. Manley regarded prose fiction as a form inferior to poetry. She started her career by writing one of the worst tragedies of her or any other age and continued writing for the stage. In her preface to *The Power of Love*, she compared what she had done with Dryden's *Fables*, but quickly added that her work was as inferior to Dryden's as prose was to poetry. Even allowing for a reluctance to deal with ideas in fiction, her work suffers from major intellectual inconsistencies. She presents a world governed by self-interest, and she quotes La Rochefoucauld with generous approval. When women fall through uncontrolled passion, she speaks of them with pity; when they act from self-interest, she criticizes them. Justice and Virtue function as characters in *The New Atalantis*, but their judgments are anything but consistent. When she comes to a moral crux, she refers it to the "Casuists" and lets it go at that. Defoe would have devoted pages to the same problem.

Whatever influence social events may have had on the *best* writers of fiction, whether a plague in Marseilles or the Licensing Act of 1737, they never abandoned their roles as moral critics. Probably nothing I can think of underscores this point so well as Penelope Aubin's version of a Robinsonade, a ten-page episode in *The Strange Adventures of the Count de Vinevil and his Family*, published two years after *Robinson Crusoe* in 1721. Mrs. Aubin describes how "Necessity taught them what to do in a Place where there was neither House nor Marker," how after receiving some comfort from a priest among them "they slept as sweetly as if they had lain in Palaces on Beds of Down." When another ship is wrecked they discover that "the Ruin of others procured their Preservation, as is frequent in this World." They also find that "Gold, that causes Men to sell their Souls, and change their Faiths was here less valuable than a Crust of Bread." They live off milk from a goat, but eventually grow weak from hunger. Finally they are rescued.[52]

The richness of *Robinson Crusoe* as a commentary on these themes and on man and society in general was obvious enough in its own day, and Golding's *Lord of the Flies* has successfully exploited a similar theme for our society. But for Mrs. Aubin, the episode was merely an opportunity for stating some commonplaces and another adventure in a work with as many as a Greek romance. That Mrs. Aubin's intention was moral and religious is

[52] Penelope Aubin, *A Collection of Entertaining Histories and Novels* (London, 1739), II, 49–59.

spelled out mainly in the gaps in the story, when a character can state a specific religious moral. Defoe solved this problem in *Robinson Crusoe*, not by a process of circumstantial realism, as Ian Watt believes, but by his willingness to render in fictional form the same ideas that he thought worthy of a treatise, whether on an economic, political, or religious theme. Crusoe was not merely a random example for economists like Marx and Böhm-Bawerk. They were able to see him as an embodiment of certain economic characteristics because Defoe built into *Robinson Crusoe* an economic parable.[53] And the meaning of that parable is not to be found in an analysis of business opportunities in York during the seventeenth century but in the broader implications of social and religious problems in Defoe's day.

Defoe may have been responding to specific problems. We now know that *The Family Instructor* was influenced by a bill that would have prevented the Dissenters from educating their children.[54] Defoe's solution was a withdrawal into the family as a moral and social unit.[55] In the same way, *Robinson Crusoe* is probably, in part, a response to some of the quarrels that shook the Church of England and the Dissenters between 1717 and 1719. In fictionalizing a scene of complete isolation, however, Defoe was able to construct a story that embodied a new social myth. What he had to say about man in nature, about money, and about government was submerged into a coherent fiction.

If we are to look for realism as a clue to Defoe's uniqueness, we should look to his psychological realism, for we never get a total view of society in Defoe's fiction; we can perceive only the fragment of experience that concerns the narrator. As Rousseau realized in *Emile*, Crusoe's real relationships, once he is in isolation, are with the objects and the physical nature of his island. To send a hero off to a cave on an island or anywhere else was a clue to the reader to expect either religious fervor or romantic excess, whether in *Guy of Warwick*, *Don Quixote*, or *Simplicissimus*. We get

---

53 See Maximillian E. Novak, *Economics and the Fiction of Daniel Defoe* (Berkeley and Los Angeles, 1962), pp. 32–66.

54 B. G. Ivanyi, "The Schism Act Explain'd," *TLS*, 7 April 1966.

55 Defoe maintained that the concept of "family" was inherent in each man. A transition from the family unit, with which he was concerned in the two volumes of *The Family Instructor* (1715, 1718), to the isolated individual is hardly surprising in view of his belief that the Schism Act would force the Dissenters to lead a secret religious life in the home while preserving a mask of conformity for the social and political world. See Defoe, *A Condoling Letter to the Tatler* (London, 1710), pp. 13–14; *Wise as Serpents* (London, 1712), pp. 40–46; and *The Schism Act Explain'd* (London, 1714), pp. 15–17, 32–40.

some religious meditation from Crusoe, but we are also told of his experiments in making bread. Both romance figures and hermits could ignore such trivial concerns even if an occasional skeptic like Sir Charles in *The Female Quixote* might protest against a hero's living on sighs and tears for ten months and Defoe might ridicule the idea that the desert fathers had to be fed by angels.

In *Moll Flanders* and *Colonel Jack*, Defoe blended the picaresque with the fictional memoir as practiced in France by Sandras. For *Roxana*, Defoe worked a variation on the novella as it appeared in the form of a secret history. The pictures of life among the poor, of social institutions like the mint, of a debtor's sanctuary, and of the glasshouses where beggars slept were unique in English fiction up until that time. The excellence of Defoe's treatment, however, rests not in physical description but in moral comment. The glasshouses are where Jack slept. The warm ashes kept him alive, and he was not unhappy there; but, as Defoe makes clear, it was no way for children to live. The same is true about Moll's picture of life in the mint. For Moll and Jack, as even for the poorest man or woman, Defoe held out the possibility of success in America, appealing to the fantasy of financial success which Adam Smith described as the "desire of bettering our condition, a desire which, though generally calm and dispassionate, comes with us from the womb, and never leaves us till we go to the grave."[56]

Defoe's vision was his own, and however tempting the desire for continuity may be, there is no reason to see the torch being passed from Defoe to Richardson and then to Fielding and Smollett. Richardson's desire to introduce "a new species of writing . . . different from the pomp and parade of romance-writing," his hatred of the "French Marvellous," and his desire to instruct were embodied in the form of a new romance.[57] More than Defoe, he was influenced by the texture of the old romances and the novellas. Like those works, his were concerned with love and passion, which he believed dominated younger persons. What Defoe did not believe capable of being sustained in a narrative, what went into works like *Religious Courtship* and *The Family Instructor* (fiction in the shape of moral dialogues), Richardson did manage to sustain. Taking a Christian marriage rather than passionate love as his ideal, Richardson turned Miss Betty, the typical servant, in-

---

[56] *The Wealth of Nations*, Everyman Library ed. (London, 1954), I, 305.
[57] Samuel Richardson, *Selected Letters*, ed. John Carroll (Oxford, 1964), pp. 41, 53.

to Mrs. Pamela Andrews, transforming her into a critic of a society that allowed justices of the peace to wink at the rape of servant girls. Like the speaker in Defoe's *Poor Man's Plea for a Reformation of Manners* in 1698, or like Steele's footman with whom we began, Pamela casts a cold glance at the manners of the great, even at monarchs like George II who she felt encouraged polygamy by keeping courtesans. She institutes family prayers and reforms all about her. The art historian, Robert Rosenblum, remarks that the "moralizing plane of Greuze's painting rejects not only the amorality of Boucher's interpretation of erotic goals but also the amorality of his style."[58] Richardson's effect on contemporary fiction was roughly the same. Instead of perusing collections of aphorisms about love extracted from romances and novellas, readers could turn to *A Collection of the Moral Sentiments, Maxims, Cautions, and Reflections, Contained in the Histories of Pamela, Clarissa, and Sir Charles Grandison*, where they might read attacks on self-love and on the passions that had been the very basis of the novellas, pithy comments on the qualities of a true gentleman, and a complete manual on the subject of virtuous love and marriage. Mary Wortley Montagu may have believed that *Pamela* and *Clarissa* would "do more general mischeif than the Works of Lord Rochester,"[59] but Richardson for the first time made fiction truly respectable and thereby socially responsible.

Smollett and Fielding profited from the new respect for fiction. Both avoided the older appellation of "romance" and "novel." Fielding preferred "history" and associated his work with the epic. Smollett, who was still strongly influenced by the style of contemporary novellas, preferred to follow in the footsteps of Mrs. Manley and claim *Roderick Random* as a satire. Smollett benefited greatly from the now acceptable surface realism, but that is hardly his claim to greatness, which lies in his powers of comedy and his vivid portrayal of the venality and general incompetence of those who rule society, from idiot politicians to homosexual captains. Fielding's picture of clergymen and justices of the peace is no less bitter, even if his satire is more gentle.

It has been pointed out that names of characters become more realistic, but picaresque fiction always had realistic names, and Mrs. Haywood, who goes over to the new fiction in *Betsy*

---

[58] Robert Rosenblum, *Transformations in Late Eighteenth Century Art* (Princeton, 1967), p. 52.
[59] *Complete Letters*, ed. Halsband, III, 9.

Thoughtless, merely picks up the typical names of stage comedy like Trueworth and Saving. In involving her heroine, Betsy, in a near rape she comes close to her usual lubricious manner, and a scene she views through a crack in the wall has some of the voyeuristic qualities of *Fanny Hill*. But we are not rushed on from adventure to adventure; we are forced to stop and observe the values of the society in which Betsy lives. Obviously Mrs. Haywood could have done it before, if she had thought that her audience wanted anything but scandal and scenes of passion presented at a rapid pace. The very range of her technical experiments with fiction shows that her reaction to the demands of her audience was immediate. Defoe, who was in the pay of the government and comfortably situated in Stoke Newington, and Richardson, who had grown wealthy as a printer, were both in a better position to experiment. Even though Mrs. Haywood had abandoned the novella, the basic nature of the form, its quick narrative and précieuse style, its dreamy landscape filled with woodbines and jasmines, continued in a multitude of forms until the end of the century.

The historical model with which I started this final section may work well enough as a general framework, but it is difficult to see how it helps our understanding of individual works very much. Defoe, Richardson, Fielding, and Smollett, the writers usually associated with the novel during this period, were all involved in the world in a way that women of the time (and most writers of novellas were women) could never be. This is also true of Swift, who must be taken into account in any general consideration of the fiction of this period. Swift was a controversial divine; Defoe thought of himself as an economic journalist; Richardson was a printer; Fielding, a judge; Smollett, a physician. They were all very much concerned with the moral nature of their society. It helps to know the social tracts of Defoe and Fielding when reading their fiction, but it is also important to recognize that Fielding was right in listing humanity as one of the four requirements of a writer of fiction; humanity mitigates whatever is harsh in Fielding's attitude toward the poor and whatever is cynical in Defoe's attitude toward the gentleman. None of these writers made the mistake of turning fiction into a social tract, but all were deeply, consciously engaged in making fiction morally responsive to the society around them.

IV

THE MOOD OF THE CHURCH
AND *A TALE OF A TUB*

Robert M. Adams

Professor of English, University of California, Los Angeles

Hate is a kind of "passive suffering," but indignation is a kind of joy. "When I am told that somebody is my brother Protestant," says Swift, "I remember that the rat is a fellow creature." That seems to be a joyous saying.—W. B. Yeats

Satires, especially large, complicated English satires published in the year 1704, often seem to have two faces because, as a genre, they direct their vision two different ways. On the one hand, they see or sense the way things ought to be under the law of rational decorum, disciplined allegiance, traditional order, which was our forefathers' seemly style of living; on the other hand, they are painfully aware of the many outrages and indignities daily perpetrated against this standard by the knaves and fools into whom our race has degenerated. Men of longsighted, judicious, and scholarly vision naturally take the nobler and more positive view; and, apart from our superior wisdom, we are often assisted in doing so by convenient circumstances, such as a relatively secure income, an established place in an established hierarchy, a set of values that (if not wholly unchallenged) we feel confident of being able to defend. Unfortunately, we are not usually the people who pen great and unsettling satires. In this paper I propose to look at *A Tale of a Tub* as if it were the work of a distinctly bitter young man who had reached the age of thirty or so without finding a settled position in the world; who had, indeed, attached himself to a hierarchy and to a set of values, but just as they were undergoing ferocious attack from outside, severe questioning from inside, and the sort of erosion (not to call it dry-rot) that angry young men often find deeply distressing. Such a young man is more likely to be impressed by knaves and fools than by high ideals; faced with deadly evil, he does not seek the lofty, wide-minded compromise, but drives for the jugular.

Implicit in the view I am taking of *A Tale of a Tub* and its circumstances is a polemical position, not very radical or fierce, but which had better be faced directly. A great many discussions of the book have quietly taken for granted that it was written in and for the eighteenth century; that its attack upon abuses in religion and learning may be understood as a way of clearing the ground for that broad, shallow, and somewhat somnolent structure, the eighteenth-century establishment.[1] When apologizing for the book in 1710, Jonathan Swift himself said explicitly that it "Celebrates the Church of England as the most perfect of all others in Discipline and Doctrine";[2] and of course, as time passed, as a sense of the book's brilliant, brittle wit prevailed over a sense of its immorality, and as Swift himself became established in Anglican hagiography as a great though eccentric churchman, the *Tale* was (quite naturally) domesticated, so far as that proved possible. I

---

[1] See, for example, R. Quintana (*Mind & Art of Jonathan Swift* [London, 1953], pp. 85–86): "It would seem that Swift worked out an allegory expressing the moderate and reasonable position maintained by the church of England between the two extremes of Roman Catholic presumption and error on one hand and dissenting enthusiasm on the other"; J. Middleton Murry (*Jonathan Swift* [New York, 1955], p. 86): "The *Tale* is primarily a manifestation of the comic spirit. Its dominant temper is genial, not savage; exuberant, not destructive"; and I. Ehrenpreis (*Swift* [Cambridge, Mass., 1962], I, 189–190): ". . . behind the book stands not a list of philosophical propositions but the idea of a good man. This idea belongs to the tradition usually called Christian humanism. . . . Swift sets before us the Christian gentleman, a landed proprietor educated in humanist culture, conscious of his duties as a subject and a master. This model conforms cheerfully to the Established Church; he willingly supports the government of England as redesigned in 1688–9, and he is a responsible head of a family." The book described by Ehrenpreis as proposing the ideal of a paterfamilias is *A Tale of a Tub*.

[2] *A Tale of a Tub*, ed. A. C. Guthkelch and D. Nichol Smith, 2d ed. (Oxford, 1958), p. 5. Subsequent references are to this edition.

propose to look at it for a moment as if it were a book assembled, if not written, between 1697 and 1702; as if it were a book composed by a man who had some reason to doubt that there was going to be an eighteenth-century establishment in which he would be a distinguished dean, who did not know and could not guess that the English church was going to drone and drowse peacefully (undisturbed save by a few errant Methodists) through a long Hanoverian summertime. Looking at it in this way, we may find an irony or two in the word "celebrate" as used to describe the *Tale*'s attitude toward the English establishment, and perhaps even elsewhere in the book.

Toward this end I have assembled a number of little things— episodes, assertions, happenings, clusters of revealing social artifacts, an insinuation or two—in the hope of representing certain moods within specific social strata of the late seventeenth century, out of which, I believe, *A Tale of a Tub* sprang. I have not tried to give a fully detailed account of any of the events, and I do not mean to put most of them into a direct causal relationship with the *Tale*. They are not, for the most part, "sources"; sometimes chronology itself precludes that. Yet they are never without a rather close relation to Jonathan Swift and people in his immediate ambience; if one allows them to build toward a picture of a state of mind, I think they will do a good deal to relate some extraordinary features of the *Tale* to some extraordinary features of an extraordinary historical era.

Toward the end of Jack's section of the *Tale* (Sec. XI), the author, while professing to have mislaid his papers, offers the reader a quick summary of what they contained:

> ... there was a full Account, how *Peter* got a *Protection* out of the *King's-Bench*: and of a Reconcilement between *Jack* and Him, upon a Design they had in a certain *rainy Night*, to trepan Brother *Martin* into a *Spunging-house*, and there strip him to the Skin. How *Martin*, with much ado, shew'd them both a fair pair of Heels. How a *new Warrant* came out against *Peter*; upon which, how *Jack* left him in the lurch, *stole his Protection, and made use of it himself*. How *Jack*'s Tatters came into Fashion in *Court* and *City*; How *he got upon a great Horse, and eat Custard*.[3]

And that is the last we ever hear of the three brothers; Martin having fled into the rainy night, Peter and Jack are left trying to

[3] *Tale of a Tub*, pp. 204–205.

flimflam each other, a contest that Jack, as the greater rogue, is evidently going to win. That this passage celebrates the Church of England is not impossible; but it is evidently a celebration that mingles hilarity with despair in about the proportions of an Irish wake. It is my argument in this paper that if we set ourselves in the painful position of an English clergyman of the conservative persuasion about the year 1697, we are likely to see the raw nerves and tight sinews of the *Tale* better than if we smooth the book with plastic historical hindsight. Here is a case in point.

In the passage where the brothers are vigorously double-dealing one another, we do not have to consult many footnotes to see in capsule allegory a decade of English religious history from James II's Declaration of Indulgence (1687) to Sir Humphrey Edwin's curious performance as the first avowedly Presbyterian lord mayor of London (1697). Jealous resentment controls the tone; Jack and Peter maneuver and connive to such effect that all Martin can do is make his escape in a rainstorm. Thus the establishment (Martin) is pushed aside by Presbyterianism (Jack), which makes use of a toleration stolen from the Roman Catholics (Peter) to usurp an unjust and illegitimate power. Sir Humphrey Edwin, who became lord mayor in 1697, provides a crucial image here, and it may be useful to revive briefly the scandal that flared during his administration. By the terms of the Test Act, Sir Humphrey was obliged, as a condition of his office, to show that he had attended the Anglican communion at least once in the past six months. He duly did so, and was properly sworn into office—he sat on the great horse and ate the ceremonial custard; but then, before he had been in place a month, he proceeded on two consecutive Sundays (31 October and 7 November 1697) to don the robes of office, command the official sword-bearer to precede him, and thus in his official capacity to attend a conventicle at Salters' Hall. The sword-bearer, evidently a traditionalist, had to be locked in his pew to keep him from leaving in indignation; and the pamphleteers and balladmongers had a field day.[4]

To be sure, occasional conformity, looked at from a modern perspective, is no very terrifying phenomenon; it is simply one step on the way to establishing an Englishman's right to hold pub-

---

[4] George Ridpath (*A Rowland for an Oliver: or, a sharp rebuke to a sawcy Levite, in answer to a sermon preach'd by Edward Oliver* [London, 1699], p. 24) speaks feelingly of the way the Lord Mayor was "abused in the street by Balladsingers, Hawkers, and rascally fellows."

lic office regardless of his religious views. And that hardly suggests the end of the world. In 1697, however, the issue was not so clear. The Test Act was on the books; occasional conformity was a patent device, a barefaced contradiction in terms, to circumvent it.[5] That the chief magistrate of the kingdom's major city should hold office by subterfuge and circumvention of the law he was sworn to uphold was by no means an easy thing to accept. The fact of nonconformity was an admitted, an established, social circumstance. As a private citizen Sir Humphrey was free to attend any meeting he wanted, or none at all, but that he should evade the penalties attached to his position, and publicly flaunt his evasion of them, in order to acquire an office to which only his interest called him was deeply distressing. It was particularly distressing to the Church of England clergy to find their communion reduced not only to a rubber stamp, but to a rubber stamp used in flagrant bad faith, and made a mockery and a laughingstock. And to have all this happen within ten years of the Church of England's finest hour, when Anglican bishops had stood as leaders of the national mood against James II (while Jack and Peter paltered and compromised on the sidelines), was of all humiliations the hardest to swallow. Seen against a background of complaint about notorious public immorality and of widespread contempt of the clergy, the bitterness aroused by Sir Humphrey Edwin's maneuver becomes understandable. The classes and the communions for whom he stood were united in blaming the established church for its failure to purify English moral life; yet here they deliberately acted to undermine the church's authority and bring it into ridicule and public contempt.

It is clear that the practice of occasional conformity was eroding a position of privilege held or claimed by the Anglican establishment, but in the discussion that surrounded this public social event, another erosion took place which was quite as significant for the *Tale*. It was an erosion of vocabulary, or rather, the capture of a vocabulary originally used in one context and with one meaning for use in another context. A key word here is "modera-

---

[5] See *The Case of Moderation and Occasional Communion Represented* (London, 1705), p. 26: "*Occasional Communion* is nothing . . . because there is a contradiction in the terms: *Occasional* is one thing, and *Communion* is the direct contrary. *Communion* is a fixed and stated thing, *Occasional* only by the bye: *Communion* is a Habit, *Occasional* only a single Act. They may be joynd together in a Proposition, but the Things themselves can never agree, nor be made one; like Rebellious Loyalty, Orthodox Heresie, the North South Wind."

tion," and the controversy over it, which had been a long time brewing, came to a head about the year 1703. *Moderation* is of course a very valuable word in time of controversy. The power of the English church to claim that word for itself had roots as deep as the Reformation; the English church had long claimed to represent a via media, a quiet, rational middle course between Presbyterianism and popery. Then in 1703 a certain James Owen published, under the bland title of *Moderation a Virtue*, a little argument to the effect that true moderation consisted, not in adhering to a moderate position, but in adhering to it moderately, that is, occasionally. When Owen chose his title, he can scarcely have been ignorant of the fact that as recently as 1683 the identical title, *Moderation a Vertue*, had been used to describe the position of the liberal Anglican clergy. What the 1683 author meant by moderation was what the word had traditionally meant: a submissive and uncontentious disposition, an emphasis on the broad grounds of moral agreement, an ardent devotion to Christian unity.[6] But Owen, like a true cuckoo bird, took over the title, using it as he clearly proposed to use the Anglican institution itself, for his own ends, and only so far as it suited those ends.

According to Owen, the occasional conformist was the true moderate because he recognized that there was good in the Church of England and good in the dissenting communions, and he would conform with them both. Such a man "judges himself obliged to get the best Helps he can for his Soul, and thinks he ought not to be more restrained in the Choice of a *spiritual Guide* for the benefit of his *Soul*, than he is in the Choice of a *Lawyer* or *Physitian* for the preserving of his *Estate* and *Bodily Health*." [7] In thus communing indifferently with church and conventicle,

---

[6] It is an interesting stylistic note that the 1683 author casts his traditional views of moderation in a gentle, semiepigrammatic balancing of catchphrases, a grave playing with formulas. The moderate man "is neither fond of needless Ritualities, nor yet molested with groundless Scruples, neither worships Images nor Imaginations, but submits to the Customs of the Country, tho not to the Iniquities of the Times. . . . He takes more pains to make good his Baptismal Covenant, than to wrangle about the Mode of its Administration, as if he were baptized with the Waters of Strife. And he is more concerned to prove himself a good Christian than to prove who is Antichrist" (*Moderation a Vertue*, by a Lover of Moderation, Resident upon his Cure [London, 1683], *ad finem*). By contrast, Owen is an edgy casuistical writer who trims his argument artfully to look as open-minded and judicious as he can. A detailed comparative study of the two styles would be of great interest.

[7] James Owen, *Moderation a Virtue* (London, 1703), p. 12.

the occasional conformists were, Owen held, convinced they were following the example of John the Baptist, Jesus Christ, and Saint Paul,[8] all of whom worshiped occasionally in the established religious groups of their day and occasionally in groups of their own devising. (It is characteristic of Owen that he uses these parallels, which he knows and says are specious, on the score that some nonconformists believe in them and are therefore not hypocrites in their occasional conformity; he does not entertain the alternative that, if not knaves, they must be fools.)[9] When Dissenters visited the Church of England only every so often (say, every six months, or just often enough to qualify for public office and thus keep Christ and Mammon comfortably hand in glove), they were not only following the example of the primitive Christians; they could claim to be particularly true and orthodox sons of the Church of England. For whereas many of the avowed supporters of that church had divided over the interpretation of its articles, no such troubles assailed the Dissenters; for them, the vaguer the articles, the better. "The Dissenters generally assert the Ancient and Orthodox Doctrine of the Church of *England*, and subscribe her Articles in the natural and genuine Sense of the Words." [10] It is a nice trick, indeed, to dissent on Monday from a church as dangerous to your salvation, and to pronounce yourself on Tuesday a believer in, and a judge of, its ancient and orthodox doctrine, a subscriber to all its articles "in the natural and genuine sense," as if the people who attend that church day in and day out are in no position to judge of what its articles mean and what its doctrine is.

Such complacent pronouncements by men whom they regarded as gross interlopers did not, of course, sit well with Anglicans of the old persuasion, and a series of polemical pamphlets appeared in answer to Owen. Rumors and reverberations of the quarrel over the word *moderation* persisted for a long time in the

---

[8] *Ibid.*, pp. 7–8.

[9] "I am not concern'd to prove the Case of our Dissenters to be parallel with these before us, 'tis sufficient to vindicate 'em from the Imputation of *Hypocrisy* and *Atheism*, that they think it so" (*ibid.*, p. 9). This shiftiness is characteristic of Owen; having raised the objection, "If there be so great Agreement between 'em [Dissenters] and the Church, how came they to be separate from it?" he answers simply: "It's none of my Business to enquire into the Reasons of their Separation here, that has been done by other Hands, particularly by Mr. *Baxter* ... and lately by Mr. *Calamy*." That is the answer we get to the question of how Dissenters can uphold separation with one hand and agreement with the other.

[10] *Ibid.*, p. 20.

periodical literature of the early century, and Jonathan Swift, in *The Sentiments of a Church of England Man* (1708), defined the word as a polite cover phrase for soliciting the cooperation of "Atheists, Libertines, Despisers of Religion and Revelation in general." [11] A frequent implication of the Anglican partisans was that moderation was being used, not just to blur, not just to equivocate, but actually to conceal a program of deliberate sabotage. Charles Leslie, for instance, implied exactly that in the title of his pamphlet against Owen, *The Wolf Stript of his Shepherd's Cloathing, in Answer to a Late Celebrated Book Intitul'd Moderation a Virtue* (1704). What Leslie implied was said explicitly in another tract, *Moderation Display'd* (1704): that behind the smoke screen of the word "moderation" a "New Sett of Men" were pushing toward a seizure of power in church and state. [12]

If it had been simply a matter of encroachment from below or pressure from outside, the situation would have been a familiar one for the established church, and would have given no particular cause for anxiety. High Church loyalists suspected, however, and even denounced, collusion and complicity with the church's traditional enemies by high authorities within the church itself. And it was to this wing of the church that both Thomas and Jonathan Swift—first cousins, intimate acquaintances, and certainly loyal associates as late as 1693, not to be open enemies until 1710— were passionately attached by training, by family tradition, by professional instinct. "Treason!" is precisely the cry that Charles Leslie, brilliantly articulate controversialist, raises in *The Wolf Stript.*[13] Leslie really does not care much about Owen, who is only a sheep at best; the wolves he wants to denounce are already in the fold: they carry pastoral crooks and wear miters. Ten years ago, he says, a plot concerted by Queen Mary and Tillotson, Archbishop of Canterbury, threatened to deliver English episcopacy into the hands of its enemies in the name of unity, harmony, comprehension, and moderation. The plot collapsed in 1694, Leslie says, because the principals in it died within a month of each other, but he is convinced that the same interests are still at work in the same direction, that the "moderation" proclaimed by nonconformists, occasional conformists, and their allies in the Whig party is simply a cloak of unction behind which they are

---

[11] Jonathan Swift, *Prose Works*, ed. Herbert Davis (Oxford, 1939), II, 3.
[12] See preface to *Moderation Display'd* (London, 1704).
[13] Charles Leslie, *The Wolf Stript* (London, 1704), pp. 38–47.

preparing to grasp ecclesiastical and then political power, objectives for which they are ready to reduce the Christian religion itself to a hollow shell.

In dealing with lucid, intransigent men like Charles Leslie (or the cousins Swift), it is not always easy to draw the line between realism and paranoia. The plot Leslie denounced could well have existed simply as an idealistic scheme for reconciling the fratricidal sects. But on whose terms would the reconciliation be made? What concessions would it require? Jealousy and suspicion lay heavily upon the mood of that wing of the English church to which the two Swift cousins adhered and from whose point of view *A Tale of a Tub* was written.[14] A revealing little phrase in Deane Swift's account of his cousin Jonathan slips out in the course of a casual mention of their mutual cousin Thomas. Thomas was "a man of Learning and Abilities; but unfortunately bred up like his Father and Grandfather, with an abhorrence and

[14] See Robert M. Adams, "Jonathan Swift, Thomas Swift, and the Authorship of *A Tale of a Tub*," *Modern Philology*, LXVII (1967), 198–232; and Denis Donoghue, *Jonathan Swift* (Cambridge, 1969), App. A, pp. 222–225. The argument in my article is that Thomas Swift did in fact, as was claimed in the 1710 *Key* issued by Edmund Curll, have a hand in writing the "Fragment" (i.e., "The Discourse on the Mechanical Operation of the Spirit") and also some part in writing the "Tale" proper (as distinct from its prefatory matter and digressions). At the risk of sounding a bit querulous, I would like to propose that this argument comes closest to claiming positive conclusions in the matter of the "Fragment" and ought to be refuted or endorsed there, rather than on its periphery. If Thomas did not have a hand in the "Fragment," then there is no reason to think he had a hand in the rest of the book; he is an envious liar, and there's an end to it. On the evidence, this seems a hard case to make; at least I have not yet seen it made. Denis Donoghue lays some weight on an unpublished article by Dipak Nandy (I have not seen it) which makes it a logical flaw to attribute Section XI to Thomas Swift on the ground that its materials are like those of the "Fragment," while attributing authorship of the "Fragment" itself to Thomas Swift on the ground that its style is inferior to that of Section XI. But the hypothesis proposed answers these facts perfectly. It is, in effect, that Thomas wrote the "Fragment"; the printer expressly says it came to him "in a different hand," and Thomas's annotations explain that otherwise enigmatic footnote. Section XI uses the same materials but in a superior way because it was written on the basis of the "Fragment" by a better writer, Jonathan. Style different; materials similar. And how to escape the matter of timing? Section XI was written after 1697—it had to be. Did Jonathan write the inferior version of all these parallel jokes after, or at the same time as, he wrote the superior version (Sec. XI)? If not, then Section XI must have been written well after the time when Jonathan himself says the book was completed. The hypothesis about Jonathan, Thomas, and these two units of the book may be right or wrong, but I cannot yet see an inconsistency in it or a better way of accounting for the hard historical facts.

contempt for all the *puritanical Sectaries*; [and therefore] continued *Rector* of *Putenham*, without any the least hope of rising in the Church for the space of three score years."[15] A man of learning and abilities, we see, held for sixty years in an inferior position because he was too hostile to the open enemies of the church he was sworn to defend and uphold. A remarkable situation indeed. Men are likely to become bitter when their ardor for the institution to which they owe allegiance is made a charge against them by superiors who profess the same allegiance. We recall that Jonathan Swift's aspirations toward the episcopacy were blighted by his association (hazy as he tried to keep it) with the *Tale*. Was it the book's bawdiness or its ferocious anti-Calvinist bias that most shocked Archbishop Sharp? We do not know, but the two considerations may well have gone hand in hand.

In close proximity to this "political" jealousy lie those economic and social grievances of the established clergy pointed up by the diagnostic treatises of witty Dr. Eachard. There is no need to recite this story at length. Eachard's argument (first published in 1670) was that the general contempt for the clergy was due essentially to the poverty and ignorance of the clergymen.[16] Under the first heading, it will suffice to point out that inflation had for several hundred years been doing to the established clergy what it generally does to men on fixed incomes. Consequently, a man often had to be a pluralist to live, and a natural consequence of giving several livings apiece to a number of men was giving none at all to a number of others. Jonathan Swift, like all other men who cared for the cloth, was much distressed at the sight of raggle-taggle clergymen drifting around London without regular employment or sufficient income to keep them from contemptible occupations.[17] He and his fellow Anglicans were particularly humiliated because Calvinist lecturers and sectarian preachers often found more comfortable maintenance outside the establishment than beneficed clergymen could find within it. Tom Brown, that loquacious, "gentlemanly" rascal, has an interesting dialogue between a couple of university scholars, one of whom

15 Deane Swift, *Essay upon the Life of . . . Swift* (London, 1755), App. XV, note *b*. The bracketed phrase is not in the original but is clearly understood.

16 John Eachard, *The Grounds and Occasions of the Contempt of the Clergy and Religion* (1670), and *Some Observations upon the Answer to an Enquiry into the Grounds and Occasions of the Contempt of the Clergy* (London, 1671).

17 *A Project for the Advancement of Religion*, in *Prose Works*, ed. Davis, II, 54–55.

has determined to turn fanatic preacher.[18] The advantages, as this young scamp enumerates them, are impressive. You don't have to know anything; a whine, a twist of the features, and a set of cant phrases will serve all turns. The living is good, the brothers are rich, and the sisters are sympathetic; there is no crusty old bishop breathing down your neck; you don't have to pay and pay and pay to get into your living; you aren't expected to lay out money for every charitable enterprise in the parish. A man is a fool to enter the establishment, says Brown's persuasive mouthpiece, when he can do so much better for himself with the Dissenters at the price of only a little self-contempt, a modest quantum of hypocrisy.

(Let me repeat the warning: it is not social reality that counts here. We are not interested in how things really were, but in the mood, the tone of feeling, pervading the milieu out of which *A Tale of a Tub* sprang. Tom Brown is a relevant witness here: though only a fake gentleman, he has a rather surprising set of Tory and even High Church principles, just as John Eachard, for a churchman, had a rather surprising strain of sparkish wit. Jonathan Swift read them both assiduously, and paid them the further compliment of borrowing some of their better strokes for use in the *Tale*.)

The learning of the clergy poses a different problem. The bookseller of the *Tale* says, in his dedication to Lord Somers, that when the manuscript was found it contained a dedication of sorts—*Detur Dignissimo*—which, says he, "for all I knew, might contain some important meaning." [19] So, to translate the arcane text, he had recourse to a number of authors, all of whom professed to be baffled by it, though in fact, the bookseller says, he had often paid them to make translations from the Latin language. Finally he consulted the curate of the parish, who managed to turn the phrase into English and so solve the problem. The passage suggests what is confirmed throughout the *Tale*, that Swift was vigorously hostile to literary men. He attacks them again and again, sometimes through the mask of the Hack, sometimes directly. Their faults are many. They pretend (as here) to knowl-

---

[18] Tom Brown, *Works*, 9th ed. (London, 1760), I, 1. The original issue of the dialogue is in the Clark Library; it was printed anonymously and without a date "for H. H. and T. J. near *Temple-Bar*"; I cannot estimate the time of its original appearance.

[19] *Tale of a Tub*, p. 23.

edge they do not really possess; they flatter the "modern" taste for self-sufficiency; they resort (for lack of genuine literary ability) to obscenity as the easiest path to literary success; they are politically unprincipled and venal; and they are always mocking the clergy. Describing the condition of the Anglican clergy after the accession of William III, Swift makes the contempt of the wits for clergymen the ultimate disgrace:

Nothing was more common in Writing and Conversation, than to hear that Reverend Body charged in gross with what was utterly Inconsistent: Despised for their Poverty, hated for their Riches; reproached with Avarice, and taxed with Luxury; accused for promoting arbitrary Power, and resisting the Prerogative; censured for their Pride, and scorned for their Meanness of Spirit. . . . Their Jurisdiction, Censures and Discipline trampled under Foot, yet mighty Complaints against their excessive Power. The Men of Wit employed to turn the Priesthood itself into Ridicule. In short, groaning every where under the Weight of Poverty, Oppression, Contempt, and Obloquy.[20]

In the ironic argument against the abolishing of Christianity (1708), Swift makes it a strong point in the clergy's favor that they provide a cheap, handy, and safe target for the exercise of the wits who, if they had no clergymen upon whom they could, with perfect safety, discharge their mockeries, might do a more important social agency, or themselves, a real mischief.[21] The *Tale* itself mentions a great "Academy of Wits" that is being projected; by a curious coincidence, it will have room for just as many wits as there are presently clergymen in the nation, and it is evidently designed to supplant them.[22]

Modern wits not only ridicule and belittle the clergy, but actually threaten to replace them by substituting sophistry for wisdom. The root of this change is a new relation to the reading public, with which we are familiar as the transition from the age of patronage to the age of booksellers. Under the former system the client stood to his patron, however tenuously and nominally, in a relation of honor; both were taking part in the pageant, the ceremony, of everyday life. The writer wrote for fame, for immortality, and by his praises bestowed that gift on the patron; he was no vulgar tradesman peddling a commodity. Sir William

20 *Examiner*, no. 21 (28 December 1710).
21 *Prose Works*, ed. Davis, II, 35–36.
22 See preface to *Tale of a Tub*, p. 42.

Temple, who had lived through the change, described it as a shift from honor to avarice as the prime motive of learning, adding that its effect was unfortunate: " 'Tis no wonder, then, that Learning has been so little advanced since it grew to be mercenary." [23] In fact, England possessed for the first time, in the late seventeenth century, a regular literary marketplace where traders cultivated the demand for certain staple commodities and speculated on the chance of striking public favor with a novelty. The way in which Mrs. Anne Baldwin, for example, served the dissenting interest gave new meaning to the word "patronage"; the patrons were a faction, a political interest, and they bestowed their patronage, through the medium of the publisher-bookseller, on authors who spoke to their convictions of the moment. The *Tale* is acutely conscious of how writings are now commissioned by booksellers to suit current market conditions, that is, the whims of clients. In this crucial respect it mirrors Shaftesbury's distinction (in *Soliloquy*, 1708) between modern authors who must flatter the fads and fancies of the fickle multitude and classical authors who assumed it was their task to discipline and reform those whims in the light of a chaste and rational taste founded upon general human nature.[24]

The treason of the clerks is thus, in a double sense, a theme of the *Tale*; modern authors are renegades from the classical standards of authorship as well as traitors to the austere ideals of clerkship maintained by the established clergy. The Hack says in his preface that he knows very well what a preface ought to do— entice the reader—but he is quite incapable of doing it himself. "Not so my more successful Brethren the Moderns"[25]—a most interesting phrase because the Hack is himself not only chronologically but spiritually a modern. Only a few pages earlier he was pleading before Prince Posterity the merits of the modern age as if it were his own; only a few pages later he will be calling the society of Grub Street authors "our society." If, momentarily, he is not one of the modern brotherhood, we may perhaps be entitled

---

[23] *Of Ancient and Modern Learning*, in *Miscellanea II* (1697), p. 68.

[24] *Soliloquy, or Advice to an Author*, Sec. III: "Our modern Authors, on the contrary, are turn'd and model'd (as themselves confess) by the publick Relish, and current Humour of the Times. They regulate themselves by the irregular Fancy of the World; and frankly own they are preposterous and absurd, in order to accommodate themselves to the Genius of the Age" (*Characteristicks*, I [1711], 264).

[25] See preface to *Tale of a Tub*, p. 42.

to think that the mask has slipped for a moment, that the jealous and contemptuous Jonathan Swift has glanced out for an instant at his "more successful brethren the moderns," masters of the unctuous, ingratiating preface and the obsequious, irrelevant compliment, as well as of the book cooked up to serve an interest or an occasion. In this whole connection it may not be amiss to recall Jonathan Swift's almost sacred horror of money made from writing, his rage with Harley and St. John when they tried to "tip" him £50 for pamphlets of special service to the government,[26] his proud assertion that he never received a farthing for any of his writings except *Gulliver*, and that only through Pope's management.

Perhaps, too, we can pause for a suspicious second glance at the Bookseller's dedication to Lord Somers, which has passed itself off rather too easily as the Hack's dedication or even as Jonathan Swift's dedication of the *Tale* to Lord Somers. But it is the Bookseller's dedication; he specifically says that the author had penned a long dedication to Prince Posterity (dedicating his work, that is, in the old-fashioned way, to immortality), but as there was more money to be made out of a dedication to Somers, he, the Bookseller, has taken it upon himself to overrule the author. What he has written sounds more like a burlesque of dedications than a real one; when we find the dedicator touching rather heavy-handedly on such delicate matters as Lord Somers's physical prowess (he was short and sickly) and his noble lineage (he was the son of a country lawyer), and find Jonathan Swift voicing in *The Examiner* a ferocious personal attack on Somers for these very qualities,[27] we may suspect the complete and simple sincerity of Swift's attachment to Somers in 1704. Somers was a patron of Toland, and Swift never had good words to say for that gentleman; Somers was president of the Royal Society from 1698 to 1703, and the *Tale* burlesqued the society with cruel and scathing buffoonery; Somers was a power among the moneymen, the so-called New Whigs, whom Swift hated with a passionate hatred. It is really time that we cast a fresh look at the Bookseller's dedication to Lord Somers, which has sometimes been described as a piece of obsequious flattery.

One of the worst things about the men of letters, from the point of view of the High Anglican clergy, was their connection with

26 *Journal to Stella*, 6 and 7 February 1710/1.
27 *Examiner*, no. 27 (25 January 1710/1).

the new philosophers. Authors, of whom Dryden often stood as a representative, were generally accused, throughout the age, of diffusing Hobbist ideas; gentlemen picked up a smattering of these ideas at the playhouse, the tavern, or the university (three equally disreputable sources of insidious ideas) and then used them to deride the parson. Eachard describes a scene that must have been many times enacted: "Comes rattling home from the Universities the young pert *Soph.* with his Atoms and *Globuli*; and as full of defiance and disdain of all *Countrey Parsons*, let them be never so learned and prudent, and as confident and magisterial as if he had been *Prolocutor* at the first *Council of Nice.*"[28] On a somewhat more reputable intellectual plane, a direct conflict between a philosopher and a bishop of note has left a clear mark on *The Battle of the Books*. The occasion of this controversy between Edward Stillingfleet, the aging Bishop of Worcester, and John Locke was the publication, in 1696, of John Toland's *Christianity not Mysterious*. For the purposes of his argument Toland had adopted, and pushed beyond their previous bounds, various principles drawn from Locke's *Essay Concerning Human Understanding*. In the autumn of 1696 Stillingfleet published *A Vindication of the Doctrine of the Trinity*, charging Locke with responsibility for Toland's views. Locke replied; Stillingfleet retorted; Locke responded; Stillingfleet riposted; and Locke's answer would infallibly have been followed by a counter from the bishop had not the latter unfortunately died in the last year of the century. The engagement was prosecuted with great keenness on both sides, and with extreme punctilio. It is possible to feel that the bishop's position was harder to defend than the philosopher's, and that he saw less clearly into Locke's mind than Locke did into his, without ceasing to admire the strictness of the old gentleman's swordplay or the tautness of his style. Both combatants wielded a sharp and weighty irony, and both appreciated the art of cutting compliment.

As one might expect, a controversy comprising so many episodes ranged across a wide variety of topics, but the general thrust of argument was simple. Locke's philosophical approach lay

---

[28] *Some Observations upon the Answer to an Enquiry*, pp. 119–120. With a very different tonality but to the same general effect we find a man like Halifax writing (*The Character of a Trimmer*, 3d ed. [1697], p. 45) that "men are become so good judges of what they hear, that the Clergy ought to be very wary how they go about to impose on their Understandings."

through a critique of his own power to form clear ideas and relate them coherently; by analyzing their clarity and defining their agreement with one another, he felt he could reach a sufficient notion of what he was and what he was not capable of understanding. In his emphasis on the clarity of basic ideas and on the need for relating them coherently by eliminating contradictions, he was doubtless following in the footsteps of Hobbes. But Locke placed less emphasis than Hobbes on external verification of ideas; he was more ready to take clarity and mutual agreement as a basis for accepting or rejecting them. His method was widely known, in its early days, as "the way of ideas"; that was what Stillingfleet called it. The core of the bishop's argument against Locke was that the new emphasis on clear, distinct ideas eliminated, almost a priori, the mysteries of the Christian faith and all concepts derived from them. On the side he tried to show that Locke's criteria did not in fact separate truth from error; but at bottom Stillingfleet was distressed that these criteria, in the hands of men like Toland, seemed to dismiss all the central doctrines of the Creed as semantic or ontological fantasies.

There is no need to go into all the nooks and crannies of what has become known as the "Socinian controversy"; enough to note that it is this controversy to which the Hack alludes when he says buoyantly that the learned in his illustrious age have no occasion for memory because they "deal entirely with *Invention*, and strike all things out of themselves, or at least, by Collision, from each other."[29] The first alternative refers to Locke's statement that his *Essay Concerning Human Understanding* had been "spun out of his own coarse thoughts,"[30] a phrase recurring again and again in the controversy, usually at the instance of Stillingfleet, who used it to impeach the philosopher of complacency and presumption. The second alternative alludes to the collision, not of authors, but of ideas; it is by reconciling conflicts among ideas, by forcing the ideas to clarify themselves, that Locke believes we can improve our understanding. The whole view of modern authorship as the spinning of insubstantial cobwebs out of one's own bowels, under the influence of self-sufficiency and contempt for others, finds an expression, so obvious that it is unnecessary to explore its details, in the spider-and-bee episode in *The Battle of the Books*. A sug-

[29] *Tale of a Tub*, Sec. VI, p. 135.
[30] See the "Epistle to the Reader" preceding the *Essay Concerning Human Understanding* (Oxford, 1894), I, 11.

gestive clue to the mood evoked by Locke's "way of ideas" is provided by the title of a book that appeared in 1697—*Solid Philosophy Asserted against the Fancies of the Ideists*—with the author designated by the interesting initials J. S. The initials probably referred to John Sergeant.

A particular peril of Locke's position (as traditionalists saw it) was the importance he placed on the analysis of his own private consciousness and the self-sufficiency this approach seemed to imply. Perhaps for John Locke such a procedure worked all right; but to set each man in the London streets a-building philosophical systems out of the jumble in his head could appear to authoritarian minds only as dangerous folly. And it seemed the more dangerous because something like this process was in fact under way. Voluntary associations—economic, practical, social, moral, and religious—were all the rage in the late seventeenth century. With the end of a fully national church (national in the sense that all men at least professed to share belief in a few ultimate values), each man had become free to set his own ultimate values, to league together with other like-minded men, and to define (or abstain from defining) his ultimate ends, just as he chose. Looking ahead a few years, we find Gay and Fielding mocking the new relativism in *The Beggar's Opera* and *Jonathan Wilde the Great*, where highwaymen become heroic as a result of their unusual ferocity and treachery; we find Defoe making his heroine a thief and a prostitute who displays extraordinary dexterity and assiduity in both callings, and Pope creating an authentically heroic figure out of Cibber because of his surpassing dullness. There is no longer one society in which all men are held to the same standards of right and wrong, good and bad; there are several societies, and it is a matter of skill or luck to find the one within which a man's special talents (for murder, lechery, moneygrubbing, or some other insanity) will earn him distinction.

The anonymous author of a penny pamphlet published near the turn of the century[31] under the provocative title *The Danger of Moderation* gave this familiar notion a new twist. The danger he warned of was not danger to the public weal but to the moderate man himself; his scene was set in the always interesting locale of Bedlam. Walking through that institution, he tells us, he encoun-

---

[31] The British Museum gives the date 1708 with a question mark, but this date is unlikely because the first page of *The Danger of Moderation* refers to *Moderation a Virtue* (1703) as lately published.

tered a sober, sensible man who seemed to know a great deal about
the patients and their problems. In fact, said the man, he had a
specific cure for all forms of madness and had taken up residence
in Bedlam simply to study more closely and treat more effectually
the various forms of mental disorder. At this point he was tapped
on the shoulder by a keeper and bidden to return to his cell for
breakfast. Without laboring the point the teller of this story gives
us to understand that it does not pay to be too different from one's
surroundings, even if that difference is for the better. No doubt it
could be moralized in other ways too. The anonymous author then
leads our reflections toward the demise of an objective standard;
for him, Bedlam clearly figures the new society:

> *Right* and *Wrong* have always been esteem'd, till lately, of an Ancient
> Family, that, Time out of Mind, has made a great Figure in the
> World; and 'twas thought by some of the Learned, that they were of
> one side at least, near a-kin to *Melchisedeck, King of Salem*, and Orig-
> inally belong'd to his Country. But of late years, all their Ancient
> Titles and Bearings have been erased, and their very Arms revers'd,
> and nothing was allow'd to bear the Name of *Right* or *Wrong*, but
> what had a *Patent* or *Decree* to be so call'd by some Prince, State, or
> other Supreme Magistrate of a Country.
>   This Pretence did not hold long; For the People being duly ap-
> priz'd that their Governors and Magistrates had no sort of Power or
> Authority, but what they deriv'd from them, they assum'd to them-
> selves this Privilege of creating *Right* and *Wrong*. But not being able
> to manage it so conveniently in a Body, they Farm'd it out to certain
> Commissioners, for a Term not exceeding three Years at a time. And
> now *Right* and *Wrong* is whatever is declar'd so to be by the major
> part of the Commissioners, or Farmers for the time being.[32]

The reference to Melchizedek points plainly to members of the
priesthood as the original custodians of right and wrong. The
Reformation transferred power of moral decision to monarchs
and the Revolution gave it to the people; the farmers who now
exercise it are members of Parliament, limited to three years'
tenure by the Triennial Act of 1694 and deciding right and wrong
by majority vote. It is the fracturing of truth and its replacement
by interest and opinion (both frankly temporary and provisional
in character) which make relevant a comparison with Bedlam and
make apparent the danger of moderation. For the conspiracy of

[32] *The Danger of Moderation*, pp. 2–3.

Bedlam (as of the new society advancing under the catchword "moderation") is to make each man his own measure of his own truth. When everyone else makes lunatic assumptions about his own capacity to determine right and wrong, the single individual who knows that the others are all crazy is still no better than a lunatic himself. (It is a dilemma familiar to anyone who happens to think the society in which he lives is psychotic; naturally, I am thinking of *Le Misanthrope*, not of modern America.) The parallels with Swift's "Digression on Madness" in the *Tale* are so many and obvious that I will not bother canvassing them, but will simply pause to note that the Hack is continually glancing at this problem of moral relativism; for example, one of the books he boasts of having written is *An Universal Rule of Reason: or, Every Man his Own Carver*.[33] That title bears a suggestive relation to a passage of Shaftesbury's *Miscellaneous Reflections*, where the metaphor of "every man his own carver" is carefully explained and explored and related to the very problem I have been discussing.[34]

I cannot offer a positive conclusion here; I can only gesture at a large, dark problem that needs much careful study: that is, dating the composition and finding out what we can about the circulation of Shaftesbury's writings during his lifetime. They were published, mostly for the first time, after his death (1711) in the volumes of *Characteristicks*, but they had no doubt been accumulated and reworked over a period of time. Many of them must have circulated in manuscript within a restricted circle. Shaftesbury was relatively young when he died, but he had been precocious. For example, the *Letter Concerning Enthusiasm*, though first published in 1708 and influenced by the agitations of the French "prophets" in 1707, had been seen in an early form by a member of the family in the early 1690s, when Shaftesbury was barely twenty years old.[35] This chronology causes me to cast an-

[33] "A Digression in the Modern Kind," in *Tale of a Tub*, p. 130.

[34] Anthony Ashley Cooper, third Earl of Shaftesbury, *Miscellaneous Reflections*, in *Characteristicks*, III (1727), 112–113.

[35] Benjamin Rand, ed., "Life Sketched by his Son the Fourth Earl," preceding *Life, Unpublished Letters, and Philosophical Regimen of . . . Shaftesbury* (London, 1900), p. xxvi. The *Inquiry after Virtue*, we are specifically told, was "surreptitiously taken from a rough draft, sketched when he was but twenty years of age" (p. xxiii). Shaftesbury was born in 1671, and so the first draft of *Inquiry after Virtue* must date from the early 1690s. The *Letter Concerning Enthusiasm* need not have been as early as that to have exerted some influence on *A Tale of a Tub*.

other suspicious glance at that passage in the *Apology for the &c* (1710), where Jonathan Swift protests that not only is he innocent of writing the *Letter Concerning Enthusiasm*, but he has not even read it. We know this last statement is not true, because in a letter to Ambrose Philips, written two years earlier (14 September 1708), Swift described the *Letter Concerning Enthusiasm* as "very well writ" and asked if Philips did not write it himself. On 12 January 1708–9 he wrote to Colonel Robert Hunter, then a prisoner of war in Paris, to assure him that he (Swift) had not written the *Letter* and to ask whether Hunter is perhaps the author.[36] All this behavior looks very much like overacting, and the name of the part is innocence. As early as 12 July 1708 Shaftesbury himself told Lord Somers, to whom the *Letter* was addressed (though without any names attached), that the names of both author and addressee had been very widely circulated by a certain club.[37] Swift's guesses were not only late, but particularly wild. Neither Ambrose Philips nor Colonel Hunter was in a social position to address Lord Somers with the casual, gentlemanly familiarity of the *Letter*, and Hunter, as a prisoner of war, was far out of the way of writing such a document. We might entertain the devious possibility that when he asked Philips and Hunter if they had written the *Letter*, Swift (who knew very well that they had not) was seeking to establish his own distance from the *Letter*, its author, and its addressee. He wanted to seem to know less about Shaftesbury and his writing than he actually did know; that fact, together with verbal resemblances and parallel turns of thought which struck contemporary readers and can still strike us, poses an interesting problem.

Whatever the truth at the bottom of this dark pocket, the fact is that among the varied atmospheres in which the *Tale* grew to maturity was the rather *désabusé* and worldly tone that men like

---

[36] *Correspondence of Jonathan Swift*, ed. Harold Williams (Oxford, 1963), I, 100, 122. Swift's exact words to Hunter are: "I cannot forbear telling you of yr. Mechancete to impute the Letter of Enthusiasm to me; when I have some good Reasons to think the Author is now at Paris." This comment does not apply to Shaftesbury, who was busy in England getting married; it has always been taken as applying to Hunter himself.

[37] *Life, Unpublished Letters*, ed. Rand, pp. 386–387. Swift was in London uninterruptedly from 29 November 1707 to 29 June 1709. He had not broken openly with Somers, and certainly had as good a chance as anyone in England to make an informed guess as to the author and the addressee of the *Letter Concerning Enthusiasm*.

Somers, Shaftesbury, and Shrewsbury (a close-knit club intimately acquainted, until his death, with Sir William Temple) carried
through the world. They were tough, worldly, secular-minded
men; and Swift clearly plumed himself on managing their dry,
sophisticated wit as well inside the church as they did outside it.
"Writing like a gentleman" and "going to heaven with a very
good mien"[38] were very much a part of his ambition; and that
style included a superiority to the pruderies and pendantries of
morality. The *Tale* seemed abominable to William Wotton largely because of its outspoken language; his reaction was, in some
measure, a class reaction. If I may recall Miss Mitford for a moment, "U" people often tend to be outspoken: it is the William
Wottons of this world who find it necessary to call cocks roosters
and to provide pianos with limbs. As a jealous and resentful victim
of usurpers, Swift held an ecclesiastical position that prevented
him from feeling any gentlemanly complacency; but he did find
gentlemanly strong speech a sharp weapon to use against his and
the church's enemies. When the unco guid have captured the vocabulary of unction and moderation, there is obviously a special
pleasure in not soft-mouthing things—in the ferocious articula-
tion, for example, of Peter persuading his brothers that a crust of
bread is really a roast of mutton. Somewhere or other the author
or authors of the *Tale* picked up this fullmouthed accent. And it
is perhaps one of the really "original" things about the book that
for the first time it put the coarse, enraged dialect of a fox hunter,
let us say, whose favorite hound has just been killed by an anonymous pitchfork, into the service of the English church.

   The mood of outburst, of exasperated rage, in the great book
is no accident. *A Tale of a Tub* grew, I am convinced, out of a
mood in which it seemed that truth, reason, and logic had collapsed (in the public sense, except as private idiosyncrasies), that
society was turning into a madhouse of monomaniacs, associated
only insofar as a few of them might happen to share the same lust
or mania. No doubt hindsight does not show it that way; but the
hard wing of the church felt it was so. One has only to look at
the tone of their polemic, the quality of their rhetoric, to see how
sharply men like the cousins Swift felt that whatever reason,
learning, and the power of persuasion could do against the Calvin-

---

[38] Steele wrote these phrases in *Tatler*, no. 5 (20 April 1709), apropos of
Swift's *Project for the Advancement of Religion*.

ist creeds had long since been done, and in vain. A man like
Thomas Beverley the millenarian[39] was absolutely impervious to
rational discourse. He had neither read nor was he capable of
understanding a fraction of what had been written to undermine
his daily assumptions by a thousand earnest, charitable, and learned
divines; yet every other day a new pamphlet appeared from his
hand, proving out of Revelation and Daniel that August 1697 was
the time of the wounding of the beast, the sealing of the gates, and
the downfall of the dragon. Reason was powerless to deal with a
man like Beverley, and it always had been; it was powerless to
deal with a specious, unctuous tricky man like Owen, the author
of *Moderation a Virtue*; it was powerless to deal even with Richard Baxter. Behind the pressing, pullulating *schwärmerei* of non-
conformism lay (the Anglicans tended to believe) the irrational
impulses of enthusiasm, personal inspiration, and the will to believe. Behind them lay pride and self-will, the arrogance of men
who define for themselves the rules of right and wrong, and the
meaning to be assigned to the laws of God. And finally behind all
that lay interest, naked self-interest, greed, and lust.[40] We have
seen how Leslie was less concerned to refute Owen logically than
to demonstrate that he was fronting for a conspiracy. The coming
to social power and independent status of the commercial and
moneyed classes whom Jonathan Swift denounced bitterly in his
very first *Examiner* was linked in his mind with the rise to independent power and coordinate status of the Calvinist sects, with
the effect, if not the purpose, of rending the seamless garment of
Christ and making impossible the application of Christian norms
to social conduct. The major problem confronting those who
would preserve the appearance of Christian values amid the English nation was clearly and simply money. "My discourse," says
the *Argument against abolishing Christianity*, "[is] intended only

[39] Beverley was not only an enthusiast for August 1697, comparing the course
of international politics with the Book of Revelation to prove the imminence of
the beast during that exact month; he would have attracted Swift's notice because he dedicated in fulsome terms to Sir Humphrey Edwin.

[40] "Whatever is pretended, Vice only breeds the Schism, and Vice only nour-
ishes it. Conscience is the Pretence; but (whatever some well-meaning and
sincere Men may be led to believe), Conscience hath nothing at all to do in the
matter. 'Tis Pride, Passion, Self-love, Envy, and such other *immoral* Principles
that are the Grounds and Causes of Schism and Confusion: And what has Conscience to do with such things, or such things to do with Conscience, except it
be to use it for a Cover, or Stalking-Horse?" (*The Case of Moderation and Occasional Communion Represented*, p. 13).

in Defence of *nominal* Christianity; the other having been for some Time wholly laid aside by general Consent, as utterly inconsistent with our present Schemes of Wealth and Power."[41]

Throughout its history the Christian church has been heard to remonstrate, from time to time, that men are too fond of money. The problem is a constant, and certainly there is no reason to think that eighteenth-century men were any fonder of money than other men. Yet there were special aspects of the money problem peculiar to that age. Broad classes of newly rich and socially untutored citizens had been created by the Civil Wars, the wars of empire, and an expanding mercantile economy. Banks, credit institutions, insurance companies, national debts, sinking funds, and joint-stock enterprises (all new social devices) made capital available, in fluid form and previously inconceivable quantities, for those who knew how to use it, thereby confusing a generation of theologians whose knowledge of economic sin was limited to medieval prescriptions against usury and corn engrossing. The churches themselves were divided in their attitudes and doctrines. Even if they had not taken different views of economic behavior, the mere fact that there were so many of them made sanctions difficult. X (let us suppose) is complained of for grinding the faces of the poor. The parish priest approaches to admonish him. But, he avers, he is a Quaker, he is a Muggletonian, he is in a state of honest doubt seeking light where he may find it—who is to discipline him, and how? Or perhaps he is a Presbyterian, and keeps a devout, painful, edifying divine in his house as a private lecturer —who shall control this godly man in his care of a conscience to which he alone has access? Who will question that very convenient argument, that the more money the virtuous patron has, the better position he will be in to do good? Meanwhile, the Anglican church was in a particularly poor position to control economic sin because, without its landed estates, it was wholly at the mercy of men with money and the power to control it. Who presented parsons to livings, who paid tithes (and could, if he chose, withhold them, or make their collection diabolically difficult)? Who but the squire? And who was the squire, more often than not, but a man grown rich in the city, with city lawyers and bankers and wholesalers and factors and agents and middlemen and parliament men, and the whole tangled bramble patch of county connections, to keep him in sympathetic contact with the central power of

41 *Prose Works*, ed. Davis, II, 28.

money? Swift, at least, tended to see the whole process as of a piece (he had a notably agglomerative imagination). The rise of a money power was linked to the rise of sects and nonconformists; for reasons of their own, both were hostile to a national church, above all one with the power of independent moral criticism (not to speak of moral discipline). The differing measures of right and wrong promulgated by independent sects drew upon the assurance of the new philosophers that the analysis by a single man of his own ideas is the surest path to truth.[42] Neglect of the traditional truths founded upon general human nature leads to the deterioration of cultural and literary, as well as religious, standards. The result is the unleashing of the beast of appetite. Instead of trying to follow their father's clear and simple will, the three brothers deck themselves in flaunts and tatters and scramble off trying to please that trio of French whores (or great ladies, if you will), the Duchesse d'Argent, the Comtesse d'Orgueil, and Madame de Grands Titres. Swift puts the process in a nutshell:

Hence began the early Practice of caressing the Dissenters, reviling the Universities as Maintainers of Arbitrary Power, and reproaching the Clergy with the doctrines of Divine-Right, Passive-Obedience, and Non-resistance. At the same time, in order to fasten wealthy People to the New Government, they proposed those pernicious Expedients of borrowing Money by vast *Premiums*, and at exorbitant Interest. . . . This introduced a Number of new dextrous Men into Business and Credit . . . [until now], through the Contrivance and Cunning of *Stock-Jobbers* there hath been brought in such a Complication of Knavery and Couzenage, such a Mystery of Iniquity, and such an unintelligible *Jargon* of Terms to involve it in, as were never known in any other Age or Country of the World.[43]

Living as we do in an era when money rules pretty freely—not wisely, it seems, nor yet well, but at least without immediate cataclysms, or a final cataclysm, as yet—we may not appreciate how awesome the juggernaut of frank plutocracy looked at its advent, how it seemed to crush and devour the very elements of human-

---

[42] In his *Sermon upon the Martyrdom of Charles I*, Swift describes the Dissenters explicitly as an "upstart sect of religion that grew out of their own Bowels" (*Prose Works*, ed. Temple Scott [London, 1895–1908], IV, 197). In this connection, it is not always appreciated that even a free, Whiggish fellow like Shaftesbury had major misgivings about the effect of Locke's aseptic philosophical presumptions (see *Letter to Michael Aynsworth*, dated 3 June 1709, in *Life, Unpublished Letters*, ed. Rand, p. 403).

[43] *Examiner*, no. 13 (2 November 1710).

ity. My last little vignette has to do with a man very close to the *Tale*, Dr. Charles Davenant, cousin to Thomas and Jonathan Swift, son of the poet laureate, economist, journalist, political thinker, and sometime political servant. After an education at Balliol and a fling at writing opera, he made his debut as social satirist in 1701 with a sharp, funny pamphlet titled *The True Portrait of a Modern Whig*, in the form of a dialogue between a knowing scoundrel happily named Honest Tom Double and an ignoramus calling himself Mr. Whiglove. Despite its title, Davenant's pamphlet is not political so much as social; the emphasis in the title should fall on the adjective "modern" rather than on the noun "Whig." "Whig" and "Tory" used to have some meaning, says Davenant; the terms used to imply some principles. A modern Whig, however, is simply a thief in league with a gang of similar thieves. Tom Double is so articulate and so blatant a rascal that he merits a quotation. After describing a career of shameless effrontery, he perorates:

And now I am at my Ease, I have my Country-House, where I keep my Whore, as fine as an Empress. You know how I am lodg'd in Town, where I am serv'd all in Plate. I have my *French* Cook, and Wax Candles; no Butchers Meat comes upon my Table; I drink nothing but *Hermitage, Champagne*, and *Burgundy: Cahors* Wine has hardly admittance to my side-board; my very footmen scorn *French* Claret. I keep my Coach and six, and out of my fine Chariot I loll and laugh to see gallant Fellows, Colonels and Admirals, trudging afoot in the Dirt. Poor silly Rogues! Their Honour forsooth led 'em to fight for England abroad, but I play'd a much wiser Game, by joining with those who in the mean while were plundering their Country at home. . . .

My life . . . may serve as a Looking-Glass in which most of the Modern Whigs may see their own Faces. In describing my self, I have drawn most of their Pictures, and there are few of 'em that do not resemble me in some of my Features. Look generally into their Originals, and you will find 'em full as mean as mine. Who was such a Great Man's Father? A scandalous barrater. What was such a Lord not long before the Revolution? A little Jackanapes that People shunned because he could not pay his Club. Did they rise by Virtue or Merit? No more than my self. How did they behave themselves in their Offices? Just as I did; they got what they could, no matter how. Did I cheat the King and his People? So did they; but with this difference only, I was a small Retailer, they dealt by Wholesale. . . . If I could but have got into the House, with my Impudence and fluent way of Speaking, with my abandon'd Principles, with my Cringing and my Flattery, no Body knows how far in those Days I might have advanc'd my self.[44]

Davenant's view is obviously extreme, but it is by no means peculiar to him. That little anonymous pamphlet already cited, *The Danger of Moderation*, said much the same thing about the New Whigs. Jonathan Swift in *The Examiner*, no. 43 (31 May 1711), can find no meaning for the word "Whig" except that it signifies someone who believed in the late ministry: an atheist, a Dissenter, a money trader, or an accomplice of one of those types. (All these indignant Whig baiters, we may suspect, were having trouble adjusting to the idea of a party united by interest rather than by principle; but that did not alter the way they felt, or the fact that they all felt about the same.) In any event, Davenant's slashing attack was deservedly successful, and in 1702 he pressed it further in a second dialogue, *Tom Double Return'd out of the Country*, in which Honest Tom Double exposed even more of his games and explained to Mr. Whiglove all the techniques of sanctimonious swindling.

But in 1704 Dr. Davenant abruptly reversed his field. In contrast with his previous slashing, scathing satires, the collection entitled *Essays upon Peace at Home and War Abroad*[45] was a hesitant, mealymouthed volume; in presenting a straight Whig version of recent English history, it said nothing whatever about corruption or money but recited in all apparent seriousness the sort of diffuse profession that Davenant's previous pamphlets had denounced as a smoke screen. Section XI is a shamefaced, underhanded argument for "moderation," defined after much paltering as occasional conformity, which is recommended as good for trade. Literally, the man had turned overnight into a Modern Whig.

Of course Davenant's volte-face did not go unnoticed. The pamphleteers fell on him with glad cries, accused him of playing a role as double as that of his satiric spokesman, and discussed in remarkable detail the amount of the bribe responsible for his turnabout. One figure assigned was £2,400 and an office; others thought the office alone was enough. Everyone remarked how ill

---

[44] Charles Davenant, *The True Portrait of a Modern Whig* (London, 1710), pp. 31–32.

[45] A promised second volume was never published.

Davenant wrote, how hesitantly and confusedly, when he wrote against his own convictions. Charles Leslie put it in a sentence: "He has Dully *Acted* that *Character* [Tom Double], which himself had before so well *Describ'd*. And writing for a *Bribe*, against his *Convictions*, has Verify'd the *Proverb*, How *Deform'd* that *Child* must be, who is Got against his *Father's* will."[46] About the cash bribe we do not know (such practices leave no traces), but Dr. Davenant was promptly appointed secretary to the committee treating for the Scottish union, and in 1705 he conveniently became inspector general of exports and imports.

In this story of a man intimately known to Jonathan Swift, a man who sold his personal honor and political faith in the very face of the sun to get an office, we see dramatically displayed the working of those forces against which the *Tale* set its satiric teeth. In such matters as the quarrel over occasional conformity, the High Church position could be seen as simply a jealous defense of ancient privilege, a gritty but not particularly elevated posture. But beyond that stance lay the larger and perhaps nobler fear that men, when they could no longer be distinguished by the words they spoke or the principles they confessed, would act merely as animated appetites, as gangs of ruthless, crafty freebooters surrounded by crowds of hired bravos and hired liars. The story of Dr. Davenant was not likely to set at rest the minds of men like Swift, who already felt the riptide of money running irresistibly against them. As a matter of fact, Swift's reaction to Davenant's betrayal of their common principles is an interesting one. Swift had a reasonable command of the invective mood; he took loyalty very seriously; he despised money and men who grubbed for it. Yet against Dr. Davenant he had only a very mild sentence to pronounce: "He was used ill by most ministries; he ruined his own estate, which put him under a necessity to comply with the times."[47] Even the author of *The True Tom Double*, whose point sounds pretty vindictive, concedes that Dr. Davenant did as well as he could as long as he could, against hopeless odds: "The Dr. himself writ some tolerable good Books, while he was Poor and Honest, worthy of Imitation, And yet how few writ after him? He hath now writ an Ill One, against his Judgement, but for his

[46] *The Wolf Stript*, p. 48.
[47] *Prose Works*, ed. Temple Scott, X, 282.

Interest; I fear the Last Example he hath set, will have most followers."[48]

These, then, are some of the circumstances expressing or conditioning (as I see it) the mood of the church at the time when *A Tale of a Tub* was experiencing the pleasures of conception and the pangs of birth. At other periods of its history the British church has enjoyed a serene reputation and a placid, almost somnolent, existence, but not in the closing years of the seventeenth century, not in the circles frequented by the cousins Swift. The currents ran fast and deep; men drowned in them. Reason did not enable one to contemplate the future as a calm expanse for the flow and counterflow of reconciling opinion, for the construction of a noble compromise; reason was a rag in the storm. There has been perhaps a tendency among some of Swift's biographers and commentators to make him look like a good man, at the cost of making him look a little stupid, a little remote from the crosscurrents of passion and interest which swirled around the church, its Jacobite friends (who were really its enemies), and its nonconformist enemies (who protested so loudly that they were its dearest friends). I accept the dilemma, but propose to take hold of it by the other horn. For the longer I look at Jonathan Swift, the less he answers to my notion of a good, stupid man. I think he was incredibly alive to the offensive and defensive values of ideas and words; I think he wrote hardly a line that was not vibrant with the instinct of lunge and parry. Sometimes, I am afraid, he was not very nice. Every now and then he was capable of being just a little bit mean. But that, after all, is the book we are talking about —a great, vicious, funny, cruel, yet somehow noble book. One reason for its greatness, I think, is the richness with which the men who contributed to it experienced, and expressed in its many shadings, the Christian rage of a church in extremis, at the end, so to speak, of its rope. I do not mean that Swift's attitude was permanent and unvarying, or that it was the attitude of the church as a whole during his entire lifetime. Like most moods, it had its ups and downs. After 1710 his own personal success, his growing maturity, and a new assurance about the church's future helped soothe the raw edges of some of Swift's nerves, and in *The Examiner*, no. 21 (28 December 1710), we find him giving thanks to God that, so far as the safety of the church is concerned, the worst

---

[48] *The True Tom Double* (London, 1704), p. 23.

of the storm has blown over. But the book that took shape in the full blast and rage of that storm is not really to be read or understood from the perspective of the calm that followed. It is more a crisis book than a compromise book; and the closer we get to the immediate circumstances, the exact details surrounding the book's creation, the better our chances to see and evaluate the precise contours of the book itself, to know (in other words) what we are talking about.

V

POPE, THE "APOLLO OF THE ARTS," AND HIS COUNTESS

James M. Osborn

Research Associate in English, Yale University

From the time when Alexander Pope's poetical precocity established him as a public figure he was fortunate in the genuine friends he made among the nobility. The names of Lord Bolingbroke, Lord Oxford, Lord Peterborow, Lord Bathurst, and Lord Burlington come immediately to mind. Of Pope's relationships with these men, the happiest for the longest span of years was perhaps his intimacy with Richard Boyle (1694–1753), third Earl of Burlington as well as fourth Earl of Cork in the Irish peerage. Burlington, dubbed the "Apollo of the Arts" by Horace Walpole,[1] was a devoted and active reformer of taste in architecture and interior design. George Vertue the engraver, speaking for the generation of artists of Burlington's time, described him as a "noble Lord" with "great Judgement in Architectonical Knowledge & true manner & Tastes," the "Instar omnia of Noblemen."[2] Walpole, writing with the perspective of the next generation, had high praise for Burlington: "Never was protection and great wealth more generously and more judiciously diffused than by this great person, who had every quality of a genius and artist, except envy."[3]

---

[1] Horace Walpole, *Anecdotes of Painting in England*, ed. James Dallaway and Ralph L. Wornum, 2d ed. (London, 1862), III, 776.

[2] *Vertue Note Books* (*The Walpole Society*, XXII [1933–34]), III, 139.

[3] *Anecdotes of Painting*, III, 773.

A modern art historian names Burlington as the "most influential of those members of the English nobility whose enlightened patronage made possible the artistic achievement of the eighteenth century."[4] Rudolph Wittkower, in a special study of the Burlington Papers, points out that his lordship's own plans and drawings clearly establish Burlington's ability to "draw and design as well as pay the bill." Wittkower's investigations led him to conclude that Lord Burlington "must be assigned a decisive share in the development of English neo-classicism, not only as a patron of artists but . . . as a practising architect."[5] It is generally agreed that Burlington shifted the direction of architecture for public buildings and country houses to the Palladian style, thereby saving England from the excesses of baroque and rococo architecture and design which were fanning out from Italy and France. Another recent historian of architecture has also spoken of Burlington's influence:

[With few possible exceptions] England had never known an academically correct Classical Architecture. She was now to receive it in full measure. . . . Burlington . . . is certainly one of the most important figures in the history of art and taste in eighteenth-century England. By the unsparing use of his great wealth and the prestige of his social position, and, it is to be presumed, by reason of personal qualities of no mean order, he continued to erect himself into a position that can almost be described as a dictatorship in the Arts, certainly of Architecture. . . . Burlington's dictatorship was founded on the fact that he represented a growing body of the upper classes whose taste had been formed on the Grand Tour. . . . In justice to Burlington it must be enforced that his teaching was not merely a negative academicism, but he himself was prepared to go behind Palladio himself direct to Rome.[6]

The date of Pope's first meeting with this young Apollo cannot be established exactly, but it probably occurred soon after Burlington's return in 1715 from a winter in Italy. The Earl, who had succeeded to the title while still a ten-year-old boy in 1704,

[4] H. M. Colvin, *A Biographical Dictionary of English Architects, 1660–1840* (London, 1954), pp. 86–87.

[5] R. Wittkower, "Lord Burlington and William Kent," *Archaeological Journal*, CII (1945), 161.

[6] Geoffrey Webb, "The Letters and Drawings of Nicholas Hawksmoor Relating to . . . Castle Howard," *The Walpole Society*, XIX (1930–31), 114–115.

was then only twenty. Apparently his winter on the grand tour had aroused his interest in the arts, though not yet in the architectural style of Palladio. (That interest soon developed, however, as a consequence of his reading, in 1715, the first volume of Colin Campbell's *Vitruvius Britannicus*, and of a return visit to Italy in 1719 to see examples of Palladian buildings.) The young lord's parts and promise, combined with his vast properties in Yorkshire and Ireland, prompted the government to thrust many official honors and titles upon him, beginning even before he left on his Italian journey. On 9 October 1714, a mere fortnight after George I landed in England, Burlington was sworn in as a member of the Privy Council. In May 1715 he was appointed Lord Lieutenant of the East Riding of Yorkshire; in June the appointment was extended to include the West Riding. Two months later he became Lord High Treasurer for Ireland. Fortunately, the actual responsibilities of these dignified offices were assumed by deputies and clerks.

The spring of 1715 saw Pope well launched on the second phase of his career. The *Essay on Criticism* was four years behind him, as were various other early poems that brought Pope the attention of the great in both literary and political circles of influence. For a year he had been laboring tediously on the translation of the *Iliad* and correcting proofs of the first volume, delivered to subscribers early in June. The earliest evidence of his friendship with Burlington is found in "Farewell to London. In the year 1715," one of Pope's most endearing occasional pieces. He was about to return to the rural home of his parents at Binfield, Berkshire, after five months of hectic life in London; while seeing the *Iliad* volume through proof into print, he was suffering the newspaper barbs of detractors and trying to keep up the heavy social schedule to which his literary fame exposed him. The delightful "Farewell to London" was written sometime between 19 May, when the Marquis of Halifax died, and 12 June, when Pope's painter friend, Charles Jervas, mentioned the poem in a letter. Because "*Homer* (damn him!) calls" (i.e., work on the second volume of the *Iliad*), Pope addressed his farewell to the "Dear, damn'd distracting Town." The penultimate stanza reveals his established relationship with the young Earl of Burlington, who had recently celebrated his twenty-first birthday. Pope himself had just passed his twenty-seventh birthday.

> Laborious Lobster-nights, farewell!
> For sober, studious Days;
> And Burlington's delicious Meal,
> For Sallads, Tarts, and Pease!

That Pope was also a visitor at Burlington's country residence, Chiswick House, is clear from John Gay's poetical epistle, "A Journey to Exeter," occasioned by his visit there later in the summer of 1715. In describing the gardens at Chiswick House, Gay wrote: "Pope unloads the boughs within his reach / The purple vine, blue plum and blushing peach." (One is touched by this intimate, affectionate allusion to Pope's crippled figure, less than five feet tall.)

The earliest reference to Lord Burlington in Pope's extant correspondence occurs in a letter he wrote to Martha Blount in March 1716. The passage echoes the quatrain quoted above: "I am to pass three or four days in high luxury, with some company at my Lord Burlington's; We are to walk, ride, ramble, dine, drink, & lye together. His gardens are delightfull, his musick ravishing."[7] Five months later, in a letter written to Thomas Dancastle on 7 August, Pope reports that a "journey into the North, which my Lord Burlington proposed I should take with him this month," has been deferred.[8] The expedition to Burlington's Yorkshire sphere of activity, which finally took place early in November, was relatively short, for within the month Pope was home again scheduling a visit to friends in Oxford.

The degree of intimacy that developed between the two friends on the Yorkshire jaunt appears in the well-known letter from Pope to Burlington, probably written later in November 1716, which describes Pope's ride to Oxford on a mare borrowed from his lordship. During the journey Pope was overtaken by Bernard Lintot, the mercenary publisher with whom he had contracted for publication of his translation of the *Iliad*. A decade later Pope openly quarreled with Lintot over publication terms of the *Odyssey*, calling him a scoundrel and a fool,[9] and ridiculed him both in *The Dunciad* (1728) and in *An Epistle to Dr. Arbuthnot* (com-

---

[7] *The Correspondence of Alexander Pope*, ed. George Sherburn (Oxford, 1956), I, 338. All references to Pope's letters are to this edition, hereafter cited as *Correspondence*; page references are usually omitted for dated letters.

[8] *Ibid.*, p. 351. For a similar reference see Pope's letter written on the same day to Teresa Blount (*ibid.*, p. 350).

[9] *Ibid.*, II, 287–288.

pleted in 1734). In 1716, however, Lintot was a necessity to be tolerated, a "dull dog" but a profitable promoter who paid more for Pope's poetry than his rival Tonson or any other publisher was willing to do.

Beginning with Lintot's *Miscellaneous Poems and Translations* (1712), to which Pope contributed seven pieces (including the first version of *The Rape of the Lock*) for a payment of £26.19.0, the relationship continued to benefit both parties. In February 1713 Lintot paid £32.5.0 for *Windsor Forest* and, in July, £15 for the *Ode on St. Cecilia's Day*. In February 1714 Lintot gave another £15 for the "Additions" to *The Rape of the Lock* and, a year later, £32.5.0 for *The Temple of Fame*. In April 1715 he paid Pope £10.15.0 for *The Key to the Lock*. Sometime after March 1714, when he signed the agreement with Lintot to translate the *Iliad*, Pope began to enjoy the subscription money; it amounted to about £680 for each volume, plus approximately £215 each which Lintot paid him. Pope could well object to Lintot's lack of manners and his unpleasant personality, but no previous poet had ever had a publisher who rewarded literary labors so well.

Pope's letter to Burlington describing the jogging journey with Lintot has been called by George Sherburn "one of Pope's most finished performances . . . doubtless subjected to much revision before printing."[10] Evidence that the letter was warmly admired in Pope's day as well as by later generations is found in one of a small group of Burlington-connected manuscripts now in the Osborn Collection in the Yale University Library.[11] Hitherto un-

---

[10] *Ibid.*, I, 371.

[11] The manuscripts, the property of a Mrs. Davenport, were purchased at Hodgson's sale of 2 June 1955. They include the following items: (1) The versified letter to Burlington, written in an unknown hand. (2) A copy of Pope's letter of 21 December 1731 to Burlington, in the hand of Lady Burlington. (3) The verses on "Cutting" printed below, in Pope's hand. (4) Verses entitled "On receiving from the Countess of Burlington Mr. Gray's Poems with Drawings by Mr. Bentley," signed "Ed. Bedingfeld" and ostensibly in Bedingfield's hand. Since the volume of Gray's poems was published in 1753, the poem was probably written within the following year but definitely before 1758 when the Countess died. Probably the writer was the Edward Bedingfield born in 1730, friend of Thomas Gray (*Horace Walpole's Correspondence with the Rev. William Cole*, ed. W. S. Lewis [New Haven, 1937], I, 234), rather than the Edward Bedingfield who helped Pope distribute copies of *The Rape of the Lock* in 1712 (*Correspondence*, I, 141–142, 145). (5) A poem and an accompanying note by one M. D. Blachett, apparently addressed to one D. Gisborne. The poem has no clear connection with the Burlingtons.

known, the manuscript contains a versified version of Pope's letter. To assist the reader the versified version[12] and the prose text of the letter are printed on facing pages, matched as closely as possible (see below).

POPE'S LETTER TO BURLINGTON DESCRIBING
HIS JOURNEY WITH LINTOT

My Lord,

If your Mare could speak, she would give you an account of the extraordinary company she had on the road; which since she cannot do, I will.

It was the enterprizing Mr. *Lintott*, the redoutable rival of Mr. *Tonson*, who mounted on a stonehorse, (no disagreeable companion to your Lordships mare) overtook me in *Windsor-forest*. He said, he heard I design'd for *Oxford*, the seat of the muses, and would, as my bookseller, by all means, accompany me thither.

I asked him where he got his horse? He answer'd, he got it of his publisher: "For that rogue, my printer, (said he) disappointed me:

---

[12] Quotation marks have been supplied or deleted in order to conform to modern usage.

To the right Hon: Earl of Burlington
Mr Pope's Epistle Versified.

———————

Sermoni propiora.

———————

If, as in *Aesops* days, when Brutes coud speak
And moral Pigs methodically squeak,
Your Mare, My Lord, her Company cou'd tell,
And what diversions on the Road befell;
No doubt she on the story wou'd refine;
But since she cannot; let the Task be mine.

Thrô Windsor Forest as I jogg^d along
Tracing Ideas of my former Song,
Loud Neighings from behind invade my Ear:
Musick, that better pleas'd your Lordships Mare.
When lo! on stonehorse mounted, the renown'd,
And lofty Lintot prances o'er the Ground,
Who thus with Hat in hand.—"Sr When I heard,
For Oxford you design'd, away I spurr'd,
In Hopes, as Town is thin, & Weather fair,
Your Bookseller might humbly wait you there."

But, *Bernard*, whence this Horse?—"Oh S^r, that Dog,
My Printer is no better than a Rogue:
He promis'd me, he woud a Horse procure;
So I, not doubting but to make all sure,

I hoped to put him in a good humour by a treat at the tavern, of a brown fricassee of rabbits which cost two shillings, with two quarts of wine, besides my conversation. I thought my self cock-sure of his horse, which he readily promis'd me, but said, that Mr. *Tonson* had just such another design of going to *Cambridge*, expecting there the copy of *a Comment upon the Revelations*; and if Mr. *Tonson* went, he was preingaged to attend him, being to have the printing of the said copy."

"So in short, I borrow'd this stonehorse of my publisher, which he had of Mr. *Oldmixon* for a debt; he lent me too the pretty boy you see after me; he was a smutty dog yesterday, and cost me near two hours to wash the ink off his face: but the Devil is a fair-condition'd Devil, and very forward in his catechise: if you have any more baggs, he shall carry them."

I thought Mr. *Lintott*'s civility not to be neglected, so gave the boy a small bagg, containing three shirts and an Elzevir *Virgil*; and mounting in an instant proceeded on the road, with my man before, my courteous stationer beside, and the aforesaid Devil behind.

Mr. *Lintott* began in this manner. "Now damn them! what if they should put it into the news-paper, how you and I went together to *Oxford*? why what would I care? If I should go down into *Sussex*, they would say I was gone to the Speaker. But what of that? if my son were but big enough to go on with the business, by G——d I would keep as good company as old *Jacob*."

Besides my Conversation, gave a Treat,
Of five & four pence, but, ifaith, was bit;
For Brother *Jacob*, on another Scent,
Seiz^d on my Promise, & to Cambridge went.

"Thus, S^r, unhors'd my Publisher I tried,
My Publisher more kind a Horse supplied;
Ev'n This; 'twas fabulous *Oldmixon*'s, he said,
Purchas'd by Scandal, & for Debt repaid.
He lent me too this Boy, so fair & trim,
Tho yesterday a Devil, black & grim,
But sure a fair-condition'd Devil it is,
And very forward in his Catechise."

This said, we journey'd on an easy Pace,
And each in manner following took his Place,
Beside me went the Stationer, so civil,
My Man before us, & behind the Devil.

Till he again—"Now d——n 'em. What care I, ⎫
If Hawkers vile about the streets shou'd crie, ⎬
Or Journalists this our Design belie? ⎭
So if to *Sussex* I should take my way,
A Journey to the Speaker, they wou'd say.
And what of that? by G——d, was once my son,
A Blessing on him! fit for Business grown.
Let *Jacob* keep what Company he wou'd,
Were it the *Kit-cat*, I wou'd keep as good."

Hereupon I enquir'd of his son. "The lad (says he) has fine parts, but is somewhat sickly, *much as you are*—I spare for nothing in his education at *Westminster*. Pray don't you think *Westminster* to be the best school in *England*? most of the late *Ministry* came out of it, so did many of *this Ministry*; I hope the boy will make his fortune."

Don't you design to let him pass a year at *Oxford*? "To what purpose? (said he) the Universities do but make Pedants, and I intend to breed him a man of Business."

As Mr. *Lintott* was talking, I observ'd he sate uneasy on his saddle, for which I express'd some sollicitude: Nothing says he, I can bear it well enough; but since we have the day before us, me-thinks it would be very pleasant for you to rest-a-while under the Woods.

Your Son! how goes he on?—"The Lad, tis true,
Has Parts, but's somewhat sickly, *much like you*—
He's now at *Westminster*, I spare no Cost
To qualify my Boy for any Post,
Either in Church, or State. What think you, S^r,
Can any School contend with *Westminster*?
Thence the late *Ministry*, & present came,
Patriots, & Poets, men of mighty Name;
Nor do I doubt, but that my Boy will climb
The highest Spoke of Fortune's wheel, in Time."—

But you intend him, I suppose, to spend
A year, or two at *Oxford*?—"To what End?
Stiff Pedants, formal Blockheads, there we find;
Mine for a Man of Business is design'd."

With that he gave a Twist, & with Sour Face
Rose gently on the stirrops.—plain the Case,
That moved my kind Concern; but he replied;
"Nothing, but what is common when I ride,
And I can bear it better than the Rays
Of the full-blazing Sun; so, if you please,
Beneath this shady Wood, we'll rest awhile."—

When [we] were alighted, "See here, what a mighty pretty *Horace* I have in my pocket? what if you amus'd your self in turning an Ode, till we mount again? Lord! if you pleas'd, what a clever *Miscellany* might you make at leisure hours." Perhaps I may, said I, if we ride on; the motion is an aid to my fancy; a round trott very much awakens my spirits. Then jog on apace, and I'll think as hard as I can.

Silence ensu'd for a full hour; after which Mr. *Lintott* lug'd the reins, stopt short, and broke out, "Well, Sir, how far have you gone?" I answer'd seven miles. "Z——ds, Sir, said *Lintott*, I thought you had done seven stanza's. *Oldsworth* in a ramble round *Wimbleton-hill*, would translate a whole Ode in half this time. I'll say that for *Oldsworth*, (tho' I lost by his *Timothy*'s) he translates an Ode of *Horace* the *quickest* of any man in *England*. I remember Dr. King would write verses in a tavern three hours after he couldn't speak: and there's Sir *Richard* in that rumbling old Chariot of his, between *Fleet-ditch* and *St. Giles*'s pound shall make you half a *Job*."

With all my Heart.—We lit.—& with a Smile,
Disdainful of his Pain, he thus began:
"Well, surely *Horace* is a charming Man!
I've here the prettiest Book,—now be so good,
As, for amusement here, to turn an Ode.
Lord! what a smart Collection you might make;
If thus at leisure Hours you'd undertake
T'oblige the World.—S^r, will you choose you one?"

Perhaps I may, said I, if we ride on;
Motion to Fancy new Ideas gives,
And nothing more than a round Trot revives
The animal Spirits; so jogg on amain,
And I will think as hard, S^r, as I can.

In silent mood we smoak^d it oer the Plain,
About an Hour, when *Lintot* lugg^d his Rein,
Stop'd, & broke out—"How far, S^r, have you gone?"—
I think seven miles—"Z——ds, S^r, I thought you'd done
At least seven *stanza*'s.—*Oldsworth* on the loose,
Trapesing round *Hampstead* Hill his patient Muse,
Wou'd a whole Ode in half the Time translate;
And (tho I lost by 'his *Tim'othy*'s) I'll say that
For *Oldsworth*, no man living did it quicker.—
And Dr *King* I've known, so full of Liquor
That for three Hours he has not spoke a word,
Write Verses, aye & good ones.—For a Third,
I'll name Sr *Richard*, who when call^d from far,
(Tuning his verses to his rumbling Car).
Wou'd with all Ease between St *Giles*'s Globe,
And *Fleetstreet* Mitre, finish half a Job."

Pray Mr. *Lintott* (said I) now you talk of Translators, what is your method of managing them? "Sir (reply'd he) those are the saddest pack of rogues in the world: In a hungry fit, they'll swear they understand all the languages in the universe: I have known one of them take down a *Greek* book upon my counter and cry, Ay this is *Hebrew*, I must read it from the latter end. By G——d I can never be sure in these fellows, for I neither understand *Greek, Latin, French,* nor *Italian* my self. But this is my way: I agree with them for ten shillings *per* sheet, with a proviso, that I will have their doings corrected by whom I please; so by one or other they are led at last to the true sense of an author; my judgment giving the negative to all my Translators." But how are you secure that those correctors may not impose upon you? "Why I get any civil gentleman, (especially any *Scotchman*) that comes into my shop, to read the original to me in *English*; by this I know whether my first Translator be deficient, and whether my Corrector merits his money or no?

But speaking of Translators, *Lintot* say,
What is your Art to manage them, I pray?
—"Vile Rogues!—S^r, in a hungry Fit, there's None
But swears that every Language is his own.
The other Day One takes down a *Greek* Book,
And cries,—Aye, This is *Hebrew*, I must look
The Title, here.—so turns him to the End.
And how I can be sure without a Friend?
For 'tis well known, that I can neither speak,
Nor Understand *Italian*, *French*, or *Greek*.
But This S^r is my Method; when we meet,
Ten Shillings I agree to give *per* sheet
Provided always, Others shall inspect
Their Doings, & with Liberty correct;
Thus many Various Judgments having past,
We to the Authors sense are led at last;
And let Translators, S^r, say what they will,
The Negative *my* Judgment shall have still."—

But the Correctors, are they always right?—
"Why, S^r, some civil Person I invite,
(Suppose a Scotchman, for they often pop,
And steal a Pamphlet-reading in my Shop,)
To read the Thing in *English*; & thus I,
Both the Translator, and Corrector try.

"I'll tell you what happen'd to me last month: I bargain'd with S[ewell] for a new version of *Lucretius* to publish against *Tonson*'s; agreeing to pay the author so many shillings at his producing so many lines. He made a great progress in a very short time, and I gave it to the corrector to compare with the *Latin*; but he went directly to *Creech*'s translation, and found it the same word for word, all but the first page. Now, what d'ye think I did? I arrested the *Translator* for a cheat; nay, and I stopt the *Corrector's pay* too, upon this proof that he had made use of *Creech* instead of the original."

Pray tell me next how you deal with the Critics? "Sir (said he) nothing more easy. I can silence the most formidable of them; the rich one's for a sheet apiece of the blotted manuscript, which costs me nothing. They'll go about with it to their acquaintance, and pretend they had it from the author, who submitted to their correction: this has given some of them such an air, that in time they come to be consulted with, and dedicated to, as the top critics of the town.

"I'll tell you, S^r—a Month or two ago,
Tonson put out *Lucretius*, you know,
So I, to rival him, as is my way,—
Agreed with S[ewell], so much Coin to pay
For so much Verse, wou'd he his Art express,
And give *Lucretius* a new *English* Dress.
He sets about it, & soon having made
A wondrous Progress, brought it, & was paid.
I gave it the Corrector to compare,
And by the *Latin* see that all was fair;
Away goes he to *Creech*, & cries, for Shame!
Save the first Page, 'tis word for word the same.
Now what d'ye think I did?—Faith, what was meet,
Arrested the Translator for a Cheat,
And because t'Other had to *Creech* applied,
And not th'*Original*, I his Pay denied."—

'Twas wisely done; but Lintot, how d'ye deal
With Critics?—"That, S^r I shall next reveal:
From Bentley down to Theobald, I can please,
And silence the most terrible with Ease;
As thus, S^r,—cheap enough—I with a sheet
Of blotted Manuscript the rich ones treat,
This they to their Acquaintance vainly shew,
As from the Author, whom they never knew.
From hence an Air of Judgment they put on,
And strut the Sovereign Critics of the Town:
The fulsome Theme of every Dedicator,
And nothing, be it Essay, *Play*, or Satyr,
Must pass, without his Lordship's *Imprimatur*.

—As for the poor Critics, I'll give you one instance of my management, by which you may guess at the rest. A lean man that look'd like a very good scholar came to me t'other day; he turn'd over *Homer*, shook his head, shrug'd up his shoulders, and pish'd at every line of it; *One would wonder* (says he) *at the strange presumption of men*; Homer *is no such easy task, that* every *Stripling*, every *Versifier*—he was going on when my Wife call'd to dinner: Sir, said I, will you please to eat a *piece of beef* with me? Mr. *Lintott*, said he, *I am sorry you should be at the expence of this great Book, I am really concern'd on your account*—Sir I am oblig'd to you: if you can dine upon a piece of beef, together with a slice of pudding—*Mr.* Lintott, *I do not say but Mr.* Pope, *if he would condescend to advise with men of learning*—Sir, the *pudding* is upon the table, if you please to go in—My critic complies, he comes to a taste of your poetry, and tells me in the same breath, that the *Book* is commendable, and the *Pudding* excellent."

—For poor ones—From one Instance may be guest
How cleverly I manage all the rest.
—Comes One who look^d a Scholar, pale & thin,
Shirtless without, & dinnerless within;
He takes up *Homer*, shruggs, & shakes his Head,
Cries, Pish, at every Line, & at last said
   'Tis strange! the great Presumption of some Men!
   When his own shoulders, knows scarce One in Ten!
   Believe me, *Homer*'s of a strain much higher,
   For *every* Stripling, *every* Versifier'—
My Wife calls Dinner, S^r, I cannot stay;
Will you be pleas'd to dine with me to day?—
   '*Lintot*, I'm sorry for you, the Expence
   Must needs be great, & you, a man of Sense,'—
S^r, I am much oblig'd t'ye;—pray, step in,
If upon Beef & Pudding you can dine.—
   'I do not say, but Mr Pope, my Friend,
   Woud he but now and then, S^r, condescend,
   To hear, & be advis'd by men more able'—
S^r, do'nt you see the Pudding's on the Table.
Down sits my Critic, & falls on so fast,
That soon he comes your Poetry to taste,
And thus in the same Breath gives his Consent,
   'The *Book* is good, the *Pudding* excellent.'

Now Sir (concluded Mr. *Lintott*) in return to the frankness I
have shewn, pray tell me, "Is it the opinion of your friends at
Court that my Lord L[ansdowne] will be brought to the Bar or
not?" I told him I heard *not*, and I hop'd it, my Lord being one I
had particular obligations to. "That may be (reply'd Mr. *Lintott*)
but by G——d if he is not, I shall lose the printing of a very good
Trial."

These my Lord are a few traits by which you may discern the
genius of my friend Mr. *Lintott*, which I have chosen for the subject of a letter. I dropt him as soon as I got to *Oxford*, and paid a
visit to my Lord *Carlton* at *Middleton*.

The conversations I enjoy here are not to be prejudic'd by my
pen, and the pleasures from them only to be equal'd when I meet
your Lordship. I hope in a few days to cast my self from your
horse at your feet.

I am, &c.

Now, S^r, (concluded *Lintot*,) I have done,
And to return the Frankness I have shewn,
As I'm concern'd about a late Report,
Pray tell me, S^r, what say our Friends at Court,
Will my Lord L[ansdowne], for I know not what,
Be brought to th' Bar?"—I told him I heard *not*,
And for that noble Lord, I wish'd it true,
As One, I'd many Obligations to.
"It may be so, but d——n it, to my Cost,
If he is not, there's a good Trial lost."

From the few Traits, my Lord, which here I send,
You may discern the Genius of my Friend:
(What Art, what Ignorance, together joind!
How wise, how dull, the mere mechanic Mind!)
At Oxford dropping him, I took my way
To good Lord *Carleton*'s, my Devoirs to pay.

My Pen wou'd only Prejudice, I fear,
The Happiness of Conversation here:
Pleasures unequal'd, but by those Delights,
To which dear *Chiswicks* Villa oft invites;
Where in few Days, my Lord, I hope to meet,
And from your Horse embrace your Lordship's Feet.

I am, &c.

The question immediately arises: Who wrote these amusing verses? Obviously, Pope is the leading candidate for the role of versifier of his own letter. He had the skill—in fact, far greater skill than any possible rival—to turn into couplets this "merry letter" (as Lintot himself called it when he first read it in 1735). Pope also had the strongest motivation, for the letter was an exercise in wit, created for the young Lord Burlington. Further, the preservation of the manuscript with a packet of Burlington-connected papers suggests that the verses were an ingroup joke, intended for the Burlington circle instead of for wide circulation.

The external evidence is meager: no author is named or hinted at on the manuscript, nor can the handwriting be identified. In contrast, the internal evidence for Pope's authorship is very strong. Certainly the poem is written in Pope's persona; for example, the versifier refers to *Windsor Forest* as "my former Song," a phrase added to the prose original. Further, it is difficult to believe that anybody other than Pope could have created the couplet describing Lintot's "genius," also added to the prose version:

> What Art, what Ignorance, together joind!
> How wise, how dull, the mere mechanic Mind!

Moreover, the line "From Bentley down to Theobald, I can please" mentions the two critics made familiar by line 164—"From slashing Bentley down to piddling Theobald"—in *An Epistle to Dr. Arbuthnot* (1735). These instances of similarity argue strongly that Pope held the pen when his epistolary *jeu d'esprit* was turned into couplets.

The date of composition of the versified version cannot be determined with certainty. Maynard Mack, whose knowledge of Pope is today unrivaled, suggests that it is more in the style of Pope's earlier light verse than in that of his later works. Mack also points out that a joke normally builds up when it is fresh, instead of later. One slight detail that supports an early date is the correct spelling of Theobald's name; after 1728 Pope chose to denigrate the critic by using the phonetic spelling, Tibald. It is possible, of course, that "Theobald" in the versified version was the copyist's preference.

Readers accustomed to thinking that the Pope–Theobald conflict grew out of Theobald's attack on Pope in *Shakespeare Re-*

stored (1726) may wonder whether ten years earlier Pope would regard Theobald as a critic. Yet in the spring of 1715 Theobald had written a series of thirty short essays, published periodically under the general title *The Censor*, which contained criticism on the drama, on translations of the classics, and on other literary subjects. The seeds of rivalry were sown at least as early as the spring of 1714, a few months after the proposals for Pope's *Iliad* had appeared, when Theobald signed a contract with Lintot to translate the *Odyssey*. And in April 1715 Pope and Gay were very much annoyed because Theobald participated in a "sixpenny criticism" of their play *The What D'ye Call It*.[13] If the poem was written about 1716, the Bentley–Theobald line would have anticipated, rather than echoed, the line from the Arbuthnot poem. Thus the possible objections to the early date by students of Pope who are familiar with his habit of utilizing earlier lines in later poems can be satisfactorily answered.

Conversely, a strong argument can be put forward for a date around 1732, when Pope was pondering schemes to get his letters published. The set piece addressed to Burlington in 1716 is the only letter to his lordship included in the 1735 collection. Although Pope may have kept a copy, it is equally likely that he asked the Earl to produce the original, for, as the Burlington archives demonstrate, his lordship habitually kept letters that pleased him. Once retrieved, the joke could be revived and enjoyed by Lady Burlington, whom he married in 1721, as well as by intimates such as William Kent, who lived in Burlington House from 1719. Hilarity over the letter would lead to the suggestion that Pope turn it into verse.

A date of 1732 or 1733 would allow Pope to borrow the Bentley–Theobald allusion from the embryo *Epistle to Dr. Arbuthnot*, which was begun early in 1732 "when Pope was smarting under assaults made upon *The Epistle to Burlington*."[14] In fact the original manuscript[15] shows that the earliest version of the line read "sanguine Milbourne," later changed to "slashing Bentley"; this authorial emendation undercuts the possibility that the Bentley–Theobald line could have been written in 1716. The poem also fits in with the other datable Burlington–Pope items in

[13] *Correspondence*, I, 288–289.

[14] John Butt, *Pope's Poetical Manuscripts* (Oxford, 1954), p. 38.

[15] In the Pierpont Morgan Library. I am indebted for this reading to Mrs. Helene Koon.

the packet of papers where it was found: a copy of Pope's letter to Burlington of 21 December 1731, transcribed in Lady Burlington's hand, and a poem in Pope's own hand (of which more later) which seems to date from about 1732. The exhuming of the 1716 letter under these circumstances would answer Maynard Mack's objection that a fifteen-year-old joke would seem stale even to Pope himself, for the enjoyment by Lady Burlington and her intimates would give it new luster. The scales of probability thus favor the later date.

To revert to the events of 1716, Pope's relationship with the bachelor, Lord Burlington, grew steadily closer, a development aided by proximity when the elder Pope sold his property at Binfield and the family moved to Chiswick. Pope's letters to John Caryll offer some details of the transition. On 20 April 1716 he wrote that, "my father and mother having disposed of their little estate at Binfield, I was concerned to find out some asylum for their old age; and these cares, of settling, and furnishing a house, have employed me till yesterday, when we fixed at Chiswick under the wing of my Lord Burlington."[16] The house was in Mawson's New Buildings, a short distance from Chiswick House, whence Pope again wrote to Caryll on 22 June:

Tho' the change of my scene of life, from Windsor Forest to the water-side at Chiswick, be one of the grand Æra's of my days, and may be called a notable period in so inconsiderable a history, yet you can scarce imagine any hero passing from one stage of life and entering upon another, with so much tranquillity and so easy a transition, and so laudable a behaviour as myself.[17]

The Pope family lived at Chiswick for little more than a year before the father died in October 1717. Having inherited a "narrow fortune," Pope began casting about for a home where he could live for the rest of his mother's and his own life. His first thought was to settle in London, and the Earl kindly offered property behind Burlington House. After long contemplation and the sketching of many plans for house and garden, Pope wrote to Burlington on 11 October 1718. This letter deserves quotation in full because it reveals the easy nature of their friendship.

[16] *Correspondence*, I, 339.
[17] *Ibid.*, pp. 343–344.

Cicester, October the 11th.

My Lord,

I would always have so much regard to the Pleasures of any one I love, as not to trouble him with Business till I needs must. Therfore I never mentioned to your Lordship the Affair of my Building during your Amusements in the Country, designing to speak of it at your return to towne. But I would not longer now defer doing it, that you may not think me so poetical as not to know my own mind & inclination, which I faithfully assure you (my Lord) is to be obliged to you, & to be yours by as many titles as I can. I therfore beg you to know, I have Piqued myself upon being your Tenant in that piece of ground behind Burlington house (which is the Situation I am fond of to the last degree) & that nothing hinderd my building there this Summer, but finding upon the exactest enquiry, the expence Mr Campbell's Proposal would have put me to, to be 200 pound above what I am pretty well assured I can build the same thing for. I promise you, my Lord, to build on the same Plan & Front with Lord Warwick's, so as not to clash with any regular design; & I beg you to believe me always in earnest in whatsoever I speak to your Lordship. I should not else in the least deserve to call myself (what upon my faith I am much more proud & pleased to call myself, than any thing else)

My Lord,
　　　Your most sincere, most
　　　obliged, & obedient Servant
　　　　　　　　　A. Pope

I went to Town a Fortnight since, in no other view than the hopes to meet you; being miserably chain'd down to finishing Homer just now, which I was never able to do near London. I've almost got over my Task, & hope to wait upon you (I hate so ceremonious a word, I mean, to be perfectly easy in your company) in a Week.

Within the next few months Pope decided against the plan for a town house, and on 2 February 1719 communicated his decision to Burlington:

I am told your Lordship is going into the Country upon some journey to morrow, & lest the affair you sent to me about should be That of my building or not, I take this method of repeating what I said when last I had the honour of seeing you; That I readily resign the piece of ground intended for me, as not being yet prepard to build, & absolutely unwilling to retard the progress of the rest who are.[18]

18 *Ibid.*, II, 2.

In his reply, now lost, Burlington evidently mentioned a house at Twickenham, and Pope responded at once: "I'm sure you shall always have me for your Neighbor, where-ever I live."[19] Within a few months he had moved into the villa on the Thames at Twickenham where he spent the rest of his life. Because it was only five miles upstream from Chiswick, Pope continued to be a frequent guest at Burlington's table when his lordship was in residence.

Most of the surviving letters between the two friends are preserved at Chatsworth and were first printed by George Sherburn in his indispensable edition of Pope's correspondence. Somewhat surprisingly, there is a gap of a decade after the last letters quoted, the next extant letter being dated 23 December 1728.[20] Aside from the happenstance usual in such matters, three other factors may help to explain the gap. First, Pope was excessively occupied during these years with literary commitments, especially the edition of Shakespeare published in 1725 and his translation of the *Odyssey*, the first fourteen books appearing in 1725 and the remainder in 1726. Second, his personal life took up a great deal of his spare time: the development of his house and garden, the illnesses of his octogenarian mother, visits of Swift to Twickenham in 1726 and 1727. Third, because Chiswick was within easy visiting distance of Twickenham letters were really unnecessary, though how often the Burlingtons were there and just when Pope visited them by water or land we have no way of knowing.

In his letter of December 1728, which revives the known correspondence, Pope thanks Burlington both for his "Humanity" to the enfeebled Mrs. Pope and for his offer to show the legal expert Nicholas Fazakerley the text and apparatus of *The Dunciad Variorum* as a guard against charges of libel.[21] In another letter written soon afterward, Pope expresses gratitude to his lordship

19 *Ibid.*

20 In this decade, sometime before 1726, Pope, as a token of friendship, gave Burlington a puppy by his Great Dane bitch, Bounce, probably the second in a series of that name (see "How many Bounces?" in Joseph Spence, *Observations, Anecdotes, and Characters of Books and Men*, ed. James M. Osborn [Oxford, 1966], II, 629–630). Pope's poem, *Bounce to Fop*, speaks of this puppy, now grown, in the lines,

> My second (Child of Fortune!) waits
> At *Burlington*'s Palladian Gates,

thus indicating that his lordship kept the dog in London rather than at one of his country homes.

21 *Correspondence*, II, 532.

for obtaining "the Decisive opinion of Mr Fazakerly" because, Pope confesses, "I am grown more Prudent than ever."[22] The two letters show the degree of easy familiarity between the two men which apparently existed from the beginning of the friendship. A few months later Burlington demonstrated his positive affection for Pope (and also his confidence in Fazakerley's legal opinion) by signing the indenture, along with Lords Bathurst and Oxford, which assigned *The Dunciad* to Lawton Gilliver. The transfer paved the way for suits against printers who had pirated the poem, suits that otherwise would have been impossible to pursue since no author or author's agent appeared as proprietor.[23]

Burlington's attitude toward Pope is made clear in the letters exchanged on this occasion. At the end of his letter of 29 October 1729 Pope wrote:

No one can be, with more Esteem & Truth, a Wellwisher . . . than I am yours. Adding to it, what all those must want, an *affection* which it would be an affront to offer to Kings, & belongs only to Friends. I am ever therefore

My Lord

Your most obliged
most faithfull humble Servant

A. Pope

Burlington replied on 2 November:

I send you the paper which I signed with that pleasure, that I shall always take, in every thing where I can be of the least use to you. . . . I am dear Sir your most affecte.

humble servant
Burlington

Aside from Burlington, the second Earl of Oxford, and the Earls of Orrery and Peterborow, Pope did not employ the words "affection" and "affectionately" in writing to members of the hereditary nobility, for such usage might have been thought presumptuous. He did use these words frequently, however, when writing to his literary friends who sprang from his own social class.

The best-known episode in the friendship between the poet and

---

22 *Ibid.*, III, 4–5.
23 *Ibid.*, pp. 37, 59, 61–62, 67.

Burlington occurred in 1731 when Pope published *An Epistle to the Right Honourable Richard Earl of Burlington*, with the subtitle, "Of Taste." Although the public did not see printed copies of the epistle until December, Pope sent Burlington a manuscript copy of the poem in a letter written 4 April 1731:

My Lord,

I send you the Inclosed with great pleasure to myself. It has been above ten years on my conscience to leave some Testimony of my Esteem for your Lordship among my Writings. I wish it were worthier of you. As to the Thought which was just suggested when last I saw you, of its attending the Book [i.e., as a prefix to his folio publication of *Palladio's Designs of the Baths, Arches, Theatres, &c. of Ancient Rome*], I would have your Lordship think further of it; & upon a considerate perusal, If you still think so, the few Words I've added in this paper may perhaps serve two ends at once, & ease you too in another respect. In short tis all submitted to your own best Judgment: Do with it, & me, as you will. Only I beg your Lordship will not show the thing in manuscript, till the proper time: It may yet receive Improvement, & will, to the last day it's in my power. Some lines are added toward the End on the Common Enemy, the Bad Imitators & Pretenders, which perhaps are properer there, than in your own mouth. I am with all truth, my Lord

> Your most obedient & affectionate
> Servant
> A. Pope

When the epistle was published on 13 December the merits of the poem as an objective discussion of the "Ballance of things" were generally overlooked. Rumor swept London that Pope was using Lord Burlington as a stalking-horse to shoot at the ostentatious Duke of Chandos (allegedly Pope's benefactor) in the character of Lord Timon. All Pope's enemies, especially the "Dunces," joined the cry against him. In vain did Pope smuggle defenses into the papers; the public clamor was too loud for him to gain a hearing. In fact, the misreading of "Timon" placed a heavy burden on Pope's reputation, a burden that remained until well into the twentieth century. In 1935 George Sherburn found documentary evidence in the Burlington Papers at Chatsworth and the Chandos Letter Books at the Huntington Library to puncture the assumptions of Dr. Johnson, the Reverend William Lisle Bowles, the Reverend Whitwell Elwin, and other moralists and divines as to the identity of Timon.[24] F. W. Bateson, in the Twickenham edition of the poem, has, by adding further details to the vindication, set the story straight for all who seek the truth.[25] Clearly Pope intended Timon to be a composite portrait instead of an individual caricature of Chandos or of anyone else.

On 21 December 1731, a mere week after the poem was published, Pope wrote Burlington an anguished letter saying that "the whole Town then, or I, have lost our Senses," and concluding with the plea:

I beg to know what are your Lordships Sentiments, that I should do in this unaccountable affair? I hope You are not abused too, because I meant just the Contrary; I can't tell, but I fancy your Lordship is not so easy to be persuaded contrary to your Senses, even tho the whole Town & Court too should require it. I doubt not the Justice, the more than justice, you will do me, on this or any other Injury: but I really want to know your Thoughts of it, being (as I perceive) a Man out of the World, & delirious: but still my dear Lord with understanding enough to Love and Adhere to you.

Exactly how Burlington responded we do not know, but the next day, 22 December, perhaps on Burlington's advice, Pope wrote to the Duke of Chandos to explain the misinterpretation. The Duke replied on 27 December saying that Pope's letter freed him from any apprehension he might have felt over what he now considered to be the unjust censures of the town. Pope followed by prefixing to the third edition of the poem, published early in January 1732, a letter to Lord Burlington in which he tried to set the record straight. He also threatened to make use, in his next satire, of "*Real* Names and not of Fictitious Ones" if the malice toward him continued. The printed letter is signed "Your Faithful, Affectionate Servant," thus publicly showing the state of his friendship with Burlington. In this new edition Pope also changed the subtitle from "Of Taste" to "Of False Taste."

The cry against Pope did not abate, however, and the verbal charges of scandal were supplemented by a graphic attack in the well-known print showing Burlington Gate with the word "TASTE" across the top of the arch. A figure representing Pope

[24] George Sherburn, "'Timon's Villa' and Cannons," *Huntington Library Bulletin*, VIII (1935), 131–152.

[25] *Epistles to Several Persons (Moral Essays)*, ed. F. W. Bateson, Vol. III-ii, Twickenham Edition of the Poems of Alexander Pope (London, 1951), pp. xxv–xxxii, 164–168.

stands on a scaffold in front of the arch, splashing whitewash on the gate and "Bespattering any Body that comes in his way," as well as the passing coach of a duke.[26] Although undated, the print was probably in circulation by the first week in January 1732. It was long attributed to Hogarth because he held a grudge against Burlington's protégé, William Kent, but William K. Wimsatt, who has investigated the subject thoroughly, believes that Hogarth was not the artist.[27] A redrawing of the engraving appeared in a volume, published on 20 January, entitled *A Miscellany on Taste. By Mr. Pope. Viz. I. Of Taste in Architecture. An Epistle to the Earl of Burlington. With Notes Variorum, and a Compleate Key, etc.* The attacks on Pope proliferated, though some are known only from the newspaper announcements of their publication.[28]

After two months the storm subsided. Professor Sherburn has placed a number of undated letters between the friends early in the same year (1732), a dating there is no reason to question. The first fully dated letter is one Pope wrote to Burlington in Yorkshire on 19 September. Again it is noteworthy that Pope signed it "Your long obliged & long affectionate grateful Servant." Burlington's answer, written on 8 October, ended as follows:

I hope you will forgive the shortness of this epistle. . . . I write in the middle of company and cards, but let me be anywhere, I can never leave off without assuring you, that no mortal can be with more affection than I am

> my dear friend
> your most faithfull servant
> Burlington

In another exchange in November, the Earl's letter, written on the last day of the month, closed in a similarly affectionate way.

And so the exchanges continued over the remaining decade of Pope's life. During these years Pope became more and more devoted to the ideal of friendship: he and his intimates developed what could be called a cult of Amicitia in the classical tradition. The eighteenth century talked a great deal about friendship, but

---

[26] The print is reproduced as the frontispiece in *ibid.*

[27] William K. Wimsatt, *The Portraits of Alexander Pope* (New Haven, 1965), pp. 115–117.

[28] See John Butt, "A Master Key to Popery," in *Pope and His Contemporaries*, ed. James L. Clifford and Louis A. Landa (Oxford, 1949), pp. 41–44.

Pope seemed almost to worship the ideal. Among a dozen friends to whom he was deeply attached, Henry St. John, Lord Bolingbroke, held a special place in his affections. Martha Blount, Warburton, and other intimates could not understand why Pope so overestimated Bolingbroke's mind and abilities, but Pope considered Bolingbroke "superior to anything I have seen in human nature." In Warburton's paraphrase of Pope's attitude, Bolingbroke "seemed to be sent down hither by Providence, from some higher Sphere."[29] When a comet appeared shortly before Pope's death he reported that he "had sometimes an imagination that it might possibly be come to our world to carry him [Bolingbroke] home, as a coach comes to one's door for other visitors."[30] Upon Pope's death the grief-stricken Bolingbroke said: "I have known him this thirty years, and value myself more for that man's love and friendship than . . . " He broke down before completing the sentence, "sinking his head and losing his voice in tears," according to Spence.[31]

The tone of the Amicitia cult is apparent in several of the letters between Burlington and Pope which go beyond the minuet of courtesy and compliment usual at the time. For example, on 3 May 1736 his lordship wrote to Pope:

I should be unworthy of the friendship you honor me with, if I coud defer the pleasure of being with you, one minute, without an absolute occasion for it. . . . [Here Burlington explains why he must postpone a meeting.] I shou'd not have been so circumstantial, if it had not been to convince you, that what I say is real, I hope you are persuaded that my affection for you is so.

Pope replied the next day to confirm the postponed date, concluding,

I should be a worse man than even Libellers can represent me, if I did not think real what ever you are pleas'd to profess, tho it be so much above my desert, as that long Friendship with which you have honour'd me. It cannot be greater than that Gratitude with which I have as long, & shall for ever receive it.

What was perhaps the ultimate accolade in the Amicitia cult

---

[29] See Spence, *Observations*, ed. Osborn, § 274 (I, 121).
[30] *Ibid.*, § 275 (I, 121).
[31] *Ibid.*, § 653 (I, 268).

appeared in Pope's letter of 19 December 1738 to the Earl. There
the poet pays Burlington the great compliment of including him
in the special intimacy that linked Pope and Bolingbroke:

If my writing to you could make you know, one tittle the more,
that I am every day in the same degree I have been these twenty years,
Yours; I would have written once a week. But all I could say is Tau-
tology: Yours I am, & yours I will be. Your Lordship may judge how
true this way of Thinking is, by examining your own breast, and I
verily believe you will find there, that you are good enough to be to
me all that you have long been, notwithstanding your Lordship has
never thought of writing to me or of me. Mr Kent could tell you how
often I talk'd of you, & wished for you; even at a time when I wish for
few or none, when I am almost constantly with the Greatest Man I
know, ever knew, or shall know [Bolingbroke]. He too is your faithful Servant; & we daily, when we meet, remember You. Our constant
Toast is, *Libertati & Amicitiae*: & we do your Lordship (tho we think
it of Few Lordships) the justice to allow you Equally Sensible of
Both.[32]

Pope's final statement on Amicitia was on his lips the day he died.
The memorable words were recorded by Spence, but were first
printed by Dr. Johnson: "In the morning, after the priest had
given him the last sacraments, as they call them, he said, 'There is
nothing that is meritorious but virtue and friendship, and indeed
friendship itself is only a part of virtue.' "[33]

Until now only passing reference has been made to Dorothy,
Countess of Burlington (1699–1758), who is generally agreed to
have been one of the most talented and colorful aristocrats of her
century. Born Dorothy Savile, daughter and coheiress of the
gifted second Marquis of Halifax, she brought both fortune and
intellect to the Earl of Burlington, whom she married in March
1721. Horace Walpole, a generation later, recorded that the
Countess "had no less attachment to the arts than her lord. She
drew in crayons, and succeeded admirably in likenesses; but,
working with too much rapidity, did not do justice to her genius.
She had an uncommon talent too for caricatura."[34]

[32] *Correspondence*, IV, 153. When Pope reported this "health after dinner"
to Spence he added that he should like his door to show the motto, "S[acra]
Amicitiae et Libertati" (*Observations*, § 279; I, 123).
[33] Spence, *Observations*, § 656 (I, 629), quoted almost verbatim in Johnson's
Life of Pope, § 247.
[34] *Anecdotes of Painting*, III, 776.

Other testimony on Lady Burlington's contemporary reputation comes from the notebooks of the professional artist, George Vertue. Here, for example, is the report of a visit in 1742/3:

Being lately to wait of the R^t Hon^{bl}. Lord Burlington I had the opertunity of seeing a room adornd with Crayon paintings heads great numbers hung all round the room done by Lady Burlington, who has painted in that way with great Success, and with much application and to be sure is a most fine and excellent Genius—these works may be esteemed an honor to the Art and a glory to this Nation when the Virtu is in so high esteem. and worthy of the regard of such a noble Lady—[35]

The Countess studied with William Kent, who lived with the Burlingtons after the Earl brought him back from Italy in 1719. From that date onward he functioned as artist, architect, and landscape designer in residence. Vertue reported also seeing at Burlington House "a picture in Crayons of M^r. Kent painter (much more like than that done by Aikman) this drawn by Lady Burlington and is in her great room adornd with many crayon painted heads—the works of her Ladyship. mostly all of them Coppyd from excellent pictures—"[36]

William K. Wimsatt, in his study of the portraits of Pope, devotes an entire chapter to William Kent and Dorothy Boyle, Countess of Burlington, though his focus is on Pope and on a rather crude drawing of Pope in his garden at Twickenham, as well as on two of Pope in his grotto. (The latter may be by either Kent or the Countess.) Wimsatt also reproduces two of Lady Burlington's drawings, one a self-portrait and the other a representation of Pope playing cards. In this chapter Wimsatt provides the fullest modern discussion of the Countess, including many details about two albums of drawings preserved at Chatsworth. The first is labeled "Lord and Lady Burlington Drawings" and the second, "Chiswick and Chatsworth Miscellaneous Drawings."

Wimsatt's taste causes him to disapprove of what he calls Lady Burlington's "fantasy style," especially "many grotesque medleys of *Dunciad*-like subjects—monkeys, dogs, owls, other birds, bats, and toads, mingled with human figures, and sometimes in multiple perspectives on a single sheet." With obvious distaste he describes several drawings in detail, calling one a "curious fancy" and an-

[35] *Vertue Note Books*, III, 115.
[36] *Ibid.* (*The Walpole Society*, XXVI [1937–38]), V, 73.

other "fairy-tale grotesque." The drawing of Pope at cards he condemns for "malicious draughtsmanship,"[37] though evil intent does not seem present to the eye of this observer. Since Pope's dislike of having to "play at cards" is well established and seems to have been one of his private jokes with Jonathan Swift,[38] despite the expertise revealed in his description of ombre in *The Rape of the Lock*, it is not improbable that Lady Burlington wanted to show Pope's attitude toward cards in his face. All evidence suggests that Pope had only the warmest admiration and affection for the Countess, that she held, indeed, a unique place among the wives of his closest friends, and that she returned the affection.

Pope's first reference to the Countess occurs in a playful letter written on 23 July 1723 to John Gay, who was then living at Burlington House but at the moment was at Tunbridge Wells with the Countess. The earliest extant letter to her is a note written in March 1729 at the time when Pope had arranged to present to the King a copy of *The Dunciad* with the frontispiece portraying an ass. Pope wrote to arrange that Lady Burlington, who was lady-in-waiting to the Queen, might see an advance copy: "If my Lady Burlington cares to be troubled with the Weight of Mr Pope, and his Dunciad, her Ladyships Coach will carry them all to day to Chiswick: and they may wait upon her, and ask Blessing of the Ass their Grandmother there, about one or two a clock."[39] The next note, written in June 1731, shows the same easy relationship and Pope's recognition that her witty mind expected wit from him:

Madam,
    As a Proof of my real Gratitude, & in full Recompence for all the Pamphlets you have preserved for my perusal, I beg leave to send you this one; which I am sure will be no small Iniquitous Delight to you, tho not the production of

Madam,
Your most obedient & faithfull
Servant
A. Pope.

[37] Wimsatt, *Portraits of Alexander Pope*, pp. 112, 122, 123, 311.
[38] *Correspondence*, II, 9; III, 91; IV, 178.
[39] *Ibid.*, III, 20.

I hope, at the end of the week, to come & receive your thanks in person.[40]

The following year, being the aftermath of the storm over the *Epistle to Lord Burlington*, proved to be an active one in correspondence between the friends. The Countess helped Pope by transcribing some of his writings, and there are several references to these kindnesses. Since her handwriting was clear and attractive, Pope was not merely flattering her when he wrote, "You shall soon have more work, but no more transcribing of this, for (whatever you think) when you do things as carelessly as you can, they will still be better than most other people's Finishd Works."[41] And again, "I do not send your Paper till I can do it effectually, a most Compleat Copy."[42] Pope, in turn, went through a great pile of Savile family papers for her. Lord Burlington mentioned them in a letter to Pope on 8 October 1732: "Lady B is very much obliged to you for the pains you have been pleased to take upon her account and begs that you wou'd put the papers into what method you please, and get some trusty person to transcribe them." Pope replied on November 6:

My Lady has found a way to give me a great deal of pleasure in her absence, in the fancying I obey her commands not unsuccessfully: For I think I clearly see all that can be done, or ought to be done, with the Papers she left me. I have got some transcribed as you directed, & might have done the same with more, but that I've found a shorter method, by figuring the Loose & Scatterd Thought first, to make one Transcription serve for all, which will at the same time reduce 'em under proper Heads. If she disapprove not of publishing Algn. Sydney's Letters, it must be Seperately: & in that case they need only be writ out just for the Press, which any Bookseller you'd employ may do himself, & save us the trouble. I think as to Lord Halifax's Works, they must be called, *Miscellanies, Political & Moral*. They will make a Volume about the size of that which was formerly printed, with the character of K. Charles added; and without any of the Letters, which should (if publishd) be in another Volume apart, with his Brothers &c. Whatever orders my Lady gives I will punctually observe.

[40] *Ibid.*, p. 201. The pamphlet has not been identified.
[41] *Ibid.*, p. 272. Among items in Lady Burlington's hand are Pope's mock satire on himself, "The Master Key to Popery," at Chatsworth and Pope's letter of 21 December 1731 in the Osborn Collection among the group under discussion.
[42] *Ibid.*, p. 273.

Pope ended the letter as follows:

My reall Services (I wish my Lord, they deserved that Epithet) attend yourself & Lady B. I hope she paints; I hope you build; I hope
you are both well & happy whatever you do, or if you do nothing:
which last is the situation (and one very much to be envyd) of

My Lord,

Your faithfull & ever

obliged Servant,

A. Pope.

According to his letter of 13 January 1733 to the Countess,
Pope returned the Savile papers soon after the turn of the new
year:

Madam,

I fully purposed to have been myself the bearer of these Papers, and
it is no small punishment to me that I am not. I believe it would be
very proper, to have as many as are thus marked ⊙ of my Lady
Sunderland's Letters, transcribed: and to joyn them with Algernon
Sydney's (if not also some of Mr Savil's &c.) which are dated in the
years, 79, & 80: as they relate to the Same Facts & Occurrencies. If
your Ladyship wants Employment, these will abundantly supply it,
till I bring you all Lord Halifax's Maxims & single Thoughts, under
their proper Heads, which I can in a few days; & if you would still
inlarge the Collection, his loose papers will furnish wherewithall. But
if this Task seems too great for your Self, I will employ an Amanu-
ensis for the rest. Your Ladyships Commands will be a better thing
than an Honour, they are really a Pleasure & Improvement to me.

The Picture is the best ornament to my New Room. The merry old
Gentleman has got a Name, which I will maintain to all Connoisseurs.
That may make it more Valuable to Them, but to me, the Hand that
painted it is Sufficient. I am with all respect & sincerity

Madam

Your Ladyship's most

obedient & oblig'd Servant

A. Pope.

The last paragraph concerns a painting of an old man which Pope
kept in his "Little Parlor" for the rest of his life. From the inventory of his estate it is clear that he had never had the painting
framed.[43]

[43] "Inventory of Pope's Goods Taken after His Death," *Notes and Queries*,
6th ser., V (1882), 364.

Only one of the Countess's drawings was celebrated in verse by Pope, and then only in a quatrain. As lady-in-waiting to Queen Caroline she saw the Queen's corpse after Her Majesty's death in December 1737 and made a sketch of her face. This drawing is preserved at Chatsworth, as are the following lines in Pope's hand:

> On a Picture of Queen *Caroline*,
> Drawn by Lady *Burlington*.
>
> Alas! what room for Flattry, or for Pride!
>   She's dead!—but thus she lookd the hour she dy'd,
> Peace, blubbring Bishop! peace thou flattring Dean!
>   This single Crayon, Madam, saints the Queen.[44]

The only other poem printed among Pope's works which he addressed to the Countess concerned her practicing of a different art, that of cutting out paper reproductions of scenes, flowers, and even portraits. This polite occupation of ladies had an honorable tradition, as we know from Edmund Waller's verses celebrating Lady Isabella Thynne's proficiency, written in the 1650's and entitled "Of a Tree Cut in Paper":

> Fair hand! that can on virgin paper write,
> Yet from the stain of ink preserve it white;
> Whose travel o'er that silver field does show
> Like track of leverets in morning snow.
> Love's image thus in purest minds is wrought,
> Without a spot or blemish to the thought.
> Strange that your fingers should the pencil foil,
> Without the help of colours or of oil!
> For though a painter boughs and leaves can make,
> 'Tis you alone can make them bend and shake;
> Whose breath salutes your new-created grove,
> Like southern winds, and makes it gently move.
> Orpheus could make the forest dance; but you
> Can make the motion and the forest too.
> A poet's fancy when he paints a wood,
> By his own nation only understood,
> Is as in language so in fame confined;
> Not like to yours, acknowledged by mankind.
> All that know Nature and the trees that grow,
> Must praise the foliage expressed by you,

---

[44] *Minor Poems*, ed. Norman Ault and John Butt, Vol. VI, Twickenham Edition of the Poems of Alexander Pope (London, 1954), p. 390.

Whose hand is read wherever there are men:
So far the scissor goes beyond the pen.[45]

Since these lines appeared in the 1668 edition of Waller's poems, Pope should have remembered them. His own poem was first printed in *Miscellanies. The Third Volume*, published in October 1732:

On the Countess of B—— Cutting Paper

Pallas grew vap'rish once and odd,
  She would not do the least right thing,
Either for Goddess or for God,
  Nor work, nor play, nor paint, nor sing.

Jove frown'd, and "Use (he cry'd) those Eyes
  So skilful and those Hands so taper;
Do something exquisite, and wise—"
  She bow'd, obey'd him, and cut Paper.

This vexing him who gave her Birth,
  Thought by all Heav'n a burning Shame;
What does she next, but bids on Earth
  Her *B——l——n* do just the same.

Pallas, you give yourself strange Airs;
  But sure you'll find it hard to spoil
The Sense and Taste of one that bears
  The Name of *Savil* and of *Boyle*.

Alas! one bad Example shown,
  How quickly all the Sex pursue!
See Madam! see, the Arts o'erthrown,
  Between *John Overton* and *You*.

Pope rushed the poem into print soon after it was written, as we learn from his letter of 19 September to Lord Burlington:

I beg my Lady's acceptance of my Services, & if in any instance relating to this, I can be of use, she may most freely command me; there is truly no man more respectfully her Servant. I hope she will forgive a Crime I've committed towards her, in putting into a Collection of Verses (which I will soon trouble you with . . .) that little

---

[45] *Poems of Edmund Waller*, ed. G. Thorn Drury (1893), p. 196.

paper-thing about her, with the Addition only of one Stanza, to show I am as ready to commend as to blame her.[46]

Pope wrote a second poem on the same subject, hitherto unprinted. The manuscript, in Pope's handwriting, is in the small group of Burlington papers previously mentioned, now in the Osborn Collection. Because these verses are more witty and playful than the poem he printed in 1732, it is possible that they were the result of a second effort, written too late to be included in the final volume of the *Miscellanies*. Or Pope may have considered the verses to be too light and familiar in tone. Here is the new poem (see illustration, p. 140):

EPISTLE of Lady B[urlington] to her Lord

The Argument.

The Lady B. having been sundry times rebuked by her Lord, & others, for cutting and snipping of Papers, to yᵉ great waste of precious Time, & loss of Conversation; writes him in Excuse, this Rational, convincing and Loving Epistle.

My Lord, the Conquest is my own,
Confess, I've fairly cut you down.
In youth, in age, in man & wife,
Cutting's the business of our Life;
How do we children first distinguish?
By cutting-Teeth, and clipping-English.
What aim we at, when we grow bigger?
At nothing but to cut a figure:
Heroes but cut their way to fame;
And wits by Snip snap get a name.
Cutting (I'l owne it to a Friend)
Brings many a Countess to her end;
But howsoever Fate shall clip
My thread of Life and Ladiship,
To the last period of my charms,
I'll clip you in my dying arms:
Let, then, my Tomb be raisd by two
Immortal Cutters, Jones & you:
You shall find marble, Pope this Ryme,
"*Learn Ladies! how to pass your Time!*"

[46] *Correspondence*, III, 314.

EPISTLE *of Lady B. to her Lord.*

The Argument.

The Lady B. having been sundry times rebuked by her Lord, & others,
for cutting & snipping of Papers, to ye great waste of precious Time, &
loss of Conversation; writes him in excuse, this Rational, ~~conjuring~~ an
Loving Epistle.

[My Lord, the conquest is my own,
Confess, I've fairly cut you down.
In youth, in age, in man & wife,
Cutting's the business of our life;
How do we children first distinguish?
By cutting – Teeth, and clipping – English.
What aim we at, when we grow bigger?
At nothing but to cut – a figure:
Heroes but cut their way to fame;
And wits by Snip snap get a name.
Cutting (I own ~~the to gain~~ Friend)
Brings many a Countess to her end;
                                      shall
But ~~whenere~~ howsoever Fate chip
My thread of life and Ladiship,
To the last period of my charms,
I'll clip you in my dying arms:
Let, then, my Tomb be rais'd by two
Immortal Cutters, Jones & You:
You shall find marble, Pope this Ryme,
"Learn Ladies! how to pass your Time!"

Manuscript in Pope's autograph, now in the Osborn Collection

The Jones mentioned is, of course, Inigo Jones, who preceded Lord Burlington as an enthusiast for the Palladian style.

Another example of Pope's pleasure in his playful relationship with the witty and accomplished Countess is a letter he wrote her on Sunday, 29 October 1738, which centers on two stock jokes in their intimate circle. The first concerned the church living of Eyam, Derbyshire, within the gift of Lady Burlington; since it carried what George Sherburn called "the luscious" income of £1,500 a year, it was naturally kept within the family. The living had fallen vacant upon the death of a kinsman in 1737, when it had been passed along to a recipient whose health was so feeble that the Burlington group speculated to whom it should next be awarded. The second joke concerned William Kent, the distinguished architect of both buildings and landscapes, who had lived with Lord Burlington since his return from Italy and served as his lordship's artistic henchman. Kent possessed a highly congenial personality and for twenty years had been a frequent crony and drinking companion of Pope's. To propose that Kent should take orders to enable him to qualify for the fat living at Eyam pleased Pope so much that he wrote the Countess as follows:

Twickenham Oct. 29th [1738]

Madam,

Having done the Ecclesiastical Duty of the Day, equally filled with good things, viz: with a Sermon, a Dinner, & strong Beer, I write in the Spirit thereof, a Letter truly Ecclesiastical; consisting of an Early Application for a Living, which I understand will speedily fall in your Ladiships Gift, (& which of the many Great & valuable Gifts, with which God hath blessed your Ladiship, seemeth not to be the least and least valuable) I mean, *The Presentation of Eyam.* Three Reasons there are, which I would offer to induce you to bestow it: The first, that my Noble Lord your excellent Consort hath promised me a Boon of this nature many years; and as it is written, that Man & Wife are One, may it not seem that your Ladyship stands hereby bound in some measure? The second reason is yet more cogent, that this Living is better worth than any of his Lordship's: And the third, to wit that the Person I reccommend is greatly meritorious, is a reason I cast at your feet, to weigh as much or as little as you think fit. Yet I will say, He is endowed with more *Edifying Qualities,* than Any below the *Pontifical* Dignity. He Should be *Pontifical,* he well deserves it, but is not allowd it under this Ministry, which he may truly call, *A Nest of Foxes.* He is as Learned, tho not so courteous as Bishop W——x; as Eloquent tho not so Courtly, as G——t; as wellbred, tho not so Bookish, as H——re, and (to sum up all) has as good a taste as R——le, & as good a Stomach as all the Clergy put together. I cannot say he is quite as accomplishd as Sh——ck, but he is more Independent; being one who hath born Testimony to the Truth, in the face of Kings, Queens, & Potentates: One who hath ever Resisted New Doctrines & Opinions, holding fast by the Pillars of sound Antiquity; by no means a Respecter of Persons, but using Sharp Speeches to the Greatest: In a word, One under whom may be expected, more than from any Prelate living, the Restoration of Churches, the ReEstablishment of Ancient Colleges, and Increase of New Foundations: till the Walls of Jerusalem shall be built up, Holocausts and Whole Burnt Offerings shall be revived, and *Calves* (to fulfill the prophecy) shall be brought unto the Altar.

I think your Ladyship begins to find the Excellent Person at whom I point, (or rather to *Smoke* him, for he is very hot, & very fat)

> Of Size that may a Pulpit fill,
> Tho more inclining to Sit still.

And (with the leave of the Otherways-Excellent the Vicar of Barrowby) I presume to name him, & defy any Objections, viz. Mr William Kent.

I protest it is my Zeal for Merit entirely (and a most disinterested one, for he will not so much as thank me for my pains) that moves me to propose him. He is totally ignorant of this Address, nor do I know any Motive he could have to accept of the Living, save to get into a Soft Pulpit, where is a Soft Cushion, to lay his Soft Head, & rest his tender Tail, from the Fatigues of a Horse, that now afflicts his Soul, moves his very Entrails (especially after dinner,) & troubles all the Bones within him; while not only the Spirit is wearyd, but the Flesh that should cleave to those bones, cleaves to the Saddle. I have sent two or three pressing Letters & Messages, to beg him to ride but one mile out of his way to Windsor, to speak to me of a Matter that nearly concerns him. He has imagind it concern'd *me* & not *him*, I suppose, & therefore will not stir. In truth it is a Matter whereby he will get some hundred pounds, & do nothing for it; but this I will not tell him, till I drag him hither: When he comes, I will very gravely acquaint him how to put a good Sum into his pocket, & after holding him in suspense, propose the Benefice of Eyam, & that several of his Friends seriously advise him to enter into Orders. It is the only revenge I can think of for his Refusal to come to me, and he will be abundantly consolated by the Money at last.

Pray be so good as to write to Lady Betty Murray, & tell her how many thousand fine things I said of her, before I guess'd Mr Murray could find them out. Because it is very necessary I should be well with her, to keep so good an Interest with Him, as I would fain do. See what an honest Reason this is, for my Civility to Other men's Wives!

Pray Madam continue to honour me with as many proofs of your Goodness as possible, but send us no more *Ale*, for my worthy Lord here is drunk, & as a mark that he is deprivd at present of his Reason, bids me to write in his stead, to assure yourself & my Lord Burlington of his sincerest Services. I durst not sign my Name so near him, but that I have prudently omitted His. However I am my Lord's, & Madam Your most Obliged Servant.

Other warm and frequently playful letters continued until Pope's final illness six years later, though how many have been lost will never be known. Because Pope dined at Chiswick regularly when the Burlingtons were there, the full story of his close relationship can only be surmised from the letters that remain. The last known letter dates from early 1744, when the poet's final deterioration had begun. The note is touching in its brevity:

If my Lord Burlington goes to Chiswick on Saturday or Sunday, & cares to be troubled with me, I will, upon his sending a warm Chariot (for I dare not go in a Chaise) put my self into his power, like a small Bird half starved, in this miserable weather.

A. Pope.

Friday night, from Twickenham.

Thus the memorable friendship of the cloth dealer's poetical son with the aristocratic "Apollo of the Arts" and his Countess came to an end. As the letters show, the Burlingtons did much to make Pope happy over three decades. In return the poet helped to make Burlington's name immortal by addressing to him the epistle that among Pope's works George Sherburn believed to be "surpassed in importance only by the *Essay on Man*, the *Essay on Criticism* and possibly the *Dunciad*." *An Epistle to Burlington* should be read, not for its personalities, but for the sound aesthetic principles it enunciates in the incisive and finished verses praising Palladian dignity and simplicity. Pope also contributed more than any other friend toward keeping alive after two centuries the name of the witty and accomplished Dorothy Savile, Countess of Burlington.

VI

THE ENGLISH PHYSICIAN IN THE EARLIER EIGHTEENTH CENTURY

C. D. O'Malley

Late Professor of Medical History, University of California, Los Angeles

My purpose in this paper is to present a picture of the English physician, particularly the London physician, during approximately the first half of the eighteenth century. Such a portrayal is not without certain complexities arising from the lack of uniformity in physicians' medical training during that period; the peculiarities of the English licensing system; the restricted areas of medicine with which the physician dealt and the related existence of nonprofessional groups performing what would today be considered functions of the physician; and finally, from the eighteenth-century concept of medical ethics. As a result some attention must be paid to the whole medical scene of that period.

A physician might obtain his training and his medical degrees at Oxford or Cambridge. At the former institution the process required, at least in theory, fourteen years, the first seven in acquiring the bachelor's and master's degrees in arts and then another seven in obtaining the degrees of bachelor and doctor of medicine. It was in accordance with this pattern, for example, that John Freind (1675–1728) received the B.A. in 1698, the M.A. in 1701, the B.M. in 1703, and the D.M. in 1707, but it is open to question whether he was finally a better physician or a better Latinist. He is in fact remembered today solely for a history of medicine.

In the eighteenth century the medical schools of Oxford and Cambridge reached their nadir. In each school official university teaching, except for anatomy, was by lecture, and the regius professor of medicine, whose duty it was to provide the lectures, was all too frequently absent, often for long periods. Anatomical studies, too, were sadly neglected even though a readership in anatomy had been established at Oxford in 1624 and a professorship at Cambridge in 1707. That any sort of satisfactory training was given was owing to teaching within the individual college of the university or through private courses for which the student paid additional fees.

In consequence, official medical training offered by the universities did not always turn out competent physicians, and the poor quality often inherent in the medical degree was augmented by degrees granted to the wholly unqualified by royal mandate or by degrees given in honor of a royal visitation to the university. In this respect it should be noted that after 1533/34 the Archbishop of Canterbury was empowered to bestow the degree of doctor of medicine—the so-called Lambeth degree. It was in this way that John Woodward (1665–1728), better known for his study of fossils than for any contribution to medicine, acquired his degree in 1695; and, as a matter of fact, in that same year he received a second degree of doctor of medicine from Cambridge, an institution with which he had never been affiliated.

A physician might also obtain a degree in Scotland. Although the second quarter of the eighteenth century witnessed the beginning of a first-class medical school in Edinburgh under the influence of Leyden and the renowned Boerhaave, and a similarly excellent school developed a little later at Glasgow (1744) through the efforts of William Cullen (1710–1790), prior to that time, and indeed well into the eighteenth century, it was possible to obtain a Scottish medical degree for little more than a request and a fee. At Aberdeen the candidate might never have to appear, but could receive the degree *in absentia* or, as it was more discreetly put, *honoris causa*.

More conscientious students could compensate for deficiencies in such university training by taking private courses in London or, as many did, by going abroad. By the opening of the eighteenth century the most famous medical school in Europe was that of the University of Leyden where Hermann Boerhaave (1668–1738) taught from 1701 to 1738, attracting many English students chiefly through the fame of his clinical teaching. Some went to Paris, or to Montpellier and other French provincial universities. Many of these provincial schools, however, were far from demanding in their requirements, offering medical degrees with the facility of the Scottish universities. Lesser numbers of students studied in Germany, Switzerland, and Italy.

Some students not only studied but obtained medical degrees abroad, and on their return sought to have their degrees incorporated at Oxford or Cambridge, if possible. Some who studied abroad without receiving degrees would often obtain them later from one of the Scottish universities; although such a degree was often meaningless, the student who received one might well have been much better trained than the graduates of Oxford or Cambridge.

Clearly, then, the quality of medical education varied widely, and a medical degree was no warranty of quality, so that there was need to distinguish between the medically qualified and the unqualified. This need had been realized early in the sixteenth century by a series of acts, all of them, despite conflicts of interest, theoretically still in force in the eighteenth century. In 1511/12 an act of Parliament empowered the bishop of the diocese, with the assistance of a panel of experts, to license physicians and surgeons. In 1533/34 the Archbishop of Canterbury was granted the power to issue medical licenses, not only for his own diocese but as well for the whole of England. A further act of 1542/43 stipulated that, in order to ensure sufficient medical care in the kingdom, certain persons who had a knowledge of herbs and an inherent healing power might practice medicine provided they accepted no fees for their services.

Most important of all was the power of the College of Physicians of London, established in 1518. Originally granted control of the practice of medicine in London through the power to license, that power was later extended to cover the provinces as well; although other licensing bodies continued to exist, the college superseded them in the later sixteenth century and throughout the seventeenth century. In the eighteenth century, however, for reasons that need not be considered at this moment, the College of Physicians pretty well ceased to prosecute unlicensed practitioners, even quacks and empirics, and devoted itself to internal college affairs.

It was desirable for one who practiced medicine in London to be a Fellow of the College, at that time located in Warwick Lane in the City of London. Because the Fellows were normally drawn from Oxford and Cambridge graduates, it was also desirable to incorporate a foreign medical degree, that is, to acquire the universities' recognition of it and so be accepted into the university body. Yet even in this matter there was inconsistency, for the King might intervene as he did in the case of Sir Hans Sloane (1660–1753). Irish by origin, graduate of the French provincial university of Orange, and without any connection with either Oxford or Cambridge, Sloane nevertheless was created a Fellow of the College of Physicians by James II in 1687.

Another complexity of eighteenth-century medicine concerned surgery. No physician practiced surgery, for that branch of medicine remained entirely within the province of the United Company of Barber-Surgeons, which had been organized as a guild in 1540. A surgeon received a seven-year period of training within the company, and although his practice was subject to its control, he was also watched by the College of Physicians to ensure that the practice of surgery did not infringe upon the practice of medicine. A surgeon was not permitted to treat a patient internally; in short, he could not prescribe medicines. In 1745 the barbers and surgeons separated and the latter formed the Surgeons' Company, the direct predecessor of the present Royal College of Surgeons of England.

Surgery remained relatively crude. Although its anatomical basis was fairly sound, few serious wounds or diseases of limbs were as yet curable. Therefore amputations were frequently performed, although with high mortality, and since stone in the bladder was then common, extraction by perineal incision was frequent, as were its septic consequences. Because all surgery had to be done on a patient who remained conscious, speed was essential; the celebrated William Cheselden (1688–1752) could amputate an arm in two minutes and extract a bladder stone in one. Better-educated surgeons were well aware of the necessary brutality of their craft, and some never became inured to it. It is said that John Abernethy (1764–1831) rarely undertook a serious operation without vomiting. Few surgeons, however, could support themselves solely by such activities, and for the most part they spent their time treating fractures, bruises, and contusions, opening veins, applying leeches and cupping glasses, and extracting teeth.

Partly related to surgery was the practice of the male midwife who invaded the field of obstetrics in the early eighteenth century. Previously the practice of obstetrics had been controlled by female midwives who, although subject to license by the local bishop, were nevertheless required to possess little more than a record for virtue and sobriety; usually, except for the knowledge they gained empirically, they were of appalling ignorance. The class of male midwives, sometimes surgeons and sometimes physicians, was a phenomenon of the eighteenth century. The group of dedicated practitioners included such men as James Douglas (1675–1742), William Smellie (1697–1763), and the celebrated William Hunter (1718–1783), who sought to approach the subject of obstetrics as a science and to write about it and to teach it to their students as a respectable field of medical study.

Nothing points up the general ignorance of obstetrics more clearly than the notorious and ludicrous incident of Mary Toft of Godalming, who in 1726 declared that she had been frightened by a rabbit and was thereafter delivered of a succession of fifteen rabbits. Although placed under observation, Mary managed to deceive Nathaniel St. André, one of the royal surgeons, into accepting further such deliveries as fact and thereafter affirming this remarkable phenomenon to the King. The deception was revealed only by subsequent observations and examinations by James Douglas and Sir Richard Manningham (1690–1759), physicians of the new school of male midwives. It was, incidentally, Manningham who set aside a few beds for lying-in women when St. James Parochial Infirmary was opened in 1739, so marking a new era in the treatment of pregnant women.

Another respectable element on the medical scene was the pharmacist or apothecary, whose task it had been to provide the ingredients for and to make up medical prescriptions according to a physician's order. Originally subservient to the College of Physicians, which had the right to enter an apothecary's shop and to examine and destroy such drugs as were considered spoiled or harmful, the apothecaries, after organizing in 1617 as the Worshipful Society of Apothecaries of London, became bolder and gradually entered upon the practice of medicine by a kind of subterfuge. Through knowledge of the prescriptions used by physicians for various ailments, the apothecary was himself able to prescribe; he was careful to avoid charging for anything except the drugs, but of course he increased that charge. Because he demanded no fee he was not liable to prosecution for the practice of medicine under the act of 1542/43.

The College of Physicians, encountering no difficulty in demonstrating the implications of the apothecary's excessive charge for his drugs, sought to counter the practice by establishing dispensaries where the poor might obtain medical advice and drugs at a minimal charge. In turn the apothecaries, outraged at this invasion of their field of livelihood, successively resorted to the law, as did also their opponents. Finally, in a shattering decision, the House of Lords recognized the right of the apothecaries to practice medicine, although without charging for their services. It was this contest that led Sir Samuel Garth (1661–1719) to compose his mock-heroic poem, "The Dispensary," as a jibe at apothecaries and at the minority of the College of Physicians who granted them favor. The fact was that there were not enough physicians to go around, and it was this lack that had led the House of Lords to make its decision.

Actually some physicians made a very good thing out of the situation. The eminent Richard Mead (1673–1754) undertook to spend a certain part of the day at a coffeehouse where puzzled apothecaries might bring him reports of their cases. Mead would listen, give his advice, and pocket a half guinea. Of course not all physicians approved of such conduct; the equally celebrated John Radcliffe (1650–1714) remarked of Mead's practice that "a man might as well draw a face as prescribe for one he did not see."

Later, in 1811, as the result of a friendly lawsuit, apothecaries became legally entitled to charge for medical advice as well as for their medicines. In time they came to be looked upon as general practitioners in contrast with the specialists of the College of Physicians.

A final medical group that enjoyed respectability comprised unlicensed practitioners who, in accordance with the parliamentary act of 1542/43, made no charge at all for their services but acted purely in the spirit of philanthropy. Usually they were kindly persons who, motivated by benevolence and charity, undertook to treat the very poor. Such was Robert Levett, Dr. Johnson's friend and once a waiter in a Paris café, who had no professional knowledge except what he had learned from casual acquaintances.

Turning to the other side of the coin, one may first note the well-meaning clergyman who sought to provide cheap medical advice and therapy for the masses or who had encountered some remedy or panacea that he believed as a good Christian he ought to share with others. For example, Bishop George Berkeley, in his book *Siris*, published in 1744, described the wonderfully therapeutic value of tar water, of which he had learned in America.

Reputedly this infusion could even cure smallpox, although it is to be hoped that no fond parent ever denied inoculation to his children because of his faith in the Bishop of Cloyne's remedy. Three years later John Wesley, the founder of Methodism, produced a book entitled *Primitive Physick*, which expounded his own unorthodox ideas of simple remedies for the masses. Fortunately, since the book went through a great many editions, the remedies were for the most part harmless, even though they might never come to grips with the particular medical problem.

England of the eighteenth century has been called the golden age of quackery, flourishing but ignored by the College of Physicians and frequently supported by the peerage or even by the crown. Thus, for example, William Read, a tailor by trade, set up as an oculist with offices in the Strand where a combination of blatant advertising and a confident and pleasing personality brought the credulous in large numbers. Addison called Read "the most successful practitioner in his way," although his way was far from professional. Eventually Read caught the attention of Queen Anne, who bestowed a knighthood upon him and made him her oculist in ordinary. Equally successful was John Taylor who, although never knighted, had no compunction about calling himself the Chevalier John Taylor and who enjoyed a successful career that was continued by his son.

Perhaps the most impertinent of this dubious class was Joshua Ward who, though a drysalter by profession, was fully prepared to grapple with any ailment since he had the support of George II and such notable figures as Lord Chesterfield, Edward Gibbon, and Horace Walpole. Ward's success and effrontery may be measured by a request in his will that upon his death, which occurred in 1761, he be buried in front of the altar in Westminster Abbey. The request was denied.

Nor was quackery limited to male exponents. A certain Mrs. Mapps of Epsom, known as "crazy Sally," was a successful bonesetter. Once or twice a week, in a four-horse chariot with outriders in splendid livery, she drove to the Grecian coffeehouse in London for the sake of her urban customers. She brought her career to an end only through excessive drinking. Mrs. Mapps appears in Hogarth's print, *Company of Undertakers*, in the top row between the Chevalier Taylor and Joshua Ward.

That great deliberative body, the Parliament of England, was induced to pay Joanna Stephens £5,000 to disclose the secret of her remedy for curing the stone. It turned out to contain a powder of calcined eggshells and snails, a decoction of soap and swine's bristles, and pills composed of snails, soap, and honey. The gullible Sir Robert Walpole is estimated to have consumed 180 pounds of soap and 1,200 gallons of limewater in the course of taking Mrs. Stephens's treatment.

The brazen boldness of such quacks, supported by the credulity of the more powerful classes of society, naturally enraged the genuine medical profession, yet the College of Physicians, despite its policing power, did nothing. Quackery flourished and its exponents continued to increase in numbers throughout the century, suffering no more than an occasional witty barb fired by Addison, Pope, Swift, or some other literary figure.

Apart from the annoyance caused by quacks, the genuine physician faced some serious medical problems. Smallpox, readily distinguished from the less lethal measles, was accepted as an inevitable epidemic disease, long known and varying in its incidence and intensity. It especially afflicted children and was seemingly more prone to attack those of the upper classes, but it became somewhat less dangerous after the introduction of inoculation. In 1713 Emanuel Timoni of Constantinople had drawn attention to this preventive procedure, long practiced in the East, by which healthy children were inoculated with the serum of a smallpox victim and thereby usually acquired the disease in a mild form with consequent immunity. But the procedure did not gain popularity in England until 1721, when Lady Mary Wortley Montagu induced George II to order the inoculation of three men and three women convicts in Newgate. After the experiment achieved results that were considered satisfactory, the Princess of Wales had her own two children inoculated, thus putting the seal of royal approval on the procedure.

Tuberculosis or phthisis, excellently described by Richard Morton in 1689, played havoc among the young of all ranks, and such other childhood diseases as chicken pox, scarlet fever, whooping cough, diphtheria, and mumps remained common, as did various kinds of coronary and gastrointestinal complaints among older patients. Many diseases, including malaria, typhoid fever, and typhus, were listed only as fevers under such names as tertian, continued, spotted, putrid, intermittent, relapsing, and brain fever, and there were frequent references to certain aspects of diseases not yet identified as entities, such as looseness, bilious colic, crudity of the stomach, and many more. The existence of typhus was dramatically advertised at the very end of the period under consideration as an aftermath of the 1750 session at Old Bailey. The court became infected with typhus, then known also as gaol fever, "killing Judges, Counsel, and others to the number of forty without making allowance for those of lower rank whose death may not have been heard of." It was in that same year that, for the first time, Dr. John Huxham (1692–1768) recognized the difference between typhus and typhoid fever. Gout was common among the male population of the upper classes, although it also incapacitated Queen Anne, and venereal diseases were all too well known.

Within limits, as a legacy in part from the great Sydenham, a fair diagnosis was often possible through observation of the patient's general appearance, his respiration and pulse, his tongue, the region of pain, and indications of fever, and also, as it was believed, from the appearance of the extracted blood. In 1707 Sir John Floyer (1649–1734) introduced the pulse watch, which had a second hand for counting the pulse beat accurately. This mechanism enabled Floyer to study the pulse quantitatively rather than according to its alleged quality, which had for the most part been used in diagnosis. Fahrenheit's thermometer, developed at Leyden for Boerhaave, was not widely used in England until the latter part of the period. Great reliance was still placed on the appearance of the urine as a diagnostic sign, and physicians convinced themselves that the blood took on a wide variety of appearances according to the disease.

Having made a diagnosis, possibly a correct one, the physician was frequently powerless to do very much for his patient. The wiser ones, in the Hippocratic tradition, put faith in rest and diet, certainly the best remedy available for gout in the eighteenth century. The treatment was also effective in other illnesses in which the most important therapeutic factor was the *vis medicatrix naturae*. This kind of treatment was more fashionably carried out at such watering places as Bath and Tunbridge, where the patient could also feel that the actual water he imbibed had had a share in his recovery, a belief often held as well by the physician, who sometimes ordered the bottled water of Bath for patients far away. The individual bath was also proposed as a therapeutic device and gained some popularity. Sir John Floyer, friend and adviser to Dr. Johnson in his earlier years, produced

An Inquiry into the Right Use of the Hot, Cold and Temperate Baths in England, which went through six editions in twenty-five years. Although intended as an exhaustive work on the subject, it made no mention of bathing for the sake of cleanliness.

There were no specifics except for Peruvian bark (the source of quinine) and mercury, for the treatment respectively of malaria and syphilis, so that such other drugs as were given—usually harmless if herbal but sometimes dangerous if metallic, such as antimony—had no influence on the course of the disease. Some physicians, such as Sir Hans Sloane, considered Peruvian bark to be a panacea, and such incredible remedies as viper's flesh and spirit of human urine were still employed even by the most notable members of the profession. One very popular remedy was Dr. James' Fever Powder, a secret, patented medicine concocted by Robert James (1705–1776), who had obtained the M.D. degree by royal mandate rather than as the reward for medical studies. The fact of a physician's patent on a drug reveals the rather different medical ethics of that day; indeed, Dr. William Cockburn (1669–1739) made an immense fortune from his similarly secret remedy for diarrhoea. Dr. James' Powder, consisting of antimony and phosphate of lime, was dangerous because of its depressant action, but it was used extensively as a febrifuge at a time when "fever" meant any condition in which the skin felt hot and the patient shivered. The powder was extolled by Horace Walpole and it may have hastened the end of Oliver Goldsmith.

Let us now observe the activities of the physician against this background, most conveniently the fashionable London physician such as Richard Mead or John Radcliffe. As a rule these men were not early risers since they had usually spent the preceding evening entertaining at home or elsewhere in conversation and wine drinking. Having risen late and, we may assume, having consumed a cup of chocolate, possibly followed by tea and toast and perhaps some slices of roast beef, the physician was next beset by the problem of shaving and dressing. His valet or a visiting barber would attend to the shaving, although Swift referred to the fact that many physicians were prone to avoid such a daily routine, with stubbly consequences. Dressing followed a strict etiquette of pompous, expansively proportioned black garments and a powdered wig of heroic size. "A physician," wrote Fielding, "can no more prescribe without a full wig, than without a fee." Properly clad, the physician was then ready to receive visitors, either friends or patients. Sir Hans Sloane made it a practice at this time of day to receive poor patients whom he treated without charge, and undoubtedly there were other humanitarian physicians who did likewise.

Finally, leaving his home, the physician was equipped with a black three-cornered hat and a cane which was used primarily as an insignia of his profession, often with a silver or gold knob in which a vinaigrette or a disinfectant was inserted, and at appropriate occasions held to the nose as illustrated in Hogarth's *Company of Undertakers*. The physician's gilt carriage was of considerable importance, too, and if possible ought to be drawn by at least four and preferably, as was the custom of Radcliffe and Mead, by six horses and accompanied by two running footmen. A tax levied on coaches in 1747 aroused considerable contention and led to some verses in the *Gentleman's Magazine* which included the lines:

> The carriage marks the peer's degree
> And almost tells the doctor's fee.

Setting out in this fashion at about ten in the morning, the physician might make the rounds of his patients, whom he saw mostly in their homes, or he might first spend an hour in a coffeehouse listening to and advising apothecaries on their patients—naturally for a fee. On Sundays some physicians were not averse, in that age of long sermons, to being called out of church from time to time through prearrangement, to ride about aimlessly in order to create the impression of an extensive practice. Advertising in this and other ways was far from uncommon and, although subject to jibe, was not considered unethical.

The ordinary day's work was ended by late afternoon and was followed by dinner anytime between four and six o'clock, after which the physician might receive friends or go to some club, tavern, or private house for an evening of conversation amply accompanied by claret or burgundy. It was at such times that the physician's primary interest often became apparent. John Arbuthnot (1667–1735), the friend of Swift, Pope, and Gay, would perhaps attend a political club when he was not writing contributions to *The Memoirs of Martinus Scriblerus*, under Pope's editorship, or writing those pamphlets against the war with France which were to appear under the title *The History of John Bull* and give birth to that English character. Such, too, would have been the activity of another distinguished physician, James Drake (1667–1707), who had the satisfaction of having one of his political pamphlets brought before the House of Lords for judgment and another publicly burned.

It should be realized that the physician of the eighteenth century frequently had had as much training in the liberal arts as he had had in medicine and that he often used his medical practice as a support for his literary interests. For example, Sir Richard Blackmore (d. 1729), Dryden's "Maurus," unhappily wrote quantities of poor verse that were a ripe target for the real literary figures of the day whom Blackmore had been so injudicious as to attack. Sir Samuel Garth, author of *The Dispensary* and awarded five pages toward his immortality in Johnson's *Lives of the English Poets*, might have been seen in the Whiggish and literary Kit-Cat Club readily mixing with Blackmore's critics. It was Garth who in 1700 made arrangements for the body of Dryden to lie in state at the College of Physicians and thereafter assembled a cortège of physicians to accompany it to Westminster Abbey where he provided a Latin eulogy of the poet to accompany the interment.

As the eighteenth century was the golden age of quackery, so, too, it may be described, but without any thought of an invidious comparison, as the golden age of the physician. The more successful physicians, such as Mead, Radcliffe, and Cockburn, enjoyed annual incomes from their practices of anywhere from £5,000 to £7,000, a very large sum in the eighteenth century. Most of these physicians managed to spend the money in various ways without much difficulty. One ready source of expenditure was the library or the museum or both; hence Pope's line "And Books for Mead and Butterflies for Sloane." After Mead's death it took twenty-eight days to dispose of his great library at auction. Sloane, as is well known, collected even more: natural history, books, and manuscripts that were to become the foundation of the British Museum.

The long years of study of the liberal arts influenced physicians in the direction of book collecting, which in time became almost a required pursuit of the physician. Dr. Anthony Askew (1722–1744), in addition to accumulating a large general collection of books and manuscripts, had the ambition to possess every edition of every Greek author. He could, moreover, read the Greek texts. James Douglas's similarly large collection contained 557 editions of the works of Horace. The most notable of all such libraries, however, was that of Francis Bernard (1627–1698). When dispersed at auction in 1698 the collection was discovered to contain better than 50,000 volumes, and although it included no more than a hundred incunabula, twenty-two of them were Caxton's publications.

Still another group of physicians had as their second interest, or even their first, a devotion to science. Sir Hans Sloane, Fellow of the Royal Society in 1687, was secretary from 1693 to 1713 and, in succession to Sir Isaac Newton, held the presidency from 1727 to 1741, the first physician to be so honored. A few others that may be mentioned were Nehemiah Grew (1641–1712), remembered today not for any medical writings but for his work on the sexuality of plants; Martin Lister (1638?–1712), one of London's fashionable physicians but chiefly noteworthy for his studies of conchology; and John Woodward, now recalled for his *Essay toward a Natural History of the Earth* (1695). Incidentally, a quarrel between Woodward and Richard Mead illustrated not only the former's quickness of wit and repartee but as well the distinction between science and therapeutics of that period. With swords drawn and combat under way, Woodward suddenly slipped and was at Mead's mercy. The latter, according to the account, haughtily declared, "Take your life," to which Woodward replied, "Anything but your physic."

In fact, however, despite the contributions to science of men like Grew, the scientific accomplishments of physicians of the first half of the eighteenth century did not compare in fundamental value with those of the preceding century, and there is some truth in Addison's remark about the "Retainers to Physick, who, for want of other Patients, amuse themselves with the stifling of Cats in an Air Pump, cutting up Dogs alive, or impaling Insects upon the point of a Needle for Microscopical Observations."

It was also at this time that a great wave of philanthropy swept over England with important effects for medicine. Notably it led to the founding of a system of country hospitals, which were badly needed, and in London to the founding of Westminster Hospital in 1720, Guy's in 1724, St. George's in 1733, the London in 1740, and the Middlesex in 1745. As a final attribute of the physicians of that time, let it be said that they, too, as men of their age, contributed to this philanthropic movement. To mention only a few instances, Dr. John Addenbrooke (1680–1719) bequeathed £4,000 "to erect and maintain a small physical hospital" in Cambridge, the beginning of what was to become the major teaching hospital of Cambridge University. John Radcliffe, who died worth about £80,000, was perhaps the most generous member of the medical profession, providing for the establishment of the Radcliffe Library, the Observatory, and the Infirmary at Oxford, as well as making a kindly bequest to St. Bartholomew's Hospital "to improve the diet of the poor patients." Sir Hans Sloane, who made sizable contributions to practically every London hospital and learned or scientific society during his lifetime, left his great collections of natural history and his books and manuscripts to the nation—for a price, it is true, but a very small price relative to their true value.

Within the time available for this presentation it has been possible to touch upon only some aspects and a few examples of the English physician and his place in medicine in the first half of the eighteenth century. Often it seems that his real interest lay in fields other than medicine, although some physicians such as Mead, Floyer, Huxham, and George Cheyne (1671–1743) made very real contributions that were, however, to find significant application only in the next fifty years or even in the nineteenth century.

The first half of the eighteenth century was decidedly picturesque, a time when the physician still wore a sword but could as well wield the pen, yet a period providing few names that stand out in the annals of medicine. In contrast with the next fifty years, which witnessed the work of William and John Hunter, Edward Jenner, William Withering, James Lind, Sir John Pringle, and William Heberden, to name but some of the major figures, the earlier period has far less claim to scientific recognition, whatever the merits of its physicians in other respects.

REFERENCES

Baragar, C. A. "John Wesley and medicine," *Annals of Medical History,* 1928, 10:59–65.
Bibliotheca Meadiana sive catalogus librorum Richardi Mead, M.D. Qui prostabunt venales sub hasta, apud Samuelem Baker. In Vico dicto York Street, Covent Garden, Londini. Die Lunae 18mo Novembris, M.DCCLIV. iterumque die Lunae, 7mo Aprilis, M.DCC.LV. N.p., n.d.
Bishop, W. J. "Some medical bibliophiles and their libraries," *Journal of the History of Medicine,* 1948, 3:229–262.
———. "Transport and the doctor in Great Britain," *Bulletin of the History of Medicine,* 1948, 22:427–440.

Brockbank, William. "Sovereign remedies: a critical depreciation of the seventeenth-century London pharmacopoeia," *Medical History,* 1964, 8:1–13.

Brooks, E. St. John. *Sir Hans Sloane.* London, 1954.

Chalke, T. B. "Tuberculosis in literature," *Medical History,* 1962, 6:301–318.

Chance, Burton. "Bishop Berkeley and his use of tar-water," *Annals of Medical History,* 1942, 4 (3d ser.):453–467.

Chaplin, Arnold. "The history of medical education in the universities of Oxford and Cambridge," *Proceedings of the Royal Society of Medicine* (Section of the History of Medicine), 1920, 13:83–106.

———. "The Oxford medical school in the eighteenth century." In *Contributions to medical and biological research dedicated to Sir William Osler* (New York, 1919), I, 16–23.

Clarke, Sir George. *The Royal College of Physicians of London.* Oxford, 1964–1966. 2 vols.

Cope, Sir Zachary. *William Cheselden, 1688–1752.* Edinburgh, 1953.

Copeman, W. S. C. *A short history of the gout.* Berkeley and Los Angeles, 1964.

Crawfurd, Raymond. *The king's evil.* Oxford, 1911.

Dobson, Austin. "Dr. Mead's library," In *Eighteenth century vignettes* (London, 1921), pp. 29–50.

Ellis, Frank H. "Garth's Harveian Oration," *Journal of the History of Medicine,* 1963, 18:8–19.

Garrison, Fielding H. "Medicine in the Tatler, Spectator and Guardian," *Bulletin of the Institute of the History of Medicine,* 1934, 2:477–503.

Gunn, Alistair. "Maternity hospitals." In *The evolution of hospitals in Britain* (London, 1964), pp. 77–88.

Halsband, Robert. "New light on Lady Mary Wortley Montagu's contribution to inoculation," *Journal of the History of Medicine,* 1953, 8:390–405.

Hazen, Allen T. "Samuel Johnson and Dr. Robert James," *Bulletin of the History of Medicine,* 1936, 4:455–465.

Hone, Campbell R. *The life of Dr. John Radcliffe, 1652–1714, benefactor of the University of Oxford.* London, 1950.

Keele, Kenneth D. *The evolution of clinical methods in medicine.* London, 1963.

Keevil, J. J. "The bagnio in London, 1648–1725," *Journal of the History of medicine,* 1952, 7:250–257.

———. "Coffeehouse cures," *ibid.,* 1954, 9:191–195.

Kett, Joseph F. "Provincial medical practice in England, 1730–1815," *ibid.,* 1964, 19:17–29.

King, Lester S. *The medical world of the eighteenth century.* Chicago, 1958.

McHenry, Lawrence D., Jr., and Ronald MacKeith. "Samuel Johnson's childhood illnesses and the king's evil," *Medical History*, 1966, 10:386–399.

McMenemey, W. H. "The hospital movement of the eighteenth century and its development." In *The evolution of hospitals in Britain* (London, 1964), pp. 43–71.

Matthews, Leslie G. *History of pharmacy in Britain*. Edinburgh, 1962.

Mullett, Charles F. *Public baths and health in England, 16th–18th century*. Baltimore, 1946.

Neuburger, Max. "John Floyer's pioneer work," *Bulletin of the History of Medicine*, 1948, 22:208–212.

Nias, J. B. *Dr. John Radcliffe*. Oxford, 1918.

Oshlag, Julius A. "The ethical practice of Sir Hans Sloane," *Bulletin of the History of Medicine*, 1947, 21:918–921.

Rook, Arthur. "Medicine at Cambridge, 1660–1760," *Medical History*, 1969, 13:107–122.

Russell, K. F. "The anatomical library of Dr. Richard Mead (1673–1754)," *Journal of the History of Medicine*, 1947, 2:97–109.

Seligman, S. A. "Mary Toft—the rabbit breeder," *Medical History*, 1961, 5:349–360.

Shelley, Harry S. "Cutting for the stone," *Journal of the History of Medicine*, 1958, 13:50–67.

Siddall, R. S. "George Cheyne," *Annals of Medical History*, 1942, 4 (3d ser.):95–109.

Sinclair, H. M., and A. H. T. Robb-Smith. *A short history of anatomical teaching in Oxford*. Oxford, 1950.

Spencer, Herbert R. *The history of British midwifery from 1650 to 1800*. London, 1927.

Thomas, K. Bryn. *James Douglas of the pouch and his pupil William Hunter*. London, 1964.

Thompson, C. J. S. *The quacks of old London*. London, 1928.

Toomey, Thomas N. "Sir Richard Blackmore, M.D. (1653–1729)," *Annals of Medical History*, 1922, 4:180–188.

Townsend, Gary L. "Sir John Floyer (1649–1734) and his study of the pulse and respiration," *Journal of the History of Medicine*, 1967, 22:286–316.

Traill, R. R. "Sydenham's impact on English medicine," *Medical History*, 1965, 11:356–364.

Wall, Cecil. *A history of the Worshipful Society of Apothecaries of London*. Vol. I: 1617–1815. London, 1963.

Wilson, T. G. "Swift and the doctors," *Medical History*, 1964, 8:199–216.

Winslow, C.-E. A. "A physician of two centuries ago: Richard Mead and his contributions to epidemiology," *Bulletin of the History of Medicine*, 1935, 3:509–544.

VII

HOGARTH'S NARRATIVE METHOD IN PRACTICE AND THEORY

Robert R. Wark

Art Curator, The Huntington Library and Art Gallery

I remember hearing a friend, who has a gift for turning a good phrase, refer to William Hogarth as "a roast beef and boiled potatoes version of the rococo." The remark, though meant to be disparaging, is also illuminating and much more penetrating than I suspect the speaker realized. It is an amusing way to suggest the combination of eighteenth-century elegance with robust, middle-class attitudes which is found in much of Hogarth's work. The remark also hints, however, at a deep-rooted and fundamental tension running through Hogarth's art which is the key to understanding his historical position. For Hogarth, to the art historian, is a complicated and puzzling figure. He stands astride one of the major watersheds in British, and indeed in European, art. He is pulled in two directions, and in the final estimate his art falls somewhere in between. In view of Hogarth's great popular reputation from his own day to ours, it would be silly to imply that he was an artistic failure. Yet there can be little doubt that he aspired to more than he accomplished. The discrepancy between his aims and his achievement is less the result of limitations in his abilities than of historical circumstances which he sensed and tried to master, but in the end was unable to control.

The tension in Hogarth's art is apparent in different ways. In this paper I wish to explore only one, which appears in his technique of telling a story. What I propose to do is to examine a series of Hogarth's narrative paintings in order to discover, simply from the viewpoint of the spectator, how the story is in fact told. This direct visual experience will then be measured against what Hogarth tells us in his writings about narration in art. Artists generally are notoriously bad critics of their own works, and it will cause little surprise that there is a discrepancy between what Hogarth actually does in his narrative pictures and what he says he is doing or would like to do. It is the nature of this discrepancy which is of interest.

As the argument to be presented concerns Hogarth's position in the history of art, it is essential at the outset to have the basic chronological facts clearly in mind. Hogarth's active career as a painter falls roughly within the second quarter of the eighteenth century. His first pictures date from the late 1720s. He lived on until 1764, but his best work was completed before 1760. With his activity falling mainly between 1730 and 1760, he is definitely in the van of the major developments in English painting. Reynolds, Gainsborough, and Wilson, with whom English painting comes of age, were all active principally in the third quarter of the century, beginning their careers just as Hogarth was coming to the end of his.

The second quarter of the century, the period to which Hogarth belongs, was the heyday of the widely based style phase that art historians call the rococo. The native habitat of the rococo was France, where it reached its fullest development. It was, however, a truly international style that appeared during the mid-eighteenth century in all countries of Europe. As subject matter rococo artists preferred lighthearted and even frivolous themes. They avoided high seriousness and drama, choosing instead the playful, witty, and amusing, often with a slightly erotic tinge. The rococo style, in the more abstract and formal sense, was perfectly adapted to this type of expression: high-keyed in color; restless and busy in design, keeping the eye scurrying about; curvilinear and two-dimensional in organization, avoiding stable, tectonic forms of composition and strong effects of depth or recession. In all these respects, Scene I from Hogarth's great narrative series, *Marriage à la Mode*, is a typical rococo painting, deserving indeed to rank among the rather select number of masterpieces of rococo art produced in England (fig. 1). It was created by Hogarth in the early 1740s, at the peak of his powers.

Examined as a direct visual experience, the painting gives the initial impression of a very busy, crowded, almost cluttered, scene. All of the many objects represented seem to be competing

Fig. 1. *Marriage à la Mode*

Fig. 2. *Marriage à la Mode*

Fig. 3. *Marriage à la Mode*

Fig. 4. *Marriage à la Mode*

Fig. 5. *Marriage à la Mode*

Fig. 6. *Marriage à la Mode*

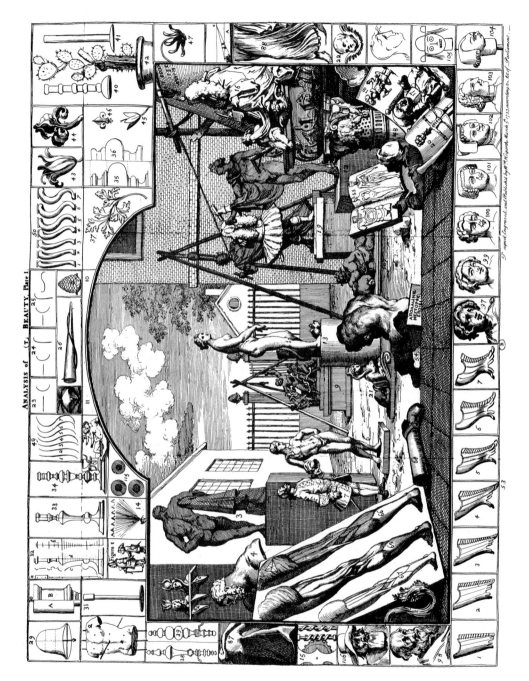

Fig. 7.
The Analysis of Beauty

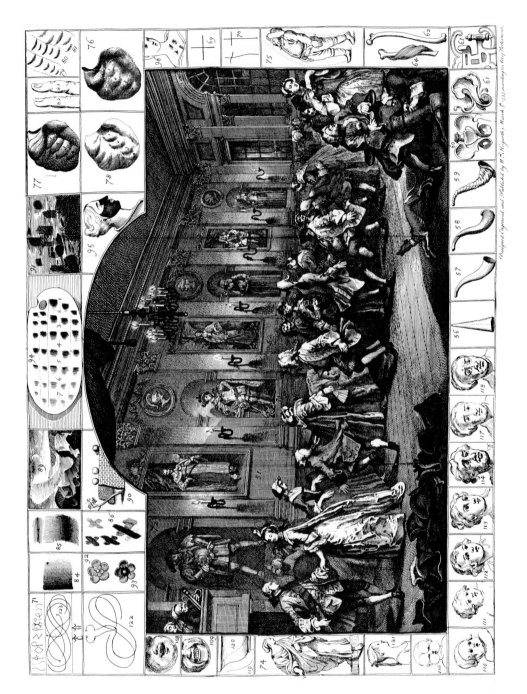

Designed, Engraved and Published by W. Hogarth, March 5, 1753 according to Act of Parliament.

Fig. 8.
The Analysis of Beauty

for the spectator's attention. Using more abstract visual jargon, one would say that the whole surface of the picture is highly animated. The spectator's eye is occupied almost equally all over the scene, with little rest or repose. Nothing dominates or attracts attention immediately; the design has no compelling focus. The reasons for this impression go beyond the mere quantity of things presented and depend ultimately on factors such as color, light and shadow, and paint application. There is no broad massing of light and shadow to direct one's attention. The colors, fairly high in intensity and value, often meet one another abruptly, with little gradation of tone to soften the transition. The individual figures, although reasonably convincing as solids in space, are not modeled with any strong shading to emphasize their bulk and solidity. Hogarth shows the corner of a ceiling receding into space and a vista seen through a window. Although these features intellectually serve to indicate depth, the idea is largely negated by the colors and the busy activity for the eye in the background areas. The paint is applied in rather crisp daubs, retaining its identity as pigment on canvas, rather than losing itself in the objects it describes. Visually the general effect of the painting is a lively and sparkling, but basically two-dimensional, surface. In all these respects Scene I of *Marriage à la Mode* is an excellent example of what is meant by the rococo style, as applied to form rather than subject matter.

Most observers, however, do not isolate their reactions to form and subject matter. Especially in a painting like this one, they immediately become concerned with what is represented. Here there is so much that asks for attention that the eye hardly knows where to begin. Anyone looking at the painting for the first time, with no prior knowledge of the subject, is likely to explore it for several minutes before reaching definite conclusions about what is going on. He sees a couple of middle-aged men seated beside a table. One, rather elegantly dressed, has his foot bandaged and resting on a stool—probably he has gout. He points to himself with one hand, and with the other to a drawing on a piece of paper beside him, which upon examination proves to be a family tree. If we look quite closely, we see that the tree is labeled as issuing from "William, Duke of Normandye." The man seated on the other side of the table holds a paper on which can be read the words "Marriage Settlement of the R^t Honble The Lord Viscount." A man standing between the two figures hands a paper labeled "Mortgage" to the first man, who also seems to be receiving some money. It appears that some kind of business transaction, involving a marriage and a mortgage, is going on.

Further detailed examination discovers several coronets scattered around the room: on the crutch beside the man with the gout, above the canopy behind him, and on the frame of a painting hanging on the wall. The particular form of coronet is recognizable as that belonging to an English earl, and thus we have a valuable clue in interpreting the scene. As the marriage contract refers to a viscount rather than to an earl, we conclude that the gouty gentleman (who must be the earl) is not the one getting married, and that the document probably refers to his son, as "viscount" is a courtesy title given to the son of an earl. There are two younger men in the painting, but as the one sharpening a quill pen is evidently some sort of clerk or lawyer, the viscount must be the dandy to the extreme left. He seems not in the least interested in the young lady seated beside him (apparently the intended bride), who is toying with her ring which is threaded on a handkerchief. This, we decide, is the young couple to be joined in holy matrimony, a state Hogarth probably expects us to equate with that of the two dogs chained together in the foreground. The clerk or lawyer seems a little oversolicitous in his attentions to the young lady, hinting at troubles to come. We conclude that the picture represents the negotiations connected with the marriage of a young nobleman to the daughter of a wealthy commoner: a frank exchange of social position for money. As the two young people exhibit no interest in each other, the prospects for a happy wedded life look grim. A good many other things might be deduced from the picture, particularly about the misguided tastes of the earl, but by now the general idea at least is fairly clear. Remember, however, the nature of the process by which we discovered what is going on. There was no dramatic, sudden revelation. The meaning of the picture developed gradually as our eyes roamed about it, picking up details, reading labels, interpreting various signs, but without following any particular order, until finally the nature of the event and its ramifications become clear.

The painting is the first of a series of six which traces the history of the marriage between the two young people shown to the left in Scene I. The whole series, entitled *Marriage à la Mode*, is usually regarded as Hogarth's finest artistic achievement. It is the culmination of a pictorial narrative technique that Hogarth developed about a decade earlier in *The Harlot's Progress* (for which the engravings were issued in 1732) and *The Rake's Progress* (1733-34). In these and several similar series, Hogarth tells a story through a sequence of pictures. His approach remains essentially the same in all of them, and *Marriage à la Mode* may safely be taken as a characteristic example of his narrative method. As Scene I is typical of the series insofar as the impact on the observer's eye is concerned, my remarks on the remaining five paintings can be much more summary.

The second scene, like the first, is lively and colorful (fig. 2). Again, the eye bounces around the picture surface with no clear sense of direction or emphasis, picking up details that are read and interpreted in order to reach a conclusion about what is represented. Apparently it is morning—daylight is streaming in through the windows and the candles are burned down or have gone out—but presumably the two young people seated by the fireplace have not been to bed. The man, dressed in coat and hat as if he has just come in from the street, gives in his whole demeanor and expression a convincing portrayal of "the morning after." His sword lies at his feet, broken in its scabbard. A little dog sniffs at something emerging from the man's pocket, which proves on examination to be a lady's bonnet. But not the bonnet of the lady in the picture, for she is wearing hers.

Apparently while the man has been carousing on his own, the lady has been entertaining at home. The remnants of a party, cards and musical instruments, lie scattered about the room. A steward who has been trying to get some household bills paid has given up in despair, having succeeded with only one. The servant, yawning in the background as he tips over a chair, suggests that the household, although clearly an opulent one, is not efficiently managed. Thus the picture represents dissipation and its aftereffects: a wealthy young couple indulging liberally, but independently, in various pleasures.

Just what the connection of this subject is to the preceding one may not be immediately clear to the casual spectator. If one compares the actors in the two paintings, however, there are a few details, like the patch under the jaw of the young man and his profile, which identify him as the young viscount who was being married off in Scene I. Although the resemblance between the young women portrayed in the two pictures is less explicit, it is probably correct to assume that Scene II is a representation of the domestic bliss that has followed the excursion into matrimony. The direct visual links between scenes in Hogarth's narrative sequences are usually rather tenuous. In the prints based on the paintings he was able to make the connection clear by appending engraved captions, often of some length, but a spectator approaching the original paintings without having the story already in mind would be at a loss to work out the direction of the narrative from the visual evidence alone. This uncertainty is particularly evident in Scene III of *Marriage à la Mode* (fig. 3), for both the scene itself and its relation to what has gone before are difficult to interpret. The viscount is visiting a doctor, seemingly a quack, but the young man's gesture and expression suggest that he is not sick himself. The trouble seems to center on the sniveling woman standing beside him and on a box of pills the viscount is holding out to the doctor. One supposes that the pills failed to work, but it is far from clear what they were supposed to have accomplished. And who is the large woman with the knife? With the direct visual evidence supplying no answers, about all we can conclude is that something rather sordid is or has been going on, and that the viscount is sinking farther and farther down the moral scale. The painting itself is lively and sparkling. The play of color, especially the bright apron against the dark skirt of the large woman, is a fine rococo touch, providing the type of surface animation that is rococo painting at its best.

Scene IV (fig. 4) returns to the activities of the other member of the duo. The lady is holding a levee, a fashionable form of entertainment consisting primarily of inviting your friends to watch you get dressed in the morning. There is a lot of amusing byplay in the picture, centered on musical activities, and it may be some time before one's attention is caught by the episode in the background, the one part that is really furthering the story. The lady is being invited by a man, apparently the lawyer of Scene I, to accompany him to a masquerade. The message is conveyed to the observer by the rather elaborate contrivance of having the lawyer offer a ticket with one hand while pointing with the other to a representation of a masquerade on a screen behind him. Any doubt about the lawyer's real motives should be dispelled by the boy servant in the foreground, who holds up a statuette of a male figure sprouting antlers—Actaeon becoming a symbol for the cuckold husband. From the earl's coronets displayed around the room it is obvious that the viscount has now succeeded to his father's title. Again, as in Scene I, the activity represented must be read and interpreted in order to discover what is going on.

Scene V (fig. 5) reveals the climax of the story. Visually the essence of what is happening is more forcefully and dramatically told than in the earlier scenes, a fact I will return to later. Nevertheless, a good deal of optical scurrying around is necessary before the episode comes clearly into focus. Apparently the countess and the lawyer retired to a bagnio after the masquerade. The young earl, exhibiting a somewhat unexpected trace of honor and chivalry, follows them there. A duel takes place, and the earl is killed. Hogarth shows us the moment when the earl is falling, mortally wounded; his wife kneels to beg his forgiveness; the lawyer attempts to escape in his nightshirt through the window as the night watch breaks in through the door.

The last scene (fig. 6) depicts the denouement of the whole sad business. The countess has returned to her father's house. She has just swallowed poison after reading the speech given by her paramour from the gallows. Her father takes the wedding ring from her finger before rigor mortis sets in; an old woman holds up a rickety child (presumably the fruit of the ill-fated marriage) for the final embrace with its mother. Scene VI is a dismal episode, but a bright and animated example of rococo painting, regardless of the events depicted.

The direct visual examination of Hogarth's paintings reveals him first as a brilliant example of a rococo artist. *Marriage à la Mode*, before it becomes a story, is a delight to the eye; bright colors spotted over the picture area make the overall surface lively and decorative. The eye dances across these spirited paintings from one color area to another; the formal organization conveys no clear sense of order, focus, or repose. Hogarth's method of telling his story fits with this staccato but diffuse effect. He fills his pictures with details, most of which have some significance for the narrative. He makes little attempt to create a path for the eye to follow through all this material, or to give emphasis to one detail over another. Our eyes move restlessly over the pictures, reading, interpreting, relating all the objects depicted as signs and symbols that eventually tell us what is happening. It is in essence a method of narration that relies almost entirely on represented details and makes little use of formal devices the artist might have at his command to give emphasis, priority, and direction to our perception of the scene.

Although Hogarth does not deal explicitly with the problem of pictorial narrative in his writings, he says enough that is related to the topic to reveal a significant discrepancy between his thinking and his practice. Hogarth sets forth his ideas in two main sources. The more important is a book, *The Analysis of Beauty*, written fairly late in his life and published in 1753. It embodies observations and thoughts that Hogarth had been accumulating for many years. The second main source, a series of autobiographical anecdotes collected and published after Hogarth's death, also contains information of value. All this material is now available in an exemplary edition prepared by Joseph Burke.[1] In his excellent introduction, Burke considers the question with which I am here concerned: the relation between Hogarth's practice and theory of painting. That he arrives at a different conclusion from mine is a circumstance depending primarily on the general context in which Hogarth's art is placed.

Probably the most remarkable feature of *The Analysis of Beauty* is its emphasis on what art historians call formal and abtract factors in painting. Much of the book is concerned with defining what Hogarth understands by "beauty." The interesting thing is that beauty, for Hogarth, has nothing to do with the subject represented and its intellectual or moral qualities. Beauty, rather, is a matter of form, consisting in essence of the presence of a particular type of S curve whose exact character Hogarth defined in a series of diagrams which accompanied his book (fig. 7). Almost anything could be beautiful, according to Hogarth, if the form followed this type of curve. As a corollary to his theory about the abstract line of beauty, Hogarth advanced the idea that any deviation from the ideal curve would have a distinct meaning for the observer. For instance, a beautiful human body naturally conforms in its contours to the ideal serpentine line. Characters differing from the ideal, however, may be represented abstractly by varying the nature of the line: "in attitudes of authority . . . more extended and spreading than ordinary, but reduced somewhat below the medium of grace, in those of negligence and ease; and as much exaggerated in insolent and proud carriage, or in distortions of pain as lessen'd and contracted into plain and par-

[1] William Hogarth, *The Analysis of Beauty. With the Rejected Passages from the Manuscript Drafts and Autobiographical Notes*, ed. Joseph Burke (Oxford, 1955).

allel lines, to express meanness, aukwardness, and submission." [2]
Hogarth worked out a second print to illustrate his point (fig. 8),
depicting a series of dancing couples; the ideal figures are at the
left with successive deviations from the ideal moving off to the
right. A diagram in the top left corner reduces the figures to a
series of lines, demonstrating in precisely what way each pair re-
lates to the ideal of beauty.

The significant fact about all this is that Hogarth clearly believed, and attempted to demonstrate, that expression in a painting
may be controlled by manipulation of abstract factors in the design, particularly line. Historically it is an idea of great interest
and significance. Although earlier writers on art had occasionally
hinted at this notion, none had been so explicit and emphatic in
expressing it as Hogarth. It must be noted, however, that Hogarth
states the idea in terms of line, rather than in terms of color, for
example, or of light and shadow. As the ideal is defined in terms
of line, so also are expressive deviations from the ideal.

When Hogarth talks about the general organization of the
composition of a painting, he also places emphasis on line. He
stresses the value of irregularity and intricacy in compositions,
and the love the eye has for what he calls "pursuing" its way
through a picture. The peculiar type of intricacy that provides
visual delight can be obtained by composing forms along Hogarth's favorite serpentine line, which "leads the eye a wanton
kind of chace." [3]

Hogarth is less conscious of the expressive value of light and
shadow, but he does point out that "objects which are intended
most to affect the eye, and come forwardest to the view, must
have large, strong, and smart oppositions." [4] Furthermore, "when
lights and shades in a composition are scattered about in little
spots, the eye is constantly disturbed, and the mind is uneasy." [5]

It would be possible to find in *The Analysis of Beauty* many
more observations that would further emphasize Hogarth's
awareness of the expressive quality of abstract factors in painting,
but enough has been said to establish the point. The question, of
course, is the extent to which this awareness is reflected in Hogarth's practice as a painter. It must be admitted that one is not

[2] *Ibid.*, pp. 145–146.
[3] *Ibid.*, p. 42.
[4] *Ibid.*, p. 123.
[5] *Ibid.*, p. 124.

immediately conscious that the abstract organization in the *Marriage à la Mode* paintings has been manipulated for expressive effect. In most of the scenes there is a satisfactory relationship between the spotty, restless organization characteristic of rococo paintings and the anecdotal, diffuse quality of Hogarth's storytelling. But on the whole one is more impressed by the lack than by the presence of formal organization for emphasis, direction, and intensity. Hogarth tells his story by represented detail rather than by expressive pictorial devices. And yet, when one studies the paintings with Hogarth's observations in mind, it is tempting and even plausible to see him making adjustments in accordance with his expressed ideas. Look again, for instance, at the climax scene of *Marriage à la Mode*, "The Death of the Earl," which portrays the most dramatic and intense moment of the story. It is here that we would expect Hogarth to drive home his moral with a strongly charged presentation that would carry his point.

I think there can be no doubt that Hogarth was quite clearly aware of the importance of Scene V for his purpose and that he is making adjustments, in accordance with his theory of expression, to heighten the emotional impact. He chooses to set the episode in a dimly lit room, which produces a much more somber coloristic effect than in the other paintings in the series. He tries to focus attention on the central episode—involving the kneeling countess and her dying husband—by making it the largest area of light in the picture. In the figure of the earl Hogarth has consciously contrived angular accents, in accordance with his theory of the expressive quality of lines, to convey a sense of the broken quality of the body. Notice how he accentuates the awkward angle of the legs as the earl falls by the position of the sword, caught in midair. Yet in spite of these efforts to increase the emotional impact and intensity of the scene, it does not in fact pack much of a punch.

The unsatisfactory effect created by the painting can be explained in at least two ways. From the point of view of the objects Hogarth has chosen to represent, there is a curious inconsistency that cancels out any nascent pathos. The figure of the lawyer scrambling through the window and the strange juxtaposition on the back wall of a female portrait on top of a mural are rather crude visual jokes that negate the drama created by the primary group of the earl and the countess. It is almost as if Hogarth was embarrassed by an emotional situation and felt obliged to retreat quickly into comedy.

If one looks at the painting more from the standpoint of form than of represented detail, a comparable inconsistency is evident. Despite Hogarth's efforts to manipulate the form of the picture for a more concentrated emotional impact, remnants of the rococo remain. The eye is not in fact permitted to rest on the principal group, but is quickly attracted to other areas of the picture, spots of light and color that draw one's attention and dissipate the focal effect.

Many explanations might be advanced for this curious state of affairs. Some critics might say simply that we are misjudging Hogarth's intentions: that his aim throughout is for comedy and raillery, and that we are mistaken in looking for pathos. This explanation, however, takes no account of the evident adjustments in form in "The Death of the Earl" to achieve a more concentrated emotional effect. Other critics may feel that Hogarth's heavy reliance on representational detail indicates a basically literary approach to the problem of storytelling, and that we are mistaken in judging the narrative by more purely visual standards. But this suggestion leaves aside Hogarth's obvious awareness in his writings of the expressive power of abstract organization. Probably the most cogent explanation comes from an understanding of Hogarth's position in the history of art.

Hogarth, as I emphasized at the outset, belongs stylistically to the rococo phase of European painting. The rococo—and this point is worth stressing again—is a style that treated the canvas as a surface to be decorated with bright colors applied in such a way as to create a brilliant but primarily two-dimensional effect. The rococo style, in its essential nature, is not capable of great variety or depth of emotion; it is a style in perfect accord with the light-hearted, witty, and titillating content most rococo artists were seeking. Hogarth aimed for a richer variety in emotion than the rococo could produce. He understood in theory, with surprising clarity, that in order to achieve the type of emotional variety he wanted he had to control and manipulate the basic abstract elements of his art: line, shape, color, light, and shade. Yet the rococo style to which he belonged was too strong to be shaken off; when he attempted a subject outside the range of expression possible to the rococo, as in "The Death of the Earl," he failed. The painting, with its overall animation leading the eye to explore the entire surface, is still essentially rococo, in spite of Hogarth's obvious efforts to modify the style toward something expressively more potent. The subject demands a more powerful and dramatic type of organization. Conversely, Hogarth is most successful when he is dealing with subjects (such as Scenes I, II, and IV of *Marriage à la Mode*) where the lighthearted and amusing theme is in complete accord with the inherent expressive character of the rococo style.

In practice Hogarth's narrative method is to accumulate representational details that the spectator reads, in a rather helter-skelter way, as signs and symbols that tell the story. In theory Hogarth shows himself very much aware of the importance of abstract organization as a means of controlling, varying, and intensifying the emotional content of a painting. His ideas on this matter, although rudimentary, are essentially valid and have subsequently become commonplaces of art criticism. There can be no doubt that nonrepresentational factors—light and shade, lines and contours, color, and suggested space—are of the greatest importance in determining the emotional impact of a picture. Hogarth's attempts to apply these principles to his own paintings failed, partly because he could not effectively shake off the rococo style, which was one of diffusion rather than of concentration, partly because he could not control his tendency to multiply representational details. The discrepancy is interesting in itself as an indication of basic tensions within Hogarth's personality. It is also significant in a broader historical context, for it demonstrates a wish on Hogarth's part to break away from the rococo idiom and develop an outlook more characteristic of the late eighteenth century. One of the few common factors running through late eighteenth-century art is the desire of artists to control a wider range of expression than any one style would allow them and consequently to regard form or style as something that could be manipulated at will. An important early theoretical statement of this idea appeared within a few years of Hogarth's *Analysis of Beauty*, with the publication of Edmund Burke's essay *A Philosophical Enquiry into the Origin of Our Ideas of the Sublime and Beautiful* (1757). At about the same time, the development of the revival phenomenon in architecture and painting led to a breakdown in the stylistic uniformity that had previously characterized the great epochs in European art. Hogarth stands astride this fundamental change in outlook. In practice he is still essentially a rococo artist; in his thinking he hints clearly at attitudes characteristic of the succeeding generation.

VIII

VERBAL AND VISUAL CARICATURE IN THE AGE OF DRYDEN, SWIFT, AND POPE

Jean H. Hagstrum

Professor of English, Northwestern University

Among the greatest achievements of English verse are the satirical lines devoted to Achitophel, Zimri, Baron Cutts the Salamander, Atticus, and Sporus. What shall we name these poetic paragraphs? Samuel Johnson called the Achitophel of *The Medall* a "picture" and referred to the "artful delineation" of character in *Absalom and Achitophel*. Of Pope's personal satires Johnson used the term employed by the author himself, by his contemporaries, and by Dryden; that term, *character*, has persisted to our own day.[1] Characters, however, are traditionally typical or categorical, not individual, and those of Pope, identified or not, are or seem to be personal. Then why not *portrait*, which Johnson in his dictionary defined as "a picture drawn from life"? Because, in spite of their many historical details and insights, the famous lines of Dryden and Pope can scarcely be regarded as realistic transcrip-

[1] "Life of Dryden," in *Works of Johnson* (Oxford, 1825), VII, 322, 324; "Life of Pope," in *ibid.*, VIII, 341; Dryden, *A Discourse Concerning the Original and Progress of Satire*, in *Essays of John Dryden*, ed. W. P. Ker (Oxford, 1900), II, 93 (hereafter cited as Ker). See Benjamin Boyce, *The Character-Sketches in Pope's Poems* (Durham, N.C., 1962) (hereafter cited as Boyce, *Pope*), a work to which, along with Professor Boyce's other works on character, I am even more indebted than appears in the annotations.

tions, and we cannot ignore Johnson's important word *artful*. It is also a challenging word, although very few have risen to tell us wherein lies the art of a form that Dryden received as brick and that left his hands as marble, an art he regarded as difficult and "severe." [2]

Perhaps one should use the plural and ask what art forms satire assumed in neoclassical Europe. Some writers created situational satires, with great skill applying epic and heroic forms to contemporary situations or adapting the highly suggestive devices of Boccalini or Quevedo. *The Tatler* and *The Spectator* made short satiric narrative effective, and Pope suggested the progresses of Hogarth in his moral tale of Sir Balaam. Pope also created short conversational dramas along lines suggested by Persius and Horace. Dryden made "beautiful turns of words and thoughts" and "sounding" and "elegant" language his especial province.[3] And from rhetoric came the ideal of vivacious imagery, of *enargeia*, of visual palpability and lifelikeness.[4]

The art of satire also consisted in the making of pictures, formal pictures; and this aspect of satiric art, which is more and other than straightforward visual vivacity, has not been much discussed. Dryden said a "man may be capable, as Jack Ketch's wife said of his servant, of a plain piece of work, a bare hanging; but to make a malefactor die sweetly was only belonging to her husband." [5] The creation of pictures was one way to do better than a plain, bare hanging.

ANALOGY WITH THE VISUAL ARTS

It is widely acknowledged that the historical situation, which always provides the artist with his choices and opportunities, was in the Restoration peculiarly congenial to the collaboration of poetry and painting. The analogy of the visual and verbal arts is a hardy perennial that grew first in classical soil and flourished in Renaissance and baroque Europe. It lived to bloom in Restoration culture because it was nourished by the most exciting and

2 "How *easy* is it to call rogue and villain, and that wittily! But how *hard* to make a man appear a fool, a blockhead, or a knave, without using any of those opprobrious terms!" Dryden also discusses how to "spare the grossness of the names, and to do the thing yet more *severely*" (emphasis added) (Ker, II, 92–93).

3 *Original and Progress of Satire* (Ker, II, 108, 113).

4 See Jean H. Hagstrum, *The Sister Arts* (Chicago, 1958), pp. 11–12, 121.

5 *Original and Progress of Satire* (Ker, II, 93).

ambitious intellectual enterprises of the period: British literary realism, philosophical empiricism, and natural science. In his ode "To the Royal Society," published in Sprat's history, Cowley refers to words as "Pictures of the Thought" and shows that he has a full-blown pictorial analogy in mind. He invokes the classical story of birds flying at painted grapes, recalls the examples of Rubens and Van Dyck, and draws a precise comparison with portrait painting, which he praises for producing "The Natural and Living Face":

> The real object must command
> Each judgment of his Eye, and Motion of his
> [the poet's or painter's] Hand.[6]

Professor Miner has said that it was natural at the time of *Annus Mirabilis* to think of the "correspondences between art and action," so natural in fact that Dryden compared Anne Killigrew's turning to classical landscape with Louis XIV's depredations upon his neighbors.[7] Since satire was where the action was, it is not surprising that satire also strove to achieve the benefits thought to be conferred upon verbal art by attempting to imitate its visual sister. Marvell, writing as a political satirist, said:

> Painter, adieu! How well our arts agree,
> Poetic picture, painted poetry.

These lines come from Marvell's *Last Instructions to a Painter*,[8] a poem that excellently represents a genre in which the painter was summoned, advised, and instructed by the poet. This genre, used by Marvell himself, by Waller, and by a number of anonymous satirists, was one of the two or three most popular forms for political poetry in the Restoration. Juvenal came into post–Civil War culture in the very year of the Restoration with sumptuous

---

[6] Stanza 7.

[7] Earl Miner, "The 'Poetic Picture, Painted Poetry' of *The Last Instructions to a Painter*," in George deF. Lord, ed., *Andrew Marvell: A Collection of Critical Essays* (Englewood Cliffs, N. J., 1968), p. 171.

[8] Ll. 942–943. The poem may be read in *Poems on Affairs of State*, ed. George deF. Lord, I (New Haven, 1963), 99–139. This volume and its sequels should be consulted, *passim*, for evidence of the pictorialism described here (see esp. I, liii; III [ed. Howard H. Schless (1968], 184). For the genre, see Mary Tom Osborn, *Advice-to-a-Painter Poems, 1653–1856* (Austin, Tex., 1949), and Hagstrum, *Sister Arts*, pp. 120–121.

illustrations by the prestigious engraver, Wenceslaus Hollar, whose engravings naïvely, suggestively, ambitiously, and vividly pictorialize the ancient satire.[9] Dryden called *Absalom and Achitophel* "a Picture to the Wast" and drew its motto (*Si Propiùs stes / Te Capiet Magis*) from the *Ars Poetica* lines that, immediately following the famous tag *ut pictura poesis*, begin Horace's influential comparison of the two arts.[10] In a lighter vein Swift uses Horace's dictum when he writes an answer for the long-nosed Dan Jackson to a libel on his face:

> My Verse little better you'll find than my Face is,
> A Word to the Wise, *ut pictura poesis*.

Swift drives on with the pictorial language and even anticipates Hogarth's aesthetics:

> Let then such Criticks know, my Face
> Gives them their Comeliness and Grace:
> Whilst ev'ry Line of Face does bring,
> A Line of Grace to what they sing.[11]

Pope, in discussing La Bruyère's characters, says: "Tis certainly the proof of a Master-Hand, that can give such striking Likenesses in such slight Sketches, & in so few strokes on each subject." [12]

We have thus summoned the poets with whom we are concerned to witness to the close association in their critical consciousness of painting with satire. Their practice follows their profession, and their satirical verses recall motifs and genres of the visual arts. In a moving night scene by Marvell which begins, "Paint last the King, and a dead shade of Night," and has for its only light a weak taper, King Charles awakens in horror, muses on "th' uneasy throne," and sees an apparition, a nude whose arms behind her are interwoven with her tresses. The King is kind, but

9 *Mores Hominum. The Manners of Men, Described in Sixteen Satyrs of Juvenal* (London, 1660). This handsome work is a revision by Sir Robert Stapylton himself of the translation and edition of 1647.

10 *Ars Poetica*, ll. 361 ff. For Dryden's statement and his use of the motto, see *The Poems of John Dryden*, ed. James Kinsley (Oxford, 1958), I, 215–216.

11 "D——n J——n's Answer," in *The Poems of Jonathan Swift*, ed. Harold Williams (Oxford, 1958), pp. 994–995.

12 Quoted from *The Correspondence of Alexander Pope*, ed. George Sherburn (Oxford, 1956), II, 142, by Boyce, *Pope*, p. 119.

he soon shrinks back, for her cold touch chills him. The airy picture vanishes, and "he divin'd 'twas England or the Peace." [13] The allegorical Virgin, so reminiscent of Botticelli's nudes, and the disturbed King meet in a tenebroso piece that also recalls Ribalta, Ribera, and the followers of Caravaggio. The poem "Advice to a Painter" (1673), perhaps by John Ayloffe, recalls the contemporary political caricature, for the Duke of York is verbally painted with the conversational balloon of the cartoon near his mouth:

> First draw him falling prostrate to the south
> Adoring Rome, this label in his mouth.[14]

Shimei appears in a formal portrait:

> His Hand a Vare of Justice did uphold;
> His Neck was loaded with a Chain of Gold.[15]

The round and liquored Og, in a kind of seascape capriccio, rolls behind his linkboy, like a stout and tossing vessel coming into harbor behind its light.[16] Sporus at the ear of Eve is less biblical or Miltonic than graphic; he resembles countless engravings of the serpent in Eden with a human or an angelic face, his body wrapped around the tree as he offers the apple to Eve from his mouth: "A Cherub's face, a Reptile all the rest." [17] Pope's "frugal crone," who is dying and is attended by praying priests, appears in a mock *sacra conversazione* which illustrates the pictorialist critic's dictum that verbal art ought to catch the single and brief dramatic action on the canvas. Even at the moment of last unction, the stingy old lady still tries from her bed "to save the hallow'd taper's end":

> Collects her breath, as ebbing life retires,
> For one puff more, and in that puff expires.[18]

These circumstances—that the poet as critic associated satirical verse with visual art and that in his practice he embodied or re-

[13] *Last Instructions to a Painter*, ll. 885–906, in *Poems on Affairs of State*, I, ed. Lord, 136.
[14] "Advice to a Painter," ll. 7–8, in *ibid.*, I, 214.
[15] *Absalom and Achitophel*, ll. 596–597.
[16] *Ibid.*, Pt. II, ll. 460–461.
[17] Pope, *An Epistle to Dr. Arbuthnot*, l. 331.
[18] Pope, Epistle I, *To Cobham*, ll. 244–245.

called specifically pictorial forms—provide historical sanction for the nomenclature now proposed: that the satirical lines attacking individual persons be called by the visual term *caricature*, and that this art (which distorts but does not destroy resemblance)[19] be divided into two subspecies, *emblematic* caricature and *portrait* caricature. The adjective in each term is intended to invoke the most closely related visual art, the emblem for the first and the portrait for the second. (1) Emblematic caricature is not primarily concerned with resemblance, although it wishes unmistakably to strike an individual. It attempts to reduce the subject to ridicule and contempt by means of insulting comparisons. These comparisons are emblematic, or hieroglyphic (to use a term Swift liked), and tend, because of the mocking reduction involved, to become grotesque. (2) Portrait caricature strives not to be monstrous but to keep the representation credible and recognizable. It too seeks to render the original reprehensible or ridiculous by means of a distorting line, but it is concerned to maintain a realistic surface.

EMBLEMATIC CARICATURE

The emblem is shorthand allegory, and allegory is an extended emblem. Among the many literary and pictorial forms that satire mocked, reduced, parodied, adapted, or subverted are both the longer and shorter versions of visual allegory. The ceilings and walls of palaces and churches, the pictorialized pages of Ovid and Spenser, and the cruder or simpler icons of the emblem books provided opportunities that a pictorially oriented satirist did not neglect. Dryden's Flecknoe sits high on a throne, with all the accouterments of dullness visually realized;[20] Pope's Dulness, though somewhat less pictorial in rendition, is surrounded by the "Four guardian Virtues" that support her throne, while Prudence bears her glass and Poetic Justice lifts her scale.[21] Pope's Obloquy dwells

[19] *Caricature* was defined in the posthumous tenth edition of Johnson's dictionary (1808) as "exaggerated resemblance in drawing" and in the edition of 1827 as the "representation of a person or circumstance, so as to render the original ridiculous, without losing the resemblance." This definition, though known from the Restoration on, does not appear in the earlier editions published in Johnson's lifetime. The term came into the official dictionaries late, no doubt because the popularity of visual caricature in England was relatively late (see M. Dorothy George, *English Political Caricature to 1792* [Oxford, 1959], Vol. I).

[20] *Mac Flecknoe*, ll. 106 ff.

[21] *The Dunciad* (A), I, 43 ff.

"Hard by a Sty, beneath a Roof of Thatch," attended by her train, her breasts marked by "ev'ry Collier's Hand." [22] Criticism in Swift's *Battle of the Books* takes her place in a pictorial stasis: "extended in her Den," her eyes turn inward but her swollen spleen extends like a dug, and she is attended by blind Ignorance and Opinion, "perpetually turning." [23]

Swift, in a witty denigration of popular imagery, outlines the method of allegorical and emblematic caricature. He refers to "mystical" writing that "enigmatically" and "cunningly" shades meaning "under Allegory." He distinguishes between "Mythology" and "Hieroglyphick" and describes verbal forms that tell fables, draw comparisons, and make visual analogues for satirical purposes.[24] Swift may have rejected the mystical and emblematic seventeenth century, but he was steeped in its visual allegories and emblems. The artistic side of his satire may be viewed as the persistence of earlier emblematic forms, which he adapted to his purpose but from whose essentially hieroglyphic qualities he never departed. Sometimes he is overtly emblematic:

> Now hear an Allusion!—A Mitre, you know,
> Is divided above, but united below.
> If this you consider, our Emblem is right;
> The B——s *divide*, but the Clergy *unite*.[25]

When Swift, in an early Pindaric, called the French king a "Tennis-Ball of Fate," [26] he was using a popular and conventional emblem. Saint Teresa saw the "devils playing tennis" with her soul, and one of Solórzano Pereira's *Emblemata* shows God dealing with kings as tennis balls.[27] Lady Acheson's thin body and face (she was Swift's friend, by the way) must have been more emblematic than realistic: chin and nose meet, the fingers are ten crooked sticks, the elbows are pointed rocks that gore a husband's side at night like the tusks of a boar.[28] The lady's portrait is drawn

[22] *Imitations of English Poets*, "II. Spenser, The Alley," ll. 28 ff., in Alexander Pope, *Minor Poems*, ed. Norman Ault and John Butt (London, 1954), p. 44.

[23] See Jonathan Swift, *A Tale of a Tub*, ed. A. C. Guthkelch and D. Nichol Smith (Oxford, 1920), p. 240.

[24] "A Digression concerning Criticks," in *ibid.*, pp. 97–99.

[25] "On the Irish Bishops," ll. 41–44, in *Poems of Swift*, ed. Williams, p. 805.

[26] "Ode to the King on his Irish Expedition," l. 121, in *ibid.*, p. 10.

[27] See Mario Praz, *Mnemosyne* (Princeton, 1970), p. 137.

[28] "My Lady's Lamentation and Complaint against the Dean," ll. 67–86, in *Poems of Swift*, ed. Williams, pp. 853–854.

in an obviously exaggerating and wittily caricaturing line that will
not disturb a friendship.

Swift's lines to Lady Acheson are a frank, spoofing, ingroup,
cease-and-desist kind of verse. He wants his friend to put on a
few pounds and to stop staying up late and abusing her health.
Even in friendship, as the *Journal to Stella* also shows, Swift finds
emblematic caricature irresistible. If this kind of caricature be
done in the green tree, what shall be done in the dry? What one
would expect. When Swift, the incorrigible maker of emblems,
fires his shots in anger, his ammunition is the inverted or perverted
emblem, the grotesque. (All emblems that carry the weight of
much meaning, even the serious ones, tend to run to the unnatural
and the grotesque. Consider Dürer's rhinoceros or the outrageous-
ly constructed woman by Ripa who symbolizes Boethian intelligence.)

Artists had for centuries reduced men to grotesques. Leonardo
created a terrible kind of visual comedy by greatly distorting his
line but always remaining within nature and sometimes even within his own family.[29] Other caricaturists reduced men to vegeta-
bles, to objects or machines, and to animals; and they did so lightly
or savagely. Arcimboldo created the head of a gardener out of
leeks, onions, carrots, cherries, apples, and rutabagas and the head
of a librarian out of books; the librarian's hair was an open book
with leaves fluttering, his nose the spine, his ear the ribbons to tie
the book.[30] Tobias Stimmer made a pontiff out of a clock, a can-
dle, and a bell. Brucelli fashioned human figures out of kitchen
utensils, as did English popular art, where maids were constituted
of mops, pails, and brooms. Staffordshire potters made women
into variously shaped bells. Hogarth saw men as periwigs, the
head of a lawyer as a mallet, the head of a bishop as a Jew's harp,
the head of a king as a guinea; he also constructed heads of weather
vanes, hands of keys, and scarecrow faces of cloth and straw.[31]
There is abundant visual precedent for the grotesques in Pope's
Cave of Spleen:

[29] See Hogarth's copy of a caricature by Leonardo in *Characters and Caricaturas* in Ronald Paulson, *Hogarth's Graphic Works* (New Haven, 1965), Vol. I,
pl. 174. See also Paulson's commentary, *ibid.*, II, 188–189.

[30] Praz, *Mnemosyne*, figs. 55, 56.

[31] I owe most of these references to Frederick Antal, *Hogarth and His Place
in European Art* (London, 1962), pp. 130–131.

> Here living *Teapots* stand, one Arm held out,
> One bent; the Handle this, and that the Spout:
> A Pipkin there like *Homer*'s *Tripod* walks;
> Here sighs a Jar, and there a Goose-pye talks.[32]

This passage, incidentally, Fuseli had no difficulty in illustrating.

Men as animals had a long visual history—from Titian's substitution of monkeys for men in a travesty of the Laocoön to Hogarth's *singerie*—which stopped well within the period under consideration. Painters had, as Sir Thomas Browne said, "singularly hit the signatures of a Lion and a Fox in the face of Pope Leo the Tenth,"[33] and Richard Flecknoe saw these same animals (surely because they were emblematic) in the face of Cromwell, whose red nose also suggested "a bloody beak" and made his countenance that of a "bird of prey."[34] Alexander Pope's head appears on a rat's body in a famous caricature, and Dr. Johnson's on an owl's, "Old Wisdom Blinking at the Stars."[35] The Scriblerians compared William Broome, Laurence Eusden, and Ambrose Philips to tortoises, who are "*slow* and *chill*, and like *Pastoral Writers* delight much in *Gardens*: they have for the most part a *fine embroider'd* Shell, and underneath it, a *heavy Lump*."[36] Count Heidegger's face was so ugly that without the ministrations of art it caricatured the human form divine, and so Pope used this "strange Bird from Switzerland," ironically the "surintendant des plaisirs d'Angleterre," the *Arbiter Deliciarum*, who rose from producing masquerades to being George II's master of revels, in a grotesque emblem: the sacred bird of the goddess Dulness is "a monster of a fowl, / Something betwixt a Heideggre and owl."[37]

Swift's animal grotesquerie—droll, savage, cruel, playful—is the most brilliant in literary history. His menagerie has weird, solemn, funny, nasty, or cute creatures, from elephants to those invisible

---

[32] *The Rape of the Lock*, IV, 49–52.

[33] Item 27 in *Musaeum Clausum*, in *The Works of Sir Thomas Browne*, ed. Geoffrey Keynes (Chicago, 1964), III, 115–116.

[34] Quoted by Benjamin Boyce, *The Polemic Character, 1640–1661* (Lincoln, Neb., 1955), pp. 53, 56–57.

[35] M. Dorothy George, *Hogarth to Cruikshank* (London, 1967), figs. 13, 119. Pope's head wears the papal crown and Johnson's has ass's ears.

[36] Pope, *The Art of Sinking in Poetry*, ed. Edna Leake Steeves (New York, 1952), p. 28.

[37] *The Dunciad* (B), I, 289–290. For Fielding's comments on Heidegger, see *Tom Jones*, Bk. XIII, chap. vii.

vermin of the fable of the fleas which inhabit the trousers of Grub Street poets. All these creatures appear *sub specie civitatis*, caught in the regularity, purity, and urbanity of the language. And they sometimes appear as though in genre prints, the verse then becoming brilliantly phrased mottoes placed under the scenes. A beau, dressed for conquest, compares his figure in the glass with a print of a monkey open before him (a print, incidentally, which prefaces one of Gay's fables). The beau's eyes move from monkey to reflection, from the printed plate to the glass, with sublime unconsciousness distinguishing all the features in common:

> The Twist, the Squeeze, the Rump, the Fidge an' all,
> Just as they lookt in the Original.[38]

Swift's emblematic grotesques appear in Ovidian allegory, Aesopian fable, satirical genre picture, or brief caricature. In all these forms Swift is a typical maker of emblems, as was Dryden before him. Both used grotesques to establish meanings. Dryden's bestiary, as we now know, was not chosen whimsically or arbitrarily; it represents a skillful application to men and their institutions of traditional beast meanings from Aristotle and Pliny, from medieval allegory, and from emblems and proverbs of the Renaissance and the seventeenth century.[39] Swift's emblems also come from tradition, and his reductions bear moral and social meanings.

Once the essential or implied seriousness of Swift's reductions has been granted, however, we do them an injustice if we do not also see them as exuberant, playful, fanciful, and personal, written in fun and pique, in exasperation and hatred, in order to give their author pleasurable relief. The compulsive linking of man and animal, the artistically just, economical, and effectual yoking of opposites in grotesque reduction—this joining is the one copulation we can be sure Swift enjoyed.

Swift's "The Description of a Salamander" (1705) is a pure example of grotesque caricature.[40] Its reduction of man and men to a single animal is a personal vendetta broadened to include large social meaning. The force of Swift's poem is revealed if it is compared with Addison's later essay on the salamander, where the

[38] "Tim and the Fables," ll. 17–18, in *Poems of Swift*, ed. Williams, p. 783.

[39] James Kinsley, "Dryden's Bestiary," *Review of English Studies*, n.s., IV (Oct. 1953), 331–336.

[40] *Poems of Swift*, ed. Williams, pp. 82–85.

animal stands for a heroine of chastity, a woman, not unlike Pope's Cloe, of the minimal frigid decencies and no more.[41] Addison's lady, like the salamander, lives in fire without being hurt, "preserv'd in a kind of natural Frost." As he generalizes the already general type, Addison tends to forget the salamander and makes assertions that are relevant intellectually but not imagistically. The frosty lady makes no distinction of sex, admits males to her bedside, is scandalized by unreasonable husbands who make physical demands, declaims against jealousy, and does not understand temptation. The reductive comparison tends to disappear in abstraction and application. The caricaturing line is there but it is not tightly drawn.

Swift's concentration on the reductive image, once it has been introduced, is fierce and unrelenting. He begins by invoking the long tradition of confusing military men and animals: mastiffs are called "Pompey" and heroes are named after brutes. Modern heroes, since the invention of gunpowder, require a new image. Buckets and pumps being too low, what could better serve than that classical creature described by Pliny, the salamander? (John Lord Cutts, a Lord Justice of Ireland and a brave soldier whom Swift hated and made his butt, had, incidentally, been called a salamander for his intrepidity under withering fire.) This image now becomes the line of distortion, the caricaturing line that bounds the whole and links part to part in an imagistic reduction of taut and brittle brilliance. The creature, gaudy and loathsome, with a shining but spotted coat, comes out of its hole in a tempest and returns to it in fair weather. So Cutts; and so other generals, peers, and beaux of the Establishment, who crawl out of their dunghills to shine in war but crawl back to mother filth in peace. The application is both individual and general: a fierce personal revenge joins a political attack on official militancy.

Salamanders not only live in flames; they also put flames out, for these creatures emit a purulent white matter that extinguishes fire. The discharge also corrupts, causing leprosy and baldness. If the sexual application that ensues is also intended for Cutts, the satire is of unprecedented and surely of unwarranted violence. When it is applied, however, to the irresponsible and predatory upper classes of Restoration and Augustan England who poisoned

[41] *Spectator*, no. 198 (17 October 1711). For Pope's portrait of Cloe, see Epistle II, *To a Lady. Of the Characters of Women*, ll. 157–180.

the flesh of English women, the emblem takes on the intensity and the cogency of Blake's attack on poisonous love in the Urizen-ic dispensation:

> So have I seen a batter'd Beau
> By Age and Claps grown cold as Snow,
> Whose Breath or Touch, where e'er he came,
> Blew out Love's Torch or chill'd the Flame;
> And should some Nymph who ne'er was cruel,
> Like *Carleton* cheap, or fam'd *Duruel*,
> Receive the Filth which he ejects,
> She soon would find, the same Effects,
> Her tainted Carcase to pursue,
> As from the *Salamander's* Spue;
> And, if no Leprosy, a Pox.
> *Then I'll appeal to each By-Stander,*
> *Whether this be'nt a* Salamander.

In 1660 an engraving by Wenceslaus Hollar represented Juvenal's satires as cloven-footed satyrs, men with goaty legs and hams, in a stroke of wit more inevitable then than now when *satyr* and *satire* were often spelled alike.[42] Before 1683 Sir Thomas Browne called the drawing of men's faces with resemblance to animals "Caricatura."[43] Both Browne and Hollar, and their readers and viewers, would have understood precisely what Swift was doing and why I have called this kind of delineation "emblematic caricature." They would also have made the proper moral response to Swift's meaning, for Browne warned his reader: "Expose not thy self by four-footed manners unto draughts, and Caricatura representations."[44]

PORTRAIT CARICATURE

At the opposite pole from the carefully selected, heavily distorted, a priori meanings and grotesque mischiefs of emblematic

[42] Second frontispiece to *Mores Hominum* (1660). Hogarth represents the satirical muses that inspire Samuel Butler as satyrs. See Hogarth's frontispiece to *Hudibras* in Joseph Burke and Colin Caldwell, *Hogarth* (London, 1968), pl. 97.

[43] Item 27 in *Musaeum Clausum*, a work originally printed in the *Miscellany Tracts* (1683). Compare Browne's statement in *A Letter to a Friend*: "When Mens Faces are drawn with resemblance to some other Animals, the *Italians* call it, to be drawn in *Caricatura*" (*Works of Browne*, ed. Keynes, I, 106).

[44] *Christian Morals*, Pt. III, sec. 14, in *Works of Browne*, ed. Keynes, I, 280.

caricature stands portrait caricature, whose drive toward realism can perhaps best be introduced by considering the scene or landscape of satire. Isaac Barrow, in a sermon that enumerates the many forms of protean wit, referred to "a scenical Representation of Persons or Things."[45] The naturally descriptive in satire can be illustrated by Pope's brilliant portrayal of the place where George Villiers was thought, mistakenly, to have drawn his last breath, a scene described late enough to have been influenced by one of Hogarth's shabby interiors:

> In the worst inn's worst room, with mat half-hung,
> The floors of plaister, and the walls of dung,
> On once a flock-bed, but repair'd with straw,
> With tape-ty'd curtains, never meant to draw,
> The George and Garter dangling from that bed
> Where tawdry yellow strove with dirty red,
> Great Villiers lies—[46]

This kind of realism portrait caricature attempted to achieve, for it was partly the art of literal appearance.

Before considering the art of portrait caricature, we ought to consider the prestige, the pride of place, and the dignity of portrait painting, whose position was fully comparable to that which the emblem had enjoyed earlier. What Richard Flecknoe claimed for his verbal "Pourtracts"—that they give the "Bodies resemblance together with the disposition of the Minde"[47]—was also claimed for the original art, after the great revolution of seventeenth-century painting had transformed languid, generalized, or emblematical representation into the achievement on canvas of the unique and living face. The body was given breathtaking verisimilitude in oil and watercolors; it was said of portraits that "if we'll credit our own Eyes, they live."[48] But the counte-

---

[45] *Sermon against foolish Talking and Jesting*, quoted by [Corbyn Morris], *An Essay towards Fixing the True Standards of Wit* . . . (London, 1744), p. viii. This essay was republished by the Augustan Reprint Society, Series One: *Essays on Wit*, no. 4 (Nov. 1947), with an introduction by James Clifford.

[46] Epistle III, *To Bathurst*, ll. 299–305.

[47] Quoted by Boyce, *Polemic Character*, p. 55. See also Flecknoe, *A Collection of the Choicest Epigrams and Characters* (1673), p. 1, for a definition of character as distinct from "Pourtract."

[48] Nahum Tate, complimenting Thomas Flatman. Quoted by William H. Halewood, " 'The Reach of Art' in Augustan Poetic Theory," in *Studies in Criticism and Aesthetics, 1660–1800: Essays in Honor of Samuel Holt Monk*, ed. Howard P. Anderson and John S. Shea (Minneapolis, 1967), p. 193.

nance on canvas also expressed the mind—*index animi vultus*; and Johnson's "Epitaph on Hogarth" closed and summarized a century-long chorus of praise for expressive *visibilia* in portrait art:

> Here death has clos'd the curious eyes
> That saw the manners in the face.[49]

In Pope's earlier years portraiture was regarded as having reached its zenith. Nowhere else, said Steele in 1711, are portraits done so well as in England: if the Virgin Mary should want to be painted once more from life (she had earlier sat to Saint Luke), she would surely come to England for a sitting.[50]

At least from the time of Richard Flecknoe on, verbal descriptions of individuals, both panegyric and satirical, were regularly called portraits. The analogy with the art of painting, besides conferring prestige, had many implications for the verbal form, particularly in verse. It implied concentration on detail, physical and otherwise; the fact that Dryden's *Absalom and Achitophel* has portraits of only twenty-seven contemporaries in 1,030 lines, while Marvell's earlier *Last Instructions* strikes at eighty-four contemporaries in 990 lines, results from a determination to render concentrated and organized detail in rich abundance.[51] The analogy also has other implications closely related to concentration and organization: verbal portraits try to achieve a stasis, in which time does have a stop, or virtually so, without narrative drive or progressive logical development. They are bounded in space; one moves clearly from a single individual to another; and they resemble a framed, not a flowing, art. Verbal portraits also achieve the simplicity, the economy, the severity (to use Dryden's term once more), the linear sharpness, of visual art, and they possess these qualities—of being framed, individual, static, and graphic —even when purely moral and mental descriptions are being made.

If we read Hogarth, we view Dryden and Pope. Something is on display, usually an individual in a portrait, sometimes an individual in a *conversazione*. The portrait of Atticus, though clearly framed and presented with unrelenting concentration, begins and progresses nonvisually, in grammar; in a brilliant series of conditions contrary to fact, one protasis after another is followed

---

49 Samuel Johnson, *Poems*, ed. E. L. McAdam, Jr. (New Haven, 1964), p. 268.
50 *Spectator*, no. 555 (6 December 1712).
51 Pierre Legouis, *Andrew Marvell: Poet, Puritan, Patriot* (Oxford, 1965), p. 169.

by a climactic and resolving apodosis, which is, however, a sad question: "Who would not weep if Atticus were he?" Yet even from this sinewy syntax a graphic setting appears, subtly, gradually, unmistakably. Atticus rules alone, tolerating no brother near the throne. Where is it he rules? Not in Turkey, although there is allusion to Oriental tyranny and fratricide, but in a place of fools and flatterers, templars and wits. And where would that be? No place else but contemporary clubland, where the pontificating, expectant, and eager dictator sits at the head of a table

> While Wits and Templers ev'ry sentence raise,
> And wonder with a foolish face of praise.[52]

The great Addison has been reduced to easy triumphs at Button's Coffee House.

The most important implication of portraits, as also of the less frequent *conversazioni*, must be more fully discussed. Whenever the art of portraiture was made exemplary by poet or critic, the claims of literal realism were being enforced. Pope, himself a painter, laughed at the dauber who, "not being able to draw Portraits after the Life, was used to paint Faces at Random" and then look around for someone on whom he could force the "likeness."[53] Pope's own satiric portraits drive relentlessly, as Professor Boyce has seen, to particularity and individuality, and his art tended to dissipate all principles of generality.[54]

From the Restoration on the art of satire, as an accompaniment to philosophic and scientific realism, attempted to be historically credible. Locke recorded in detail the physical symptoms of the first Earl of Shaftesbury, permitting a modern diagnosis of the ailment as a suppurating hydatid cyst of the liver. A surgeon operated successfully and left the wound open, inserting first a silver and then a golden tube for drainage. That pipe, nicknamed "Tapski," entered the anti-Shaftesbury literature:

> The silver pipe is no sufficient drain
> For the corruption of this little man,
> Who, though he ulcers have in ev'ry part,
> Is nowhere so corrupt as in his heart.[55]

[52] Pope, *An Epistle to Dr. Arbuthnot*, ll. 211–212.
[53] Quoted from *Guardian*, no. 4, by Boyce, *Pope*, p. 12.
[54] Boyce, *Pope*, p. 41.
[55] John Caryll, "The Hypocrite" (1678), ll. 64–67, in *Poems on Affairs of State*, II, ed. Elias F. Mengel, Jr. (New Haven, 1965), 106. See K. H. D. Haley, *The First Earl of Shaftesbury* (Oxford, 1968), pp. 201–205.

But realistic detail was not enough. The ambition was to achieve the whole man. According to Henry Gally, the great ambition of personal satire was to "draw a Character so to the Life, as that it shall hit one Person, and him only."[56] The great satirists were thought to have succeeded. Horace Walpole believed that Dryden "caught the living likeness" of Buckingham and that "Pope completed the historical resemblance."[57]

Was reality ever satisfactorily achieved? No portrait of Pope can be judged "absolutely faithful, unbiased, and complete."[58] We have doubts about most identifications, even those made in the eighteenth century. Even when we are absolutely sure of the historical original (Atticus is indubitably Addison, Zimri indubitably Buckingham), we cannot now be sure of the justness of the portrait, and, human complexity and partisanship always having been more or less what they are now, no one could ever have been sure. There are exceptions, of course; so penetrating was the realism of a Dryden that it can be counted on to guide historians into understanding contemporary characters. On the whole, however, we must conclude that the realism of the satirical portrait belongs more often to art than to history; specifically, it belongs to the art of appearance, to a desire, like that of Defoe and of Swift in *Gulliver's Travels*, to seem real and therefore to be rhetorically effective. Writers seemed impelled to act as though satire, like all the didactic art of the period, had to resemble a clear and undistorting glass before which one could adjust one's manners and morals. Yet distortion lurks in the very medium. A limited frame that sets off only a few short lines requires simplification and selection. Even Flemish portraits, for all their abundant detail, select and emphasize; and Boswell, who called his great *Life of Johnson* a Flemish picture, has cast over his subject a distorting ray. Trevelyan treated visual caricatures with rapture: "How wonderful a thing it is to look back into the past as it actually was"; but he lapsed into doubt a few months later and conceded that these drawings need not always be taken literally.[59]

Dryden and Pope give us not history but art, not literal truth

[56] Quoted by Boyce, *Pope*, p. 114.
[57] Quoted from Walpole, *Royal and Noble Authors*, by Osmund Airy, ed., Gilbert Burnet's *History of My Own Time*, 2 vols. (Oxford, 1897–1902), I, 183 n. 2.
[58] Boyce, *Pope*, p. 75.
[59] Quoted by J. Jean Hecht, "Eighteenth-Century Graphic Satire on Historical Evidence," *Studies in Burke and His Times*, X (Spring, 1969), 1258–1259.

but rhetoric, not transcriptions of reality but revealing distortions based on an appearance of reality, an appearance that is never destroyed. In other words, they have created caricatures, and we now move from the adjective, *portrait*, to the substantive, *caricature*. The term *caricature* applied to the grotesque emblems of Swift will arouse no objection, but if applied to the dignity of Dryden or to the subtlety of Pope, it may. Caricature is usually thought of as gross and greatly exaggerated. But need it be? Caricature, by historical definition, must not destroy resemblance, and the term itself should say nothing about the degree or kind of satirical distortion, whether light or heavy, comic or tragic.

Painted portraits can idealize or degrade, but in the classical age both the idealization and the degradation were lightly and delicately done. And under an austere ideal of realistic representation there is not much difference between departures up or down from the norm of nature. Hogarth's portraying pencil went in both directions. In his portrait of Simon Fraser, Lord Lovat, the leader of the Highland chiefs who wanted to restore the Stuarts, the pencil moves downward, that is, toward satire.[60] Hogarth, however, drew from life; he visited the chief after his capture and on his way to the trial that found him guilty and condemned him to death. In the etching Lovat's face is fat; his clothes bulge; he wears a wig; he gestures as though speaking and counting, the index finger touching the right thumb. Is any of this portrayal unnatural distortion? We cannot now tell, but we may venture to assert that the represented face has been touched by a sinister line. The eyes, matching the grossness of the countenance, look drunken. There is no humble fear of death, as the tongue wags and the fingers count. Surely this man is not one to be entrusted with the destinies of a nation. Not an emblem, but moving slightly in that direction, and not a grotesque either, but bearing the hint of a hostile and distorting line, Hogarth's Lord Lovat is insistently more than representation. What is it then? Even though the distortion is slight, it must be called caricature—portrait caricature—for its resemblance remains fully intact while the representation distorts to achieve satirical meaning.

So close to this technique are the great verbal portraits of Dryden and Pope that they too must be named portrait caricatures. No other term available from literary or art history will do as well. The portrait caricature in its apogee has transcended the

[60] Paulson, *Hogarth's Graphic Works*, Vol. I, pl. 178 (pp. 192–193).

sketch, that series of descriptive strokes with details from reality badly or miscellaneously organized. It is no longer the credo character, consisting of assertions about a person's beliefs and attitudes. It is not now an agglomeration of psychological details that merely add up to complexity. The remnants of these antecedent forms may still confer weight, veracity, credibility, conviction, but the lines to Zimri and Cloe are portrait caricatures of the same genre—though in a different medium—as Hogarth's Lord Lovat.

Sir Thomas Browne's definition of wit supports the application to Swift of the word *caricature*. Did Augustan England provide a foundation for Pope's art of combined representation and distortion which we have also called caricature? It did, very precisely. John Hughes in 1712 defined *caricaturas* as "preserving, amidst distorted Proportions and aggravated Features, some distinguishing Likeness of the Person. . . ."[61] Dryden, too, had a clear notion of caricature; in discussing the theory of satire, he said: "To spare the grossness of the names [fool, blockhead, knave, and the like], and to do the thing yet more severely, is to draw a full face [the ideal of resemblance], and to make the nose and cheeks stand out [the caricaturing line]."[62]

Hughes was able to define portrait caricature with precision and Dryden was able to apply its elements to his art with easy knowledge because it had been precisely defined and precisely practiced by its Italian masters. Its inventor, Annibale Carracci, not only made caricature heads but analyzed and defended his practice. Bernini also practiced the art and brought to it at least a part of the genius that transformed Counter-Reformation Rome.[63] The invention and practice of mock portraiture was vastly more

[61] *Spectator*, no. 537 (15 November 1712). Hughes is thinking of extreme forms of caricature, for he adds the clause: "but in such a Manner as to transform the most agreeable Beauty into the most odious monster." The more violent qualities of emblematic caricature were eliminated from the practice of portrait caricature; this fact did not affect the definitions until much later (see n. 19, above).

[62] *Original and Progress of Satire*, in Ker, II, 93.

[63] E. H. Gombrich and E. Kris, *Caricature* (Harmondsworth, 1940), pp. 10–15. On Bernini and caricature, Filippo Maldinucci wrote in his life of Bernini, which first appeared in 1728: "Effetto di questa franchezza é stato l'aver egli operato singolarments in quella sorta di disegno, che noi diciamo Caricatura, or di colpi Caricati, deformando per ischerzo a mal modo l'effigie altrui, senza tolgiere loro la somiglianza, e la maestá." This comment is very close to that of Hughes (see n. 61, above), but it makes more of keeping the resemblance. See *Della Notizie de' Professori del Disegno da Cimabue in Qua*, XX (Florence, 1774), 132.

than a mere trick of line and illusion. It was an attempt to grasp the truth beneath the surface through superficial distortion, to enter more deeply into nature by deforming it, to create a new kind of comic art by a new vision of deformity.

The Scriblerians asked, mockingly, "Is there not an Architecture of Vaults and Cellars, as well as of lofty Domes and Pyramids?"[64] It may be answered, seriously, that caricature, both in its Italian origins and in its later English literary manifestations, was a countertendency to the dominant idealism. High culture was capable of turning itself upside down; *The Dunciad* is the other and sometimes concealed face of *The Rape of the Lock.* The art of distortion is to the art of idealization what bathos is to hypsos: an exact inversion, to which the same techniques apply, though the direction is down and not up. The art of distorting reality is the precise reversal of *la belle nature.* It is nature consummately wrought down to a lower pitch.

Thus far I have attempted to define portrait caricature; to establish its relations to the visual art it paralleled; to disclose its historical roots; and to point out the verbal equivalents of frame, bounding line, concentration on a single individual, vivid *visibilia,* and pictorial or graphic realism. No attempt has yet been made to define the verbal equivalent of the caricaturing line, the distorting ray or linear movement which, whether gross or delicate, is at the very center of caricature, the art of distorted but not destroyed resemblance.

The equivalent in verbal portraits to the caricaturing line or ray of pictorial art is, I believe, usually intellectual or psychological or moral. Concentration on a single individual establishes a resemblance to portrait; emphasis upon a single mental trait or dominating intellectual feature within that person creates the caricature. Paradoxically, the distorting emphasis may not, to the author, have seemed to be caricature at all; in the conscious mind it may have been a serious effort to enter into both universal and particular human psychology, that is, an effort to disclose a human gestalt, to establish a doctrine about human nature, or to reflect a conviction that human evil is a central eccentricity, a departure from the divine or the human norm. The effect of caricature remains, however, whether the author strikes in daylight anger or mischief, creating a distortion with conscious malice aforethought; or whether he is expressing a seriously held doctrine of the ruling

[64] *Art of Sinking,* ed. Steeves, p. 15.

passion; or whether he is following the rhetorical practice of exaggeration for emphasis; or whether he is doing all these things under impulses of a nighttime demon in the unconscious. In the end the writer has produced not literal but caricatured resemblance, as the following examples are designed to show.

Pope's Wharton is consumed by a ruling passion, "the Lust of Praise," and on that mark alone the picture is focused, an example of distortion by excessive clarity:

> This clue once found, unravels all the rest,
> The prospect clears, and Wharton stands confest.[65]

Long before Pope made the ruling passion basic to some of his portrait caricatures, Evelyn associated that idea with the line or shape of graphic art: "And now we mention Picture, since the *Posture*, or *Stroak* of one single Line, does often discover the Regnant Passion."[66]

The caricaturing line in the initial portrait of Achitophel in *Absalom and Achitophel* reduces the complex historical Shaftesbury to an intellectual diagram. But what a diagram it is! A black-and-white, unshadowed, larger-than-life Satan, who threatens human stability because he is "Bold, and Turbulent of wit," "Restless," "fiery," "daring," "great," "Pleas'd with the Danger."[67] "Turbulent of wit": *wit* means *imagination*, and Johnson's great phrase illuminates the distortion within Achitophel: "Dangerous Prevalence of Imagination."

Zimri is also tortured out of shape by imagination. This "Blest Madman's" imagination, however, is a lightweight, dilletantish kind of thing better called *fancy*, a kind of parody of the fretting, restless imagination of Dryden's Shaftesbury. Buckingham is various, an epitome of levity, a spinning top that draws all unstable motion to itself, the whirligig of revolutionary energy. Nature's pencil had doubtless distorted the man into caricature before he ever sat to Dryden, but Dryden heightens the color and concentrates the line.[68]

---

[65] Epistle I, *To Cobham*, ll. 181, 178–179.
[66] John Evelyn, *Numismata* (London, 1687), p. 335.
[67] Ll. 150 ff.
[68] Ll. 544 ff. Dryden's portrait should be carefully compared with Burnet's prose description and Butler's character of Buckingham. See esp. Samuel Butler, "A Duke of Bucks," in A. R. Waller, ed., *Characters* (Cambridge, 1908), pp. 32–33. Butler calls Buckingham's appetite in pleasure "diseased and crazy"; Dryden

Pope's caricature of Philomedé[69] begins, "See Sin in State," and ends by displaying State in Sin. Henrietta Churchill, the Duchess of Marlborough (if indeed she is the original), is an intelligent woman and a peeress who is drunken and promiscuous in public. The incongruity distorts in two directions: the noble position of wife is prostituted and a decently placed, privately confined, so-cially stable promiscuity is also prostituted, for the woman is

> Chaste to her Husband, frank to all beside,
> A teeming Mistress, but a barren Bride.

Such a lady cannot remain even a balanced incongruity, and the caricaturing line plunges her into action, into social and intel-lectual disgrace. Philomedé lectures mankind on refined taste and soft passion; but, like the dictator at a feast who analyzes the wine and meat but eats a plain pudding at home, this peeress, falling in an instantaneous plunge to Pope's underworld,

> —stoops at once
> And makes her hearty meal upon a Dunce.

CONCLUSION

Graphically vivid details had appeared in English character sketches almost from the beginning. In 1650 Sir Anthony Wel-don, James I's onetime clerk of the kitchen, described his royal master:

His eyes large, ever rowling after any stranger came into his presence, in so much, as many for shame have left the roome, as being out of countenance; his Beard was very thin; his tongue too large for his mouth, which ever made him speak full in the mouth, and made him drink very uncomely, as if eating his drinks, which came out into the cup of each side of his mouth; his skin was as soft as Taffeta Sarsnet, which felt so, because he never washt his hands, only rub'd his finger ends sleightly with the wet end of a Naptkin, . . . his walke was ever circular, his fingers ever in that walke fidling about his codpiece.[70]

calls him a "blest madman." Butler comments on his "excess" and "variety"; Dryden calls him "So over Violent, or over Civil, / That every man, with him, was God or Devil." Burnet may be said to have drawn a historical sketch; Butler, who tries to present a "Monster" that "deforms Nature," provides a kind of emblem caricature; Dryden's, the most devastating of all, is a portrait caricature.

[69] Epistle II, *To a Lady. Of the Characters of Women*, ll. 69–86.

[70] *The Court and Character of King James* (London, 1650), pp. 178–179.

This portrait has breathtaking realism but, lacking pictorial analogues, it is perhaps not caricature.

Hudibras's beard is of the emblematic variety, like Swift's salamander. Butler elsewhere provides many visually vivacious details, often seeming to write clear libretti for his illustrator. His characters are paintable and "engravable," and we see his hero's face and features, his dress, paunch, sword, and horse. We also see his beard, with its tile and whey and orange-gray colors. That adornment, however, is more than a watercolor in subtle chromatic gradation. It is, to use Butler's—and Swift's—own term, "Hieroglyphic"; it is an emblem with many alternative meanings: a Samson head of hair, on a hairy meteor that presages the fall of scepter and crown, or a "Hieroglyphic Spade" that digs its own and the state's grave, or a martyrlike sufferer spat upon and tortured by red-hot curling irons.[71] Butler has given us an *emblematic caricature*.

Juvenal's sixth satire, the one devoted to women, is a characterization of women and their society; although mischievously unfair to the sex, as Dryden noted,[72] it is perhaps a just indictment of the society. As a social scene it has breadth, vividness, and much truth; and its tiny vignettes are as memorable as its occasional longer narratives. But this conversationally lively and flowing commentary on corrupt women in a corrupt city is not pictorial and not even very visual, for it lacks frame, living individuals,[73] and sustained pictorial concentration.

What Juvenal's satire lacks, Pope's *Of the Characters of Women* abundantly possesses.[74] The poem begins with a paragraph that recalls the motifs and poses of fashionable portraits and directly "quotes" paintings by Van der Vaart and Titian. Pope then presents himself as a painter, preparing his ground and colors. Through the rest of the poem he sustains the metaphor and gives us a gallery of twelve portraits, each bounded and framed, each portraying or seeming to portray a living person. For a caricaturing line Pope invokes the *donna é mobile* theme but sharpens that cliché into one of "Contrarieties" existing within one person. With consummate skill, varying this theme to make it adaptable to an

---

[71] *Hudibras*, I, i, 241 ff.

[72] In the "Argument" of Satire VI (*Poems of Dryden*, ed. Kinsley, II, 694).

[73] Juvenal said that his victims were all dead, their ashes safely "under the Flaminian and the Latin Road" (see Niall Rudd, *Satires of Horace* [Cambridge, 1966], p. 260).

[74] For a fuller commentary, see Hagstrum, *Sister Arts*, pp. 236–241.

individual and also keeping it uniform and clear to serve as a line of distortion running through the entire gallery, Pope paints a central incongruity into the vivid but bounded realism of each representation. He has thus achieved *portrait caricature*.

In England emblematic caricature virtually disappeared from poetry, and portrait caricature moved from couplets to the novels of Fielding, Smollett, and Dickens and also to the prints of Hogarth, Rowlandson, Gillray, and Cruikshank. After Pope, caricature declined in poetry. Although Charles Churchill achieved some power through bold and direct assertion and through descriptive strokes that can draw blood, the art of organized distortion was gone. The taut visual line of Dryden, Pope, and Swift had slackened. The brilliant Byron admired Dryden and wondered that Wordsworth,

> The "little boatman" and his *Peter Bell*
> Can sneer at him who drew "Achitophel"! [75]

And yet Byron, for all his admiration of the neoclassical masters, was not himself able to sustain a verbal caricature. He reduced Hogarth's complex portrait of Wilkes to a single line, calling him "A merry, cock-eyed, curious-looking Sprite." [76] Byron's situations are comic and, when cosmic, marvelously grotesque; his individual words ring, in and out of the teasing rhyme; his stanzas are flexible; his rhythms flow with colloquial ease. But where are the tightly drawn individual emblems of Swift? Where are the galleries of Dryden and Pope, with their framed pictures, their sharply etched and deeply bitten black-and-white engravings? They have all gone—at least out of poetry. With the disappearance of *ut pictura poesis* in satire and the languishing of the habit of looking to emblem and portrait for inspiration and example, the bounded but energetic line of caricature has also disappeared. Never, since Pope, has literary satire in verse been able to keep its eye on a single object with the same relentless pictorial concentration. Never again has a distorting poetic line been able to reduce a victim to visual incongruity. The verbal art of concurrent representation and distortion has had its day and has ceased to be.

[75] *Don Juan*, III, c.
[76] *The Vision of Judgment*, lxvi.

IX

THE TROUGH OF THE WAVE

Bertrand H. Bronson

Emeritus Professor of English, University of California, Berkeley

Every schoolboy knew that English Poetry crested three times, at intervals of about a century: in the Age of Elizabeth, *circa* 1600; in the Age of Dryden and Pope, *circa* 1700; and in the Age of Wordsworth, around 1800. Not all the greatest names conformed to this convenient pattern. Before 1600, we have to go back some two hundred years for Chaucer (who was not a galaxy). After 1800, we may have to wait until at least the year 2000 before another comparable poetic genius appears. (And, if he does, he is likely to be solitary.) Milton, again, is an awkward anachronism. As a belated Rennaissance figure, he is too early for Sutherland and Sherburn, who leave him to Bush, for whom he is almost too late, but who gladly accepts him, to bring up his rear with honor: "last of all not in time, but as perfection is last," or as, similarly, Bach is last. But Milton, despite his splendor, does not, in the sense originally suggested, constitute a "crest."

It is pertinent, therefore, to ask what it takes to establish such a phenomenon. One poet does not seem enough, though a supreme poet may be essential. If he is so, need he be recognized as such by his contemporaries, or only in retrospect, from the historical perspective? Is he the leader of a homogeneous school (*primus inter pares*), or outstanding among diverse talents? Is the situation like the Renaissance painter's atelier—*scuola di Rafaelle, di Leonardo*? Were Shakespeare's contemporaries trying to write like

Shakespeare? Were Pope's contemporaries his imitators? Did Wordsworth's fellows aspire to be Wordsworths? Surely not. Or at least, if there were such, they would have been slow to admit it. Who then determines leadership, and how is it constituted?

To shift the perspective slightly to greatness, D. S. Brewer, in *Chaucer and Chaucerians*, has this to say:

It now seems reasonable to assume that a great poet can only arise when the general culture is propitious to genius. That is, granted the genius, which is rare, standards of education must be high, at least for the relevant audience; the status of literature must be high; there must be good means of communication. A sense of the relationship between literature and the general culture, though crudely expressed, appears in the biographical and broader cultural interest in the past that began to be felt in the eighteenth century.[1]

Few of us, I think, would be inclined to deny that, in spite of the appalling ignorance, deprivation, and brutality of large masses —perhaps even the majority—of the population of Dryden's and Pope's days, Brewer's conditions, with the stated proviso, *the relevant audience*, were fulfilled. Dryden and Pope were read and appreciated by their contemporaries in sufficiently large numbers for their influence to be palpable and effective. In fact, Pope, before his death, had gradually become a *national* poet, a cultural force, and even, as Mack in his recent book, *The Garden and The City*, abundantly demonstrates, a political force as well.[2] What this implies is that, thanks to the permeating and consolidating influence of a classical education held in common and diffused among the upper classes of society beyond the privileged alumni of Oxford and Cambridge, Edinburgh, St. Andrews, Aberdeen— for Pope himself was one of the disadvantaged—allusions to the ancients, along with the English Bible, Shakespeare, and probably the seventeenth-century poets in general, English and French, were familiarly recognized and critically appreciated by most contemporary readers of poetry.

How homogeneous, then, were the poets of Pope's generation? Closest to him, one would suppose, would be those for whom his correspondence shows him to have had a friendly affinity. Some of

[1] D. S. Brewer, ed. *Chaucer and Chaucerians: Critical Studies in Middle English Literature* (University, Ala., 1966), p. 261.

[2] Maynard Mack, *The Garden and the City: Retirement and Politics in the Later Poetry of Pope, 1731–1743* (Toronto, 1969).

these he looked up to with respect as his elders, like Sheffield, Wycherley, or Walsh. These, however, were either writing with the left hand, or in a different medium from his. But because Pope was so precocious, we may allow him a handicap of ten or twelve years.

This concession would bring him level with Addison, Watts, Parnell, and John Hughes; but would still leave him a generation behind Garth, Swift, and Prior. All these, when they practiced in heroic couplets, were certainly influenced by Dryden, as was Pope himself. But they could scarcely have looked to Pope as a model, nor in fact did their work often resemble his in subject, mood, or style. Garth's *The Dispensary* (1699), topical satire after Dryden, comes nearest to what Pope would perfect thirty-odd years later; and some passages, carelessly read, might easily be mistaken for Pope's: for example,

> Into the right we err, and must confess,
> To oversights we often owe success. (IV, 64–65)

or

> Harsh words, tho' pertinent, uncouth appear,
> None please the fancy, who offend the ear. (IV, 208–209)

But Garth is incapable of Pope's stylistic involutions.

Ambrose and John Philips and Isaac Watts, all very different spirits, and all a dozen years ahead of Pope, are not numbered among his correspondents, for obvious reasons. Watts was worlds away from what preoccupied Pope. John Philips, author of delightful Miltonic burlesque verse and the more ambitious but still light blank verse Georgic, *Cyder*, was neither comparable nor akin to Pope. Ambrose Philips, the butt of Pope's devilish mischief, was capable of by no means contemptible poetry, witness the lovely picture of an ice-coated landscape in his "Winter-Piece." But he who could address Walpole in lines like what follows, could hardly have chimed with Pope:

> Wise disposer of affairs,
> View the end of all thy cares!
> Forward cast thy ravish'd eyes,
> See the gladning harvest rise:
> Lo, the people reap thy pain!

Thine the labor, theirs the gain. . . .
See, at last, unclouded days;
Hear, at last, unenvied praise.

Pope's closest contemporaries who were also his friends—Gay, Hill, and Young—were again disparate in their objectives, and their creative paths converged infrequently. Gay was seldom highly serious for long, and never successfully so. He excelled in three classic kinds not practiced by Pope: the mock pastoral eclogue, the mock Georgic, and the Fable. Pope was certainly sympathetic to Gay, and may have contributed more than we know, in lines or ideas, whether to *The Beggar's Opera* or to the pastoral operetta, *Acis and Galatea*. But Gay's lyric gift of song was out of Pope's compass. Young's orbit, again, was a very wide one. He began with tragedy, moved speedily to satire. His *Love of Fame* came early enough (1726) to have set Pope upon writing satirical epistles.

Looking at all this diversity, we may ask, would the period be a crest without Dryden or Pope? I think the answer is, No. We have, to be sure, omitted to mention a number of Pope's contemporaries, but very few who were not born at the beginning of the next century or later. These will be our proper subject-matter as we proceed.

None the less, the concept of the Augustan Age, although difficult to circumscribe within dates, or define by exclusion, is sufficiently current and generally accepted to pass in most contexts unchallenged. The same may be said of the Romantic Period. We are all agreed that these are two very high points, or crests, of English poetry. It follows, therefore, that the period falling between was on a lower level of poetic achievement, to which we may give the metaphorical designation, The Trough of the Wave. It is this relatively unspectacular period to which I wish to invite attention. Manifestly, it is only on a retrospective, historical view that we can so regard it. It is altogether likely that those who were living at that time had no clear sense that they were engulfed in such a predicament. They were well aware of the past, but they did not know what was to follow. The uncertainties of the present are always sufficiently exciting to contemporary experience, and who knows what tomorrow may bring forth? Miss Miles quotes from James Ackerman an observation which is pertinent here:

[the artist] accepts and rejects aspects of what he finds in things about him and he adds something of his own. By his choice and by his contribution he moves a step—sometimes a leap—away from the past. . . . In his terms the future is a void—how can he move toward it? [3]

At a distance, posterity is too ready to write off as dull what from its point of vantage seems relatively unexciting. And it is a disconcerting truth that evaluations of poetic merit seldom long remain constant. Pope's reputation, we well know, has itself experienced a complete revolution on the wheel of critical estimation in a couple of centuries. After dropping to the nadir about a hundred and fifty years ago, it now has risen higher than ever it stood in his lifetime.

It will be worth while to try to rid ourselves of the inbred preconception that at the death of Pope next to nothing was happening to English poetry, except an occasional flicker symptomatic of the Romantic Revival. At this point, we might briefly pursue the physical analogy. The action of water between two sea-waves is a complex phenomenon. An elementary hand-book of physics will tell us that, in general contour, the crest of the wave has a relatively sharp delineation, compared with the valley. The latter, the "trough," has no corresponding angularity at the lowest point, but a quite broad and gentle spread. There is, it is important to remember, just as much operative energy at work in the valley as activates the crest. The same force causes the water to rise as pulls it down. But the up-and-down motion is not the only one. Near the top of the crest, the particles are going forward in the direction in which the waves are travelling; but on the same slope, near the bottom of the trough, the particles are moving backward, so that an object on the surface really describes a circle like that of a hand on the face of an upright clock, down and back, up and forward, as the water alternately lifts and subsides. If the analogy holds, we should expect that the tendency of the poets in the earlier part of a transitional period will be to pull, or fall, back toward the epoch being left behind; and of those in the later stage to push up and forward toward the next crest. Something like this backwash and surge does appear to take place. But of course, movements of the spirit do not occur with the neat and tidy regularity of physical rules, and besides, the analogy reads spatial motion in temporal terms. Still, to quote my *Everyday Physics*, "it is important to

[3] "A Theory of Style," *Journal of Aesthetics and Art Criticism*, XX (1962), 231.

bear in mind that all forms of wave-motion are examples of the transmission of energy."

The cyclical wave-length of roughly a century between crest and crest appears to be a demonstrable fact. In a series of extraordinarily interesting studies, Josephine Miles has shown the periodicity of certain recurrences in the language of poetry from Chaucer's time to the present. She has collected statistics on a chronological list of two hundred poets, analyzed their vocabulary and sentence structure as these are affected by the relative proportions of three grammatical components—nouns, adjectives, and verbs—in the normal poetic practice of each poet. She is not concerned with "crests" and "troughs," but with usage: likenesses and differences objectively measured between one era and another, and one poet and another. On this basis, she discriminates three basic "modes" of statement: one predicative, one adjectival, one balanced. The first has a relatively high proportion of verbs and clausal structures, the second a relatively high proportion of adjectives in phrasal structures, the third relatively equal proportions of adjectives and verbs, resulting in clausal and phrasal structures in combination. She finds that these stylistic variations involve also verse-patterns and vocabulary as they affect purposive statement. The predicative style adopts "a strongly conceptual vocabulary of reference and a formal stanzaic sound pattern." The phrasal or adjectival style involves cumulative participial modifying, for descriptive and invocatory ends, and proceeds line by line, without stress on external rhymes. It leans to blank verse, or to freely varied line lengths characteristic of the irregular ode, with internal sound effects and a vocabulary elevated and celebrational, unargumentative. The balanced style mediates between these extremes in a classical moderation approximating an equal incidence of adjectives and verbs which, added together, equal the number of nouns employed: the average of two nouns to one adjective and one verb in a line. The balanced mode is also typical of the ancient classical poets.

Now, however, Miss Miles makes the startling discovery that since the early sixteenth century these modes have tended to move "in stages (about a generation apart) from extreme through balance to extreme"; so that, though we may find one or other extreme prolonged, we do not find a juxtaposition of opposites. Beginning with Wyatt's days, we get, according to her analysis, the following sequence of modes: clausal, balanced, clausal; clausal, balanced, phrasal; phrasal, balanced, clausal; clausal, balanced, clausal. It thus appears that the phases of balance are separated from each other by two stages. Each two intermediate ones are modally alike, but irregular in reappearance. About a third of a century is occupied by each generation of poets. If, then, we fit dates to the scheme, we find that the periods of balance coincide with the turn of the centuries. In a thousand lines of Shakespeare's sonnets, Miss Miles finds the proportions of adjectives, nouns, verbs to be 10, 17, 10. A hundred years later, Dryden's *Absalom and Achitophel* shows a proportion of 10, 19, 10. Pope's *Rape of the Lock* shows 11, 20, 11. A century later, to choose the most balanced for listing: Crabbe 11, 19, 11; Burns 10, 16, 10; Rogers 11, 20, 11; Wordsworth 9, 16, 9; Southey 10, 17, 9; Hunt 10, 19, 10; Shelley 10, 18, 9.

The phase of classical balance, then, has emerged three times, each time coincidentally with a crest of poetic achievement: the Elizabethan, the Augustan, the Romantic. In the earlier periods, exceptional cases, where the adjectives outnumber the verbs, do occur, but by Miss Miles's count they are scarce: Spenser, Sylvester, Phineas Fletcher, Waller, More, and (most pronounced of all) Milton, he with a proportion of 12 adjectives to 15 nouns to 7 verbs.

But we see a very different picture over all when we enter the eighteenth century. This is where the only two phrasal epochs occurred. From Dryden to Wordsworth, the stages are: balanced, phrasal, phrasal, balanced. This is surely a singularity that deserves to be examined. It seems to signify a willingness to leave the beaten track and follow untrodden ways. We are not in the habit of thinking of the neoclassicists as an adventurous lot, but rather as "douce folk that lived by rule." Perhaps their fault was that they aimed too high! In setting up the ancient classics, with Longinus as cicerone, and, after those, Spenser and Milton, they chose lofty models for imitation. Certainly, they did not lack ambition. Their readiness to abandon the "madding crowd's ignoble strife," the mundane daily walks, and to pitch their tents on the heights of ideal imagination, is hardly deserving of contempt, even if they were to find it difficult to breathe the rarefied air. They were dedicated converts. Let me read, for reminder, the brave declaration with which Joseph Warton (aged 24) prefaced his book of poems:

The public has been so much accustomed of late to Didactic poetry alone and Essays on moral subjects that any work where the Imagination is much indulged will perhaps not be relished or regarded. The author therefore of these pieces is in some pain lest certain austere critics should think these too fanciful and descriptive. But he is convinced that the fashion of moralizing in verse has been carried too far, and, as he looks upon Invention and Imagination to be the chief faculties of a Poet, so he will be happy if the following Odes may be looked upon as an attempt to bring back Poetry into its right channel.

The obverse of this, of course, is that logical thought, or reasoning, is not the province of poetry. *Religio Laici, The Hind and the Panther, Epistle to Arbuthnot,* simply do not belong. Keats, later, will agree.

Miss Miles, with an all-embracing, pantoscopic vision, has looked before and after:

> The outstanding classical poets to offer the model of a different mode were Pindar and Lucretius. Their cosmic and ceremonious overload of sublime epithets and phrasal constructions indicated a kind of extreme which English poetry did not reach until the eighteenth century. But Biblical richness and the Platonic tradition early offered to such poets as Spenser and Sylvester, and then Milton, the idea of a poetic language as free as possible from clausal complication, as resilient as possible in richly descriptive participial suspension. . . .
>
> This is the mode which would give us the heavens and earth of *Paradise Lost,* the cosmological reaches of Akenside, the rich details of Thomson, the personifications of Collins, the great aesthetic and social divine wars of Blake, the figure of Keats's Autumn, the vigor of symbol and celebration in Whitman and Henley. In our own day, such poets as Dylan Thomas may lead us back to it.[4]

We shall have to take a closer view of the immediate manifestations of this unfolding panorama as they relate to our present concern. What were the forces at work and how did they interact? The role of tradition: was it being repudiated? or invoked with a difference? We must try to isolate some of the factors in play.

It seems fair to say that the eighteenth century is the first century to be strongly marked by a lively awareness and sense of the Past, an historical interest in it for itself and in its broad cultural ramifications and implications. This is not only manifest in the development of historical writing, of annals, of lives other than commemorative memorials, of specialized studies of an art, e.g. Poetry, Music, but of the bearing of more exact historical knowl-

4 Josephine Miles, *Eras & Modes in English Poetry,* 2d ed. (Berkeley and Los Angeles, 1964), pp. 15–16.

edge on the critical understanding and appreciation of extant monuments, achitectural, literary, institutional, legal, political.

For the practicing poet, this meant an increasing interest in, and better acquaintance with, the accomplishments of his predecessors not merely immediate but also distant. How he would take, absorb, or repudiate, this increment of knowledge, and widened horizon, is the key to a great deal of what ensued on the literary scene of at least the next fifty years. The number of Spenserian imitations, beginning with Prior, running on through Shenstone's *Schoolmistress*, Thomson's *Castle of Indolence*, Robert Lloyd's *Progress of Envy*, Mickle's *Sir Martyn*, Beattie's *Minstrel*, Burns's *Cotter's Saturday Night*—to ignore the plentiful remainder of pieces listed by Wasserman—are sufficient evidence that Spenser was not a repressive influence on the creative impulses of that poetic generation. Even to burlesque, as Sherburn reminds us, and Wasserman tends to forget, does not mean to despise or undervalue, but may signify affection and esteem. We do not need to seek proof of the honor and attention that was given to Milton in that age. The omnipresence of Miltonic blank verse is at least as great as that of Pope's couplets, and a tribute that is inescapable, however much it may be deplored in later times. And this is to pass over the critical attention given to these poets in essays and editions. The period, as Bate has noted, "saw over a hundred editions of *Paradise Lost*, and over seventy of the complete poems."[5]

We cannot say, then, that these great ancestors were an inhibiting influence on the majority of these eighteenth-century poets. "If their ranks," Bate writes, "did not include the major minds and artists, there were enough of them to justify us in recognizing this as the first large-scale example, in the modern history of the arts, of the 'leapfrog' use of the past for authority or psychological comfort: the leap over the parental—the principal immediate predecessors—to what Northrup Frye calls the 'modal grandfather.' "[6]

In his seminal essay, "Tradition and the Individual Talent," T. S. Eliot wrote of our [Anglo–American]

tendency to insist, when we praise a poet, upon those aspects of his work in which he least resembles anyone else. In these aspects or parts

5 W. J. Bate, *The Burden of the Past* (Cambridge, Mass., 1970), p. 22.
6 *Ibid.*

of his work we pretend to find what is individual, what is the peculiar essence of the man. We dwell with satisfaction upon the poet's difference from his predecessors . . . ; we endeavour to find something that can be isolated in order to be enjoyed. Whereas if we approach a poet without this prejudice we shall often find that not only the best, but the most individual parts of his work may be those in which the dead poets, his ancestors, assert their immortality most vigorously.

Allowing that novelty is better than repetition, he continues:

Tradition is a matter of much wider scope. It cannot be inherited, and . . . you must obtain it by great labour. It involves, in the first place, the historical sense . . . ; and the historical sense involves a perception, not only of the pastness of the past, but of its presence; the historical sense compels a man to write not merely with his own generation in his bones, but with a feeling that the whole of the literature of Europe from Homer and within it the whole of the literature of his own country has a simultaneous existence and composes a simultaneous order. This historical sense, which is a sense of the timeless as well as of the temporal and of the timeless and of the temporal together, is what makes a writer traditional. And it is at the same time what makes a writer most acutely conscious of his place in time, of his contemporaneity.[7]

Familiarity with the King James Bible was doubtless even commoner than acquaintance with Milton. The better known poets of the seventeenth century habitually avail themselves of it in reference and comparison, and this habit continues well into the eighteenth. But, more than in the seventeenth, the mass of educated English in the eighteenth century was permeated, even saturated, with the great Roman poets. Why the sympathetic influence should have been so thoroughgoing, just in these years, invites partial answers. But a truism does not have to be belabored. Happen it did, and it is fairly obvious that it could not have happened earlier and was impossible later—religious, political, economic, educational reasons all conspiring to this result. Neoclassicism, to call it by its common name, was not a recurring phenomenon.

One of its manifestations for poetry was an almost universal acceptance of the classical poetic forms and a wholehearted determination, if the effort was serious, to write after those models, whichever the genre chosen. "Invention" might be one of the

[7] *The Sacred Wood*, 2d ed. (London, 1928), pp. 48–49.

chief faculties of a poet; but it did not go so far as the devising of new forms. Granted the established norms, the challenge was to give them a novel content—at least, one fresh and different—and to achieve comparable felicity of expression in a language not only less sonorous but staled by vulgar interchange and commonplace needs. But first the forms.

No doubt, many of that generation longed to write epics. Many (including Johnson) *did* write "tragedies." But the Ode was not only less formidable, even in its strict Pindaric shape, but also capable of modulations with respectable precedents, like Cowley's irregular odes, Dryden's for music, Milton's stanzaic hymns and his pair of contrasting humors in short couplets, which in due course generated an abundance of imitative odes, often quite attractive, in the mid-eighteenth century. Prior, with his Augustan Ode to William, directly modelled on Horace, early produced one of the most splendidly artful; and Pope followed Dryden with his St. Cecilia's Day Ode. Scores and scores of odes, homely and grand, were written in these middle years, but posterity has been ungrateful for all but a few, notably the Wartons', Collins's, and Gray's. The characteristic ideal of the best is happily caught by Collins in the Pindaric epigraph he affixed to the title-page of his *Odes on Several Descriptive and Allegoric Subjects*—roughly thus: "Would I might be a finder of bold and compelling words, and serviceable in the Muses' chariot." An eloquence larger than life was what they were seeking. To this Johnson vigorously reacted in his well remembered pronouncement on Gray's Odes: "He has a kind of strutting dignity, and is tall by walking on tip-toe. His art and his struggle are too visible."

But the form that was peculiarly congenial to this generation of poets was the Georgic. The reason was probably that Virgil had provided a model of extraordinary flexibility, capable of extreme modulations, *buxom* to whatever subject-matter the author chose to introduce, from the loftiest to the most homely, and capable with no loss of dignity of accommodating extreme contrasts, without the interposition of troublesome transitions or narrative filler, such as epic required. It could lend itself to invocation, descriptive detail or panoramic sweep, episodic narrative, historical analogue, explanation of process, and practical advice. It could incorporate almost any kind of matter except dramatic dialogue. It made the poet free of whatever territory he chose to occupy, and liberty to develop it according to his interests, temperament, expertise, or didactic motive. A few lines, chosen almost at random, will exhibit the diapason (in Fairclough's translation):[8]

Well I know how hard it is to win with words a triumph herein, and thus to crown with glory a lowly theme. But sweet desire hurries me over the lonely steeps of Parnassus; joyous it is to roam o'er heights, where no forerunner's track turns by a gentle slope down to Castalia. Now, worshipful Pales, now must we sing in lofty strain. (Nunc, veneranda Pales, magna nunc ore sonandum.)
    First I decree that the sheep crop the herbage in soft pens, till leafy summer soon returns, and that you strew the hard ground beneath them with straw and handfuls of fern, lest the chill ice harm the tender flock, bringing scab and unsightly foot-rot. [III, 289–99]

How tempting Virgil's supreme achievement could be as a model to any poet who had his own theme to celebrate is obvious. If the epic surpassed it, the epic was forbidding by comparison. The Georgics, besides, were comprised in four books only, and it was at least debatable whether they were not almost level with the highest possible effort. The opinion of two great judges found few opponents in this age: Dryden, translating them, called them "the best poem of the best poet"; and Addison declared that they were "the most complete, elaborate, and finished piece of all antiquity."
    In a form so liberated from predetermined and arbitrary regulation, we need not look for sustained heights of exaltation. The most we can demand is not too infrequent purple passages. And this, too, is inviting to a poet who has a congenial subject, and something more than his private sentiments to impart, yet who is modest enough to be unsure of the divine afflatus, exalting him to sail "like the Theban Eagle," "with supreme dominion thro' the azure deep of air," but confident enough of his craftsmanship, and eager to practice it. The challenge was to develop a language suitable to his needs and occasions, which should not sink too far below the Virgilian prototype to render its English counterpart contemptible by comparison. Here, Milton had shown the way which was to be diligently pursued.
    Miss Miles has characterized the style of this whole school of poets as "sublime." She makes the valuable point that there was a continuity in their use of the English vocabulary, so that their difference from their predecessors consisted not so much in their

    [8] Virgil, *Eclogues, Georgics, Aeneid I–VI*, trans. H. Rushton Fairclough, vol. 58 in Loeb Classical Library, rev. ed. (Cambridge, Mass., 1935), I, 175, 177.

innovations in diction as in the relative emphasis on qualifying epithets and the consequent shift from a clausal syntax, giving additional weight to the pictorial and descriptive elements. As to vocabulary, she finds:

In only 10 of 32 innovations by the majority (from 1550 to 1850) is there no precedent minority appearance (of familiar terms), and six of these are in the eighteenth century, a fact which suggests perhaps that more variation was going on between the 1640's and 1740's than later. The metaphysical poets created the force of *earth* and *soul*; the romantics, *light* and *spirit*; the rest are the eighteenth century's: *soft, air, friend, joy, youth, rise,* a characterizing list for which we see least evidence of preparation.

And she discovers words of especially high frequency in the 1740s, as *gay, tender, vain, divine; youth, breast, fate, maid, muse, scene, virtue; behold*: all common enough, except in the insistence put upon them in that decade.[9] Her description of the general effect of the shift to the phrasal mode has already been quoted.

Although Johnson was abused by his contemporaries for his low rating of Gray, there is undeniable truth in the charge of artificial elevation of style. But this brings us up sharply against a vital point: there are *degrees* of artificiality. The theatergoing public accustomed, for instance, to realistic drama will rebel against blank verse as a dramatic medium. The audience used to opera goes in expectation of a vastly heightened form of expression. Previous acceptance of established convention, agreement about the way things are to be done, puts us into a receptive frame of mind and has much to do with our level of tolerance. Nothing is more evident than that the desired norms of dignified poetic utterance in the mid-eighteenth century were on a higher plane than ever they have been since. That the expectation was widespread and generally approved was certain: one has only to consider the number of long and ambitious works that were published in those decades. And not only published, but republished, and frequently revised and enlarged on republication. Akenside's *Pleasures of the Imagination* is a case in point. Thomson's *Seasons* is another. Young's *Night Thoughts* is another. It would not be any trouble, with the help of Chalmers or Anderson, to compile a long list. Glover's *Leonidas*, 12 books; his *Atheniad*, 30 books; Brooke's *Universal Beauty*; Wilkie's *Epigoniad*; William Thomp-

9 Josephine Miles, *The Continuity of Poetic Language: Studies in English Poetry from the 1540's to the 1940's* (Berkeley and Los Angeles, 1951), p. 528.

son's *Sickness*, 5 books; Blair's *Grave*; georgics by the handful, usually in four books apiece, in blank verse: Philips's, Armstrong's, Somervile's, Jago's, Dyer's, Grainger's. Clearly, there was an appetite for these: they were demanded; they were approved; there was reputation and esteem to be gained thereby. Many of these poets, and others not named here, won admission into the collection dignified by Johnson's biographies. It would be hard to defend the claim that the Past sat on these voluminous poets as a perceptible "burden." Their ambition was fired by it, and much of their inspiration derived from it. The ideal of sublimity to which they subscribed and aspired was noble: it did honor to Poetry by its basic assumption that, as Virgil had exemplified in the *Georgics*, all life and thought, even the humblest, had inherent dignity, and could be celebrated, enhanced, and universalized in art. Miss Miles's name for the style ("sublime") is appropriate in the sense in which she uses it. But as an adjective it has an awkward ambiguity in that it seems to characterize the reader's response, more than to denote a class. And if the reaction is unfriendly, the term is rendered opprobrious and ironic.

F. A. Pottle has reminded us recently of the judgment passed by A. E. Housman on these poets. It went in part like this:

The way to write real poetry, they thought, must be to write something as little like prose as possible; they devised for the purpose what was called a "correct and splendid diction," which consisted in always using the wrong word instead of the right, and plastered it as an ornament, with no thought of propriety, on whatever they desired to dignify.

We can say if we will—and many have said—that all that effort and energy was misapplied and misspent. But it is an arrogant act to assume that we are the people, and wisdom will die with us; that we are possessed of ultimate truth, having a different system of values, or standards of measurement. It is disturbing to be faced with the fact that whole generations, steeped in the poetry which we still regard as the best, saw beauty where we can find little but flatulency. I for one prefer to think it historically sounder to suspect that the trouble lies in a loss of our hearing in the upper register. And I suspect—*horresco referens*—that the same is true for many of us who profess criticism in these degenerate days, when we read *The Georgics* of Virgil himself.

EXAMPLES OF POETRY IN THE TROUGH OF THE WAVE

JOHN PHILIPS, *Cyder* (1708 ed.), II, 329–362

Now also, when the Colds abate, nor yet
Full Summer shines, a dubious Season, close
In Glass thy purer Streams, and let them gain,
From due Confinement, Spirit, and Flavour new.
  For this Intent, the subtle Chymist feeds
Perpetual Flames, whose unresisted Force
O'er Sand, and Ashes, and the stubborn Flint
Prevailing, turns into a fusil Sea,
That in his Furnace bubbles sunny-red:
From hence a glowing Drop with hollow'd Steel
He takes, and by one efficacious Breath
Dilates to a surprizing Cube, or Sphære,
Or Oval, and fit Receptacles forms
For every Liquid, with his plastic Lungs,
To human Life subservient; By his Means
Cyders in Metal frail improve; the *Moyle*,
And tastful *Pippin*, in a Moon's short Year,
Acquire compleat Perfection: Now they smoke
Transparent, sparkling in each Drop, Delight
Of curious Palate, by fair Virgins crav'd.
But harsher Fluids different lengths of time
Expect: Thy Flask will slowly mitigate
The *Eliot*'s Roughness. *Stirom*, firmest Fruit,
Embottled (long as *Priameian Troy*
Withstood the *Greeks*) endures, e'er justly mild.
Soften'd by Age, it youthful Vigor gains,
Fallacious Drink! Ye honest Men beware,
Nor trust its Smoothness; The third circling Glass
Suffices Virtue: But may Hypocrites
(That slyly speak one thing, another think,
Hateful as Hell) pleas'd with the Relish weak,
Drink on unwarn'd, 'till by inchanting Cups
Infatuate, they their wily Thoughts disclose,
And thro' Intemperance grow a while sincere.

JOHN ARMSTRONG, *The Art of Preserving Health* (1744),
II, 301–385

(Climate and Diet)
   Far in the horrid realms of winter, where
Th' establish'd ocean heaps a monstrous waste
Of shining rocks and mountains to the pole;
There lives a hardy race, whose plainest wants
Relentless earth, their cruel step-mother,
Regards not. On the waste of iron fields,
Untam'd, untractable, no harvests wave:
Pomona hates them, and the clownish God
Who tends the garden. In this frozen world
Such cooling gifts were vain: a fitter meal
Is earn'd with ease; for here the fruitful spawn
Of Ocean swarms, and heaps their genial board
With generous fare and luxury profuse.
These are their bread, the only bread they know;
These, and their willing slave the deer, that crops
The shrubby herbage on their meager hills.
Girt by the burning zone, not thus the south
Her swarthy sons, in either Ind, maintains:
Or thirsty Lybia; from whose fervid loins
The lion bursts, and every fiend that roams
Th' affrighted wilderness. The mountain herd,
Adust and dry, no sweet repast affords;
Nor does the tepid main such kinds produce,
So perfect, so delicious, as the stores
Of icy Zembla. Rashly where the blood
Brews feverish frays; where scarce the tubes sustain
Its tumid fervor and tempestuous course;
Kind nature tempts not to such gifts as these.
But here in livid ripeness melts the grape;
Here, finish'd by invigorating suns,
Thro' the green shade the golden Orange glows;
Spontaneous here the turgid Melon yields
A generous pulp; the Coco swells on high
With milky riches; and in horrid mail
The soft Ananas wraps its tender sweets.
Earth's vaunted progeny: In ruder air
Too coy to flourish, even too proud to live;

Or hardly rais'd by artificial fire
To vapid life. Here with a mother's smile
Glad Amalthea pours her copious horn.
Here buxom Ceres reigns: Th' autumnal sea
In boundless billows fluctuates o'er their plains.
What suits the climate best, what suits the men,
Nature profuses most, and most the taste
Demands. The fountain, edg'd with racy wine
Or acid fruit, bedews their thirsty souls.
The breeze eternal breathing round their limbs
Supports in else intolerable air:
While the cool Palm, the Plantain, and the grove
That waves on gloomy Lebanon, assuage
The torrid hell that beams upon their heads.
  Now come, ye Naiads, to the fountains lead;
Now let me wander thro' your gelid reign.
I burn to view th' enthusiastic wilds
By mortal else untrod. I hear the din
Of waters thundering o'er the ruin'd cliffs.
With holy rev'rence I approach the rocks
Whence glide the streams renown'd in ancient song.
Here from the desart down the rumbling steep
First springs the Nile; here bursts the sounding Po
In angry waves; Euphrates hence devolves
A mighty flood to water half the East;
And there, in Gothic solitude reclin'd,
The chearless Tanais pours his hoary urn.
What solemn twilight! What stupendous shades
Enwarp these infant floods! Thro' every nerve
A sacred horror thrills, a pleasing fear
Glides o'er my frame. The forest deepens round;
And more gigantic still th' impending trees
Stretch their extravagant arms athwart the gloom.
Are these the confines of some fairy world?
A land of Genii? Say, beyond these wilds
What unknown nations? If indeed beyond
Aught habitable lies. And whither leads,
To what strange regions, or of bliss or pain,
That subterraneous way? Propitious maids,
Conduct me, while with fearful steps I tread
This trembling ground. The task remains to sing

Your gifts, (so Pæon, so the powers of health
Command) to praise your chrystal element:
The chief ingredient in heaven's various works;
Whose flexile genius sparkles in the gem,
Grows firm in oak, and fugitive in wine;
The vehicle, the source, of nutriment
And life, to all that vegitate or live.

Ibid., IV, 52–83

(On Study)
   The strong-built pedant; who both night and day
Feeds on the coarsest fare the schools bestow,
And crudely fattens at gross Burman's stall;
O'erwhelm'd with phlegm lies in a dropsy drown'd,
Or sinks in lethargy before his time.
With useful studies you, and arts that please
Employ your mind, amuse but not fatigue.
Peace to each drowsy metaphysic sage!
And ever may the German folio's rest!
Yet some there are, even of elastic parts,
Whom strong and obstinate ambition leads
Thro' all the rugged roads of barren lore,
And gives to relish what their generous taste
Would else refuse. But may nor thirst of fame
Nor love of knowledge urge you to fatigue
With constant drudgery the liberal soul.
Toy with your books: and, as the various fits
Of humour seize you, from Philosophy
To Fable shift; from serious Antonine
To Rabelais' ravings, and from prose to song.
   While reading pleases, but no longer, read;
And read aloud resounding Homer's strain,
And weild the thunder of Demosthenes.
The chest so exercis'd improves its strength;
And quick vibrations thro' the bowels drive
The restless blood, which in unactive days
Would loiter else thro' unelastic tubes.
Deem it not trifling while I recommend
What posture suits: To stand and sit by turns,

As nature prompts, is best. But o'er your leaves
To lean for ever, cramps the vital parts,
And robs the fine machinery of its play.

WILLIAM SOMERVILE, *The Chase* (1796 ed.), III, 405 ff.

     (Royal Stag Hunt, Windsor Forest)
   Unharbour'd now, the royal stag forsakes
His wonted lair; he shakes his dappled sides,
And tosses high his beamy head; the copse
Beneath his antlers bends. What doubling shifts
He tries! not more the wily hare: in these
Would still persist, did not the full-mouth'd pack,
With dreadful concert, thunder in his rear.
The woods reply, the hunter's cheering shouts
Float through the glades, and the wide forest rings.
How merrily they chant! their nostrils deep
Inhale the grateful steam. Such is the cry,
And such the harmonious din, the soldier deems
The battle kindling, and the statesman grave
Forgets his weighty cares: each age, each sex,
In the wild transport joins; luxuriant joy,
And pleasure in excess, sparkling, exult
On every brow, and revel unrestrain'd.
How happy art thou, man! when thou'rt no more
Thyself; when all the pangs, that grind thy soul,
In rapture, and in sweet oblivion lost,
Yield a short interval, and ease from pain!
   See, the swift courser strains; his shining hoofs
Securely beat the solid ground. Who now
The dangerous pitfall fears, with tangling heath
High overgrown? or who the quivering bog,
Soft yielding to the step? All now is plain,
Plain as the strand, sea-laved, that stretches far
Beneath the rocky shore. Glades crossing glades,
The forest opens to our wondering view:
Such was the king's command. Let tyrants fierce,
Lay waste the world; his the more glorious part,
To check their pride; and when the brazen voice
Of war is hush'd, as erst victorious Rome,

To employ his station'd legions in the works
Of peace; to smooth the rugged wilderness,
To drain the stagnate fen, to raise the slope
Depending road, and to make gay the face
Of nature, with the embellishments of art. . . .
    Now the blown stag thro' woods, bogs, roads, and streams,
Has measured half the forest; but, alas!
He flies in vain; he flies not from his fears.
Though far he cast the lingering pack behind,
His haggard fancy still, with horror, views
The fell destroyer; still the fatal cry
Insults his ears, and wounds his trembling heart. . . .
See here, his slot; up yon green hill he climbs,
Pants on its brow a while; sadly looks back
On his pursuers, covering all the plain;
But, wrung with anguish, bears not long the sight,
Shoots down the steep, and sweats along the vale;
There mingles with the herd, where once he reign'd
Proud monarch of the groves; whose clashing beam
His rivals awed, and whose exalted power
Was still rewarded with successful love.
But the base herd have learn'd the ways of men;
Averse they fly, or, with rebellious aim,
Chase him from thence: needless their impious deed,
The huntsman knows him by a thousand marks,
Black, and imboss'd; nor are his hounds deceived;
Too well distinguish these, and never leave
Their once devoted foe: familiar grows
His scent, and strong their appetite to kill.
Again he flies, and, with redoubled speed,
Skims o'er the lawn; still the tenacious crew
Hang on the track, aloud demand their prey,
And push him many a league. If haply then
Too far escaped, and the gay courtly train
Behind are cast, the huntsman's clanging whip
Stops full their bold career: passive they stand,
Unmoved, an humble, an obsequious crowd,
As if, by stern Medusa, gazed to stones. . . .
Soon, at the king's command, like hasty streams
Damm'd up a while, they foam, and pour along
With fresh recruited might. The stag, who hoped

His foes were lost, now once more hears, astunn'd,
The dreadful din: he shivers every limb;
He starts, he bounds; each bush presents a foe.
Press'd by the fresh relay, no pause allow'd,
Breathless and faint, he falters in his pace,
And lifts his weary limbs with pain, that scarce
Sustain their load: he pants, he sobs, appall'd;
Drops down his heavy head to earth, beneath
His cumbrous beams oppress'd. But if, perchance,
Some prying eye surprise him, soon he rears
Erect his towering front, bounds o'er the lawn,
With ill dissembled vigour, to amuse
The knowing forester; who inly smiles
At his weak shifts, and unavailing frauds. . . .
From wood to wood redoubling thunders roll,
And bellow through the vales; the moving storm
Thickens amain, and loud triumphant shouts,
And horns, still warbling in each glade, prelude
To his approaching fate. And now, in view,
With hobbling gait, and high, exerts, amazed,
What strength is left: to the last dregs of life
Reduced, his spirits fail, on every side
Hemm'd in, besieged; not the least opening left
To gleaming hope, the unhappy's last reserve.
Where shall he turn? or whither fly? Despair
Gives courage to the weak: resolved to die,
He fears no more, but rushes on his foes,
And deals his deaths around: beneath his feet
These grovelling lie, those, by his antlers gored,
Defile the ensanguined plain. Ah! see, distress'd,
He stands at bay, against yon knotty trunk,
That covers well his rear, his front presents
An host of foes. O shun, ye noble train,
The rude encounter, and believe your lives
Your country's due alone. As now aloof
They wing around, he finds his soul upraised,
To dare some great exploit; he charges home
Upon the broken pack, that on each side
Fly diverse; then, as o'er the turf he strains,
He vents the cooling stream, and, up the breeze,
Urges his course with eager violence:

Then takes the soil, and plunges in the flood
Precipitant; down the mid stream he wafts
Along; till, like a ship distress'd, that runs
Into some winding creek, close to the verge
Of a small island, for his weary feet
Sure anchorage he finds, there skulks, immersed:
His nose alone, above the wave, draws in
The vital air; all else beneath the flood
Conceal'd, and lost, deceives each prying eye,
Of man or brute. In vain the crowding pack
Draw on the margin of the stream, or cut
The liquid wave with oary feet, that move
In equal time. The gliding waters leave
No trace behind, and his contracted pores
But sparingly perspire: the huntsman strains
His labouring lungs, and puffs his cheeks in vain.
At length a blood-hound, bold, studious to kill,
And exquisite of sense, winds him from far;
Headlong he leaps into the flood, his mouth
Loud opening, spends amain, and his wide throat
Swells every note with joy; then fearless dives
Beneath the wave, hangs on his haunch, and wounds
The unhappy brute, that flounders in the stream,
Sorely distress'd, and, struggling, strives to mount
The steepy shore. Haply once more escaped;
Again he stands at bay, amid the groves
Of willows, bending low their downy heads.
Outrageous transport fires the greedy pack;
These swim the deep, and those crawl up with pain
The slippery bank, while others on firm land
Engage; the stag repels each bold assault,
Maintains his post, and wounds for wounds returns.
As when some wily corsair boards a ship
Full freighted, or from Africk's golden coasts,
Or India's wealthy strand, his bloody crew
Upon her deck he slings; these in the deep
Drop short, and swim to reach her steepy sides,
And, clinging, climb aloft; while those, on board,
Urge on the work of fate; the master bold,
Press'd to his last retreat, bravely resolves
To sink his wealth beneath the whelming wave,

His wealth, his foes, nor unrevenged to die.
So fares it with the stag: so he resolves
To plunge at once into the flood below,
Himself, his foes, in one deep gulf immersed.
Ere yet he executes this dire intent,
In wild disorder once more views the light;
Beneath a weight of woe he groans, distress'd:
The tears run trickling down his hairy cheeks;
He weeps, nor weeps in vain. The King beholds
His wretched plight, and tenderness innate
Moves his great soul. Soon, at his high command,
Rebuked, the disappointed, hungry pack
Retire, submiss, and grumbling quit their prey.
   Great Prince! from thee, what may thy subjects hope;
So kind, and so beneficent to brutes?
O mercy, heavenly born! sweet attribute!
Thou great, thou best prerogative of power!
Justice may guard the throne, but, join'd with thee,
On rocks of adamant it stands secure,
And braves the storm beneath; soon as thy smiles
Gild the rough deep, the foaming waves subside,
And all the noisy tumult sinks in peace.

JOHN DYER, *The Fleece* (1757), I, 153 ff.

   Hail noble Albion! where no golden mines,
No soft perfumes, nor oils, nor myrtle bow'rs,
The vig'rous frame and lofty heart of man
Enervate: round whose stern cerulean brows
White-wingèd snow, and cloud, and pearly rain,
Frequent attend, with solemn majesty:
Rich queen of mists and vapours! These thy sons
With their cool arms compress; and twist their nerves
For deeds of excellence and high renown.
Thus formed, our Edwards, Henrys, Churchills, Blakes,
Our Lockes, our Newtons, and our Miltons, rose.
   See the sun gleams; the living pastures rise,
After the nurture of the fallen show'r,
How beautiful! How blue th' ethereal vault,
How verdurous the lawns, how clear the brooks!

Such noble warlike steeds, such herds of kine,
So sleek, so vast; such spacious flocks of sheep,
Like flakes of gold illumining the green,
What other paradise adorn but thine,
Britannia? happy, if thy sons would know
Their happiness.

Ibid., I, 410 ff.

(Lambing)
   Ah gentle shepherd, thine the lot to tend,
Of all, that feel distress, the most assail'd,
Feeble, defenceless: lenient be thy care:
But spread around thy tend'rest diligence
In flow'ry spring-time, when the new-dropt lamb,
Tott'ring with weakness by his mother's side,
Feels the fresh world about him; and each thorn,
Hillock, or furrow, trips his feeble feet:
O guard his meek sweet innocence from all
Th' innum'rous ills, that rush around his life;
Mark the quick kite, with beak and talons prone,
Circling the skies to snatch him from the plain;
Observe the lurking crows; beware the brake,
There the sly fox the careless minute waits;
Nor trust thy neighbour's dog, nor earth, nor sky:
Thy bosom to a thousand cares divide.
Eurus oft slings his hail; the tardy fields
Pay not their promis'd food; and oft the dam
O'er her weak twins with empty udder mourns,
Or fails to guard, when the bold bird of prey
Alights, and hops in many turns around,
And tires her also turning: to her aid
Be nimble, and the weakest, in thine arms,
Gently convey to the warm cote, and oft,
Between the lark's note and the nightingale's,
His hungry bleating still with tepid milk. ...
Nor yield him to himself, ere vernal airs
Sprinkle thy little croft with daisy flow'rs:
Nor yet forget him: life has rising ills:
Various as æther is the past'ral care.

Ibid., II, 565–586

(On Dyes)

For it suffices not, in flow'ry vales,
Only to tend the flock, and shear soft wool:
Gums must be stor'd of Guinea's arid coast;
Mexican woods, and India's bright'ning salts;
Fruits, herbage, sulphurs, minerals, to stain
The fleece prepar'd, which oil-imbibing earth
Of Wooburn blanches, and keen allum-waves
Intenerate. With curious eye observe,
In what variety the tribe of salts,
Gums, ores, and liquors, eye-delighting hues
Produce, abstersive or restringent; how
Steel casts the sable; how pale pewter, fus'd
In fluid spirit'ous, the scarlet dye;
And how each tint is made, or mixt, or chang'd,
By mediums colourless: why is the fume
Of sulphur kind to white and azure hues,
Pernicious else: why no materials yield
Singly their colours, those except that shine
With topaz, sapphire, and cornelian rays:
And why, though nature's face is cloath'd in green,
No green is found to beautify the fleece,
But what repeated toil by mixture gives.

Ibid., III, 184–202

(Steeping the Wool)

Th' ingenious artist, learn'd in drugs, bestows
The last improvement; for th' unlabour'd fleece
Rare is permitted to imbibe the dye.
In penetrating waves of boiling vats
The snowy web is steep'd, with grain of weld,
Fustic, or logwood, mix'd, or cochineal,
Or the dark purple pulp of Pictish woad,
Of stain tenacious, deep as summer skies,
Like those, that canopy the bow'rs of Stow
After soft rains, when birds their notes attune,
Ere the melodious nightingale begins.

From yon broad vase behold the saffron woofs
Beauteous emerge; from these the azure rise;
This glows with crimson; that the auburn holds;
These shall the prince with purple robes adorn;
And those the warrior mark, and those the priest.
　　Few are the primal colours of the art;
Five only; black, and yellow, blue, brown, red;
Yet hence innumerable hues arise.

Ibid., IV, 591–614

(On Anson's Voyage)
Proud Buenos Ayres, low-couched Paraguay,
And rough Corrientes, mark, with hostile eye,
The lab'ring vessel: neither may we trust
The dreary naked Patagonian land,
Which darkens in the wind. No traffick there,
No barter for the fleece. There angry storms
Bend their black brows, and, raging, hurl around
Their thunders. Ye advent'rous mariners,
Be firm; take courage from the brave. 'Twas there
Perils and conflicts inexpressible
Anson, with steady undespairing breast,
Endur'd, when o'er the various globe he chas'd
His country's foes. Fast-gath'ring tempests rous'd
Huge ocean, and involv'd him: all around
Whirlwind, and snow, and hail, and horror: now,
Rapidly, with the world of waters, down
Descending to the channels of the deep,
He view'd th' uncover'd bottom of th' abyss;
And now the stars, upon the loftiest point
Toss'd of the sky-mix'd surges. Oft the burst
Of loudest thunder, with the dash of seas,
Tore the wild-flying sails and tumbling masts;
While flames, thick-flashing in the gloom, reveal'd
Ruins of decks and shrouds, and sights of death.

James Grainger, *The Sugar-Cane* (1764), I, 168 ff.

(On Soil Culture and Compost)
For tho' the clouds relent in nightly rain,
Tho' thy rank Canes wave lofty in the gale;
Yet will the arrow, ornament of woe,
(Such monarchs oft-times give) their jointing stint;
Yet will winds lodge them, ravening rats destroy,
Or troops of monkeys thy rich harvest steal.
The earth must also wheel around the sun,
And half perform that circuit; ere the bill
Mow down thy sugars: and tho' all thy mills,
Crackling, o'erflow with a redundant juice,
Poor tastes the liquor; coction long demands,
And highest temper, ere it saccharize;
A meagre produce. Such is Virtue's meed,
Alas, too oft in these degenerate days. . . .
   But, as in life, the golden mean is best;
So happiest he whose green plantation lies
Nor from the hill too far, nor from the shore.
   Planter, if thou with wonder wouldst survey
Redundant harvests, load thy willing soil;
Let sun and rain mature thy deep-hoed land,
And old fat dung co-operate with these.
Be this great truth still present to thy mind;
The half well-cultur'd far exceeds the whole,
Which lust of grain, unconscious of its end,
Ungrateful vexes with unceasing toil.
   As, not indulg'd, the richest lands grow poor;
And Liamuiga may, in future times,
If too much urg'd, her barrenness bewail:
So cultivation, on the shallowest soil,
O'erspread with rocky cliffs, will bid the Cane,
With spiry pomp, all bountifully rise. . . .
   Of composts shall the muse descend to sing,
Nor soil her heavenly plumes? The sacred Muse
Nought sordid deems, but what is base; nought fair
Unless true Virtue stamp it with her seal.
Then, Planter, wouldst thou double thine estate,
Never, ah never, be asham'd to tread
Thy dung-heaps, where the refuse of thy mills,

With all the ashes, all thy coppers yield,
With weeds, mould, dung, and stale, a compost form,
Of force to fertilize the poorest soil. . . .
  Whether the fattening compost, in each hole,
'Tis best to throw; or, on the surface spread;
Is undetermin'd: Trials must decide. . . .
  Enough of composts, Muse; of soils, enough:
When best to dig, and when inhume the Cane;
A task how arduous! next demands thy song.

JOHN DYER, *The Ruins of Rome* (1740), ll. 369–392

          (On Virgil and Poetry)
  Suffice it Now *th' Esquilian Mount* to reach
With weary Wing, and seek the sacred Rests
Of *Maro's humble Tenement*; a low
Plain Wall remains; a little sun-gilt Heap,
Grotesque and Wild; the Gourd and Olive brown
Weave the light Roof; the Gourd and Olive fan
Their am'rous foliage, mingling with the Vine,
Who drops her purple Clusters through the Green.
Here let me lie, with pleasing fancy sooth'd:
Here flow'd his Fountain; Here his Laurels grew;
Here oft the meek good Man, the lofty Bard,
Fram'd the celestial Song, or social walk'd
With *Horace* and *the Ruler of the World*:
Happy *Augustus!* who, so well inspir'd,
Could'st throw thy Pomps and Royalties aside
Attentive to the Wise, the Great of Soul,
And dignify thy Mind. Thrice glorious Days,
Auspicious to the Muses! Then rever'd,
Then hallow'd was the Fount, or secret Shade,
Or open Mountain or whatever Scene
The Poet chose to tune th' ennobling Rhyme
Melodious; ev'n the rugged Sons of War;
Ev'n the rude Hinds rever'd the Poet's Name:
But now—Another Age, alas! is Ours—

RICHARD GLOVER, *Leonidas* (1804 ed.), IX, 103–152

(Teribazus' Body Recovered from the Slain)
                                        Night retires
Before the purple-winged morn. A band
Is call'd. The well-remember'd spot they find
Where Teribazus from his dying hand
Dropt in their sight his formidable sword.
Soon from beneath a pile of Asian dead
They draw the hero, by his armour known.
    Then, Ariana, what transcending pangs
Were thine! what horrors! In thy tender breast
Love still was mightiest. On the bosom cold
Of Teribazus, grief-distracted maid,
Thy beauteous limbs were thrown. Thy snowy hue
The clotted gore disfigur'd. On his wounds
Loose flow'd thy hair, and, bubbling from thy eyes,
Impetuous sorrow lav'd th' empurpled clay.
When forth in groans these lamentations broke.
    "O, torn for ever from these weeping eyes!
Thou, who, despairing to obtain a heart
Which then most lov'd thee, didst untimely yield
Thy life to fate's inevitable dart
For her, who now in agony reveals
Her tender passion, who repeats her vows
To thy deaf ear, who fondly to her own
Unites thy cheek insensible and cold.
Alas! do those unmoving, ghastly orbs
Perceive my gushing sorrow? Can that heart
At my complaint dissolve the ice of death,
To share my suff'rings? Never, never more
Shall Ariana bend a list'ning ear
To thy enchanting eloquence, nor feast
Her mind on wisdom from thy copious tongue!
Oh! bitter, insurmountable distress!"
    She could no more. Invincible despair
Suppress'd all utt'rance. As a marble form,
Fix'd on the solemn sepulchre, inclines
The silent head, in imitated woe,
O'er some dead hero, whom his country lov'd;
Entranc'd by anguish, o'er the breathless clay

So hung the princess. On the gory breach,
Whence life had issu'd by the fatal blow,
Mute for a space, and motionless, she gaz'd;
When thus in accents firm. "Imperial pomp,
Foe to my quiet, take my last farewell!
There is a state where only virtue holds
The rank supreme. My Teribazus there
From his high order must descend to mine."
   Then, with no trembling hand, no change of look,
She drew a poniard, which her garment veil'd;
And, instant sheathing in her heart the blade,
On her slain lover silent sunk in death!

INDEX